## Praise for *Changing*

Personal experience and the harnessing of knowledge from highly regarded experts and professionals allows Chatterley to really get to grips with perceptions and misconceptions, throwing light on what drives behaviour challenges in schools and how we need to take a more sophisticated approach to how we deal with them. This is an honest and, at times, emotional read, where Chatterley allows us an insight into his own lived experiences that confirm why he is a person to listen to and learn from.

**Dave Whitaker, Director of Learning, Wellspring Academy Trust, author of *The Kindness Principle***

In *Changing Perceptions* Graham Chatterley guides us through a number of steps to better understand children's complex behaviour. Rooted in relational practice, neuroscience, restorative and trauma-informed approaches, Graham weaves in case studies to help educational practitioners develop a nuanced approach to behaviour.

**Sarah Johnson, President of PRUsAP, author of *Behaving Together in the Classroom: A Teacher's Guide to Nurturing Behaviour*, Head of Behaviour and Inclusion and Director of Phoenix Education Consultancy**

*Changing Perceptions* is an enjoyable, thought-provoking read. Teachers and leaders at every level will get so much from reading his book. He manages to hit the target without missing the point, which is that behaviour is about meeting the underlying needs of all members of schools as communities. Graham explores behaviour with authenticity and warmth and keeps the well-being of children central. Read Graham's book and behaviour will be better as a result.

**Mark Finnis, author of *Restorative Practice*, Director of L30 Relational Systems**

In *Changing Perceptions* Graham's choice to share professional vulnerability with the reader lays the foundation for a reader–author relationship within a sense of trust which is, as he says, vital for learning. Graham set out to write the book he wishes he could have read at 22, and I think anyone working in education could learn from this book.

**Dr Jess Mahdavi-Gladwell, SENCO and Head of Assessment Centre, Newhaven Pupil Referral Unit**

Chatterley takes the reader on a journey, providing them with an opportunity to understand why behaviourist approaches to the communication of distress are not simply outdated but also pointless. Utilising the most contemporary research, supplying a coherent narrative and exploring the lived experiences of families, children and young people, this book is an essential read for everyone working in the education community.

**Lisa Cherry, Director, Trauma Informed Consultancy Services and author of *Conversations That Make a Difference to Children and Young People***

*Changing Perceptions* is a must-read book for all who sit beside children and youth carrying pain-based behaviours. Graham explains how toxic stress – the 'why' – impacts behaviours and how holistic and restorative practices are critical for social and emotional well-being which leads to deepened learning. Most importantly, Graham shares his lived and often painful experiences as a father raising an autistic child. I am honoured to have this book in my hands as author Graham Chatterley shares his brilliance in working with children and youth who often dare us to love them and teach them.

**Lori Desautels, Assistant Professor, College of Education, Butler University**

Graham's book is a bold and ambitious clarion call for teachers to 'change their perceptions' of several things; to change their perceptions of what lies behind the behaviour of the students they teach; to change their perceptions of the most effective language to use when describing the behaviour of the young people in their class; to change the perceptions of what approaches work to get better behaviour; and, above all, to change their perceptions of the young people they work with, especially those young people with the most 'challenging' behaviour. And there is a clear starting point for these changed perceptions and that is with all of us being a little more 'fiercely curious'.

**Mark Goodwin, Director of Behaviour and Wellbeing, The Mercian Trust**

*Changing Perceptions* is a realistic and comprehensive discussion about how the education system can change its response to the need for emotional regulation in our schools and classrooms. Thank you, Graham, for sharing your personal story and for advocating for children throughout the country. Let's hope this book can continue the progress we are making in changing perceptions about children and families and, therefore, being more effective practitioners.

**Rachel Tomlinson, Head Teacher, Barrowford Primary School**

In *Changing Perceptions* Graham Chatterley set out to write the book he wished he'd had as an NQT when he struggled with pupil behaviour. What he has produced – the fruit of many years spent thinking, researching, observing, learning from experts and, above all, working with children in classrooms in mainstream and specialist settings – is a book I wish I'd had at any stage of my career.

**John Cosgrove, retired Head Teacher**

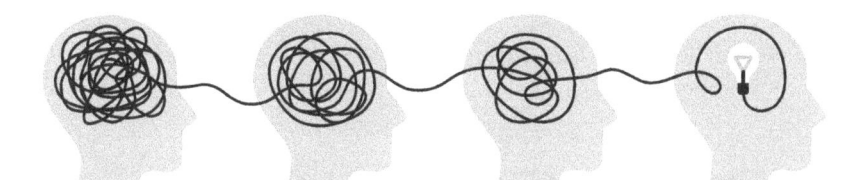

# Changing Perceptions

Deciphering the language of behaviour

Graham Chatterley

Crown House Publishing Limited
www.crownhouse.co.uk

First published by

Crown House Publishing Ltd

Crown Buildings, Bancyfelin, Carmarthen, Wales, SA33 5ND, UK

www.crownhouse.co.uk

and

Crown House Publishing Company LLC

PO Box 2223

Williston, VT 05495, USA

www.crownhousepublishing.com

© Graham Chatterley 2023

The right of Graham Chatterley to be identified as the author of this work has been asserted by him in accordance with the Copyright, Designs and Patents Act 1988.

Cover and chapter start images, © kotoffei – stock.adobe.com.

Image pages 24, 27, 28 and 30, © spline_x – stock.adobe.com. Image page 140, © Arcady – stock.adobe.com. Images pages 144 and 148, © Matsabe – stock.adobe.com.

All rights reserved. Except as permitted under current legislation no part of this work may be photocopied, stored in a retrieval system, published, performed in public, adapted, broadcast, transmitted, recorded or reproduced in any form or by any means, without the prior permission of the copyright owners. Enquiries should be addressed to Crown House Publishing Limited.

Crown House Publishing has no responsibility for the persistence or accuracy of URLs for external or third-party websites referred to in this publication, and does not guarantee that any content on such websites is, or will remain, accurate or appropriate.

British Library of Cataloguing-in-Publication Data

A catalogue entry for this book is available from the British Library.

Print ISBN: 978-178583675-6

Mobi ISBN: 978-178583679-4

ePub ISBN: 978-178583680-0

ePDF ISBN: 978-178583681-7

LCCN 2023930676

# Foreword by John Cosgrove

What if, instead of insisting that children are 'school ready' we asked schools to be 'children ready'? What if, rather than trying to eradicate undesirable behaviour by punishment, we attempted to understand where it was coming from and treated the causes as well as the symptoms? What if we thought as much about the unconscious messages we give in our responses to children as about the ways they challenge us?

In medieval times, part of the examination for master of education at the University of Cambridge involved the candidate being presented with a birch rod, a small bat for smacking hands known as a 'palmer' and a boy. When the child had been soundly beaten, he was paid a few pence for his essential part in enabling a future teacher to demonstrate the skills needed to survive in a classroom. It sometimes seems that we have not moved on very far. The tools of control may have changed but perceptions have not.

Pupil behaviour management has been a concern for teachers from the dawn of time. If a child will not listen and follow instructions, it is very difficult for learning to take place. The trouble is that whilst we may no longer hit children with canes or paddles, we still too often approach behaviour from a purely punitive stance, with demerits, detentions, focus rooms, isolation booths, exclusions and expulsion. What if, instead of seeking to 'manage' behaviour, we taught children how to behave appropriately?

Graham Chatterley is an experienced teacher, school leader, trainer and consultant. In this important book, the fruit of many years working with children, teachers and schools, he challenges everyone involved with education to re-examine the most basic assumptions we make about our work. He explores some of those 'what if' questions and, using examples from his personal experience, shows how the latest research can inform our practice and how all our dealings with young people can be informed by empathy and respect.

Some years ago, a head teacher from a different continent came to visit the school I led at the time, a large multicultural primary in what I always describe as 'a challenging urban environment'. As I showed him round, he was particularly interested in the work of our specialist resource for children with autism. Later, over coffee in my office, he told me with a sad smile: 'I am ashamed to say that in my country we don't have special needs. We just beat children.' He didn't add – but we both knew – that the beatings achieved nothing. They were not a solution; they were because that head teacher and his staff, just like the masters of education hundreds of years ago and the proponents of isolation booths today, did not – and do not – know what to do instead.

What is important, of course, is not that we shame or blame teachers and schools, but that we show them the better ways of doing things. We challenge and change perceptions. Which is exactly what Graham does in this book.

# Acknowledgements

It has certainly been a journey to get here, a finishing line I wondered whether I would ever reach. I would like to thank Mike and Kerry, without whose leadership, guidance and opportunity to develop my training this book would not exist.

A big thank you to Paul Dix and the Teacher Hug team for letting me be a part of this wonderful project, and for giving me the confidence to believe that people wanted to listen to what I had to say.

Special thanks to Dr Alec Clark, John Cosgrove, Maryse Dare, Mark Goodwin and Dr Jess Mahdavi-Gladwell for reading through drafts and offering advice and support throughout the writing of the book.

The most important thanks goes to all the children, including my own, who have taught me so much and continue to do so.

And, finally, thanks to Morgan for helping Dad with his terrible punctuation and grammar and support throughout the editing process. Unlimited high fives from here on out.

# Contents

*Foreword by John Cosgrove* .................................................. *i*
*Acknowledgements* ............................................................ *iii*

Introduction ...................................................................... 1
Chapter 1: Relationships ..................................................... 7
Chapter 2: How we respond ................................................ 19
Chapter 3: The origins of behaviour ..................................... 33
Chapter 4: Short-term survival responses ............................. 49
Chapter 5: What is the behaviour communicating? ................ 61
Chapter 6: The five responses to threat ................................. 69
Chapter 7: Prevention is better than cure .............................. 77
Chapter 8: Consequences ..................................................... 93
Chapter 9: Long-term survival ............................................. 109
Chapter 10: Shielding from shame ....................................... 119
Chapter 11: Not school ready ............................................... 127
Chapter 12: Overwhelm ....................................................... 137
Chapter 13: Lifting them up ................................................. 151
Chapter 14: Linking self-esteem and additional needs ........... 159
Chapter 15: My autism journey ............................................ 173
Chapter 16: Emotional resilience .......................................... 193
Chapter 17: The power of trauma ......................................... 201
Chapter 18: Behind the mask ............................................... 209
Chapter 19: Expectations and values .................................... 235
Chapter 20: Enforcing external control versus teaching self-control  253
Chapter 21: Less is sometimes more ..................................... 267
Conclusion ......................................................................... 275
*Bibliography* ..................................................................... 279

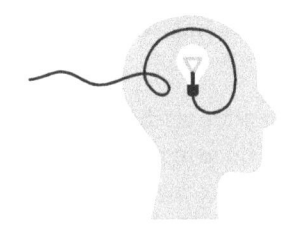

# Introduction

I started my teaching career completely unprepared. The messages I had taken led me to try to be an authority figure, but I lacked that personality. I looked around at experienced teachers, attempting to emulate their classroom management. I bought into the idea that if my pupils sat still and conformed, that was a measure of my teaching capabilities.

Every day was a struggle. I left each day thinking that I couldn't do it, my lessons weren't interesting enough, I wasn't firm enough and I wasn't liked or respected by my pupils. I was very close to failing my newly qualified teacher (NQT) year and even closer to calling it a day. In fact, in my head, I had made that decision; I just hadn't told anyone.

Then a strange thing happened. I relaxed, I stopped putting myself under so much pressure and, in order to make a little bit of extra money to save up for when I wouldn't have a teaching salary, I signed up to do three extracurricular clubs. (Yes, there was once a time when teachers got paid for extracurricular activities.) A new laid-back me engaging in activities I enjoyed gave the children an opportunity to see the personality I had been working so hard to hide because I was under the illusion that it would damage my authority. The side effect was that behaviour in my lessons improved, which prompted some overdue reflection about what I had been prioritising.

That reflection led me to analyse my teacher training and focus on the experiences I had been ignoring. I had got it all wrong: authority isn't the reason why children conform. Experienced staff don't have well-behaved pupils because of what they are doing now, but because of what they have done before. The children are conforming to their high expectations because the groundwork of building relationships and earning respect has already been done.

I had believed that the successful teaching practice I'd had in my final year was down to what I had done in the classroom, but it wasn't. It was down to the brilliant Jamie Hallett, my fellow trainee at the same school, who had dragged me onto the yard at break and lunch times to interact with the children, and also to the good luck that my teaching practice coincided with a school residential, further allowing the children to see my human side. I had been oblivious to it, but those little interactions had been my currency for better behaviour in the classroom. It was a currency I didn't have during my NQT year because the children had never seen it, but I was now building it in those extracurricular activities when I was getting out and interacting outside the classroom. I started to play to my own strengths and to be authentic, and I actually began to enjoy teaching for the first time.

Now, some people reading this will probably think that I was a bit slow to catch on, and they are probably right, but I got there in the end. I have been reflecting and learning ever since. I have taught at primary and secondary level and pupils with social, emotional and mental health (SEMH) needs, and I look back with horror at some of the mistakes I made both as an inexperienced and as an experienced educator. It was a journey from shouty NQT to occasionally putting on a performance to not shouting for the last decade. My approach has probably gone from too unfriendly to too friendly and back to the middle, hopefully balancing Kim Golding's (2017) two hands of discipline and parenting (i.e. emotional connection and nurture in one hand and discipline and boundaries in the other) to the best of my ability.

Meanwhile, I have tried to learn everything I can about the reasons behind children's challenging behaviour. I have worked to support colleagues and share my experiences whilst doing outreach support for a decade, and I devised the training course that I wish I'd had when I was training. If I'd had a better understanding of child development, additional needs, self-esteem, emotional regulation and trauma, and if I had realised the importance of safety, trust, co-regulation, belonging and happiness, I would have started out as a better teacher. I am confident that the training course has helped more staff than I can count, so now I have written the book I wish I'd had when I was starting my teaching journey.

There are a lot of books on the market from teachers supporting teachers from a strategic perspective. Equally, there are lots of books from academics exploring trauma, neuroscience and additional needs. My hope is that this is a book that bridges the two. I was a teacher first (I guess you could even call me overly traditional in style), who has searched and researched to understand behaviour. I have read extensively about the science of behaviour, each time prompted by incidents when we weren't successful with a child.

I will consistently repeat the message throughout this book that behavioural mistakes are learning opportunities – and that doesn't just apply to the pupils. If something isn't working, it is time for us all to reflect and improve. My hope is that this is the book the 22-year-old me would have picked up and read, and saved myself from feeling like a failure. It happens to too many new (and experienced) teachers, so we need to ensure that they start their careers armed with as much information as possible.

This book contains practical strategies, but on their own they will never be enough, especially if we want to be inclusive. We must have a solid understanding of the 'why' before we settle on the 'what'. The first three-quarters of this book are designed to explain the 'why' and the last quarter the 'what' and 'how'. I will share examples of individuals who have impacted on me and led my reflections, as well as real-world examples of the processes being used in practice. Everything in this book is tried and tested and has been proven successful. It also contains some insights from my own personal life, and how supporting my own children's experiences with autism have further shaped my journey.

The aim of this book is to explore every avenue of children's experiences to help us to react differently when faced with behavioural challenges. We will look at all the aspects of the conflict spiral and equip staff with the skills to de-escalate and repair situations that would otherwise deteriorate.

# The purpose of school

A few years ago, I found myself in the role of parent sat across from my own child's head teacher discussing the main purpose of school. The head teacher said: 'The most important thing is the learning.' I replied: 'No, the most important thing is well-being.' So, what *is* the main purpose of school? The question has been asked and debated for a long time, and is at the root of many discussions amongst educators. Of course, teaching, and therefore learning, is the fundamental job of a school. I have no desire to dispute that, but are we talking about academic learning or more holistic learning? Are we prioritising academic grades to achieve a higher league table position, or to produce successful adults with good jobs and happy families? Does a school see the child first, or the academic grade they can achieve?

It is very easy for academic grades to take precedence because that is what the system dictates. Children are too often viewed as their potential achievements rather than who they are. If something isn't measurable in a standardised test, then it is easy to see it as less valuable. Many school leaders don't buy into this narrative, despite the fact that it is how their school will be judged. If the priority is the individual, then we need a holistic approach for each child. One that equips them not just to contribute to society through whatever job they have, but also by providing them with the ability to be good parents, partners and friends, and to have a positive impact on their community beyond financial contribution.

See the child, not the grade. See the child, not the behaviour. Don't get me wrong: these aren't mutually exclusive (as some would have you believe). For example, my son's school didn't ignore well-being; the leadership and ethos was very inclusive. However, deciding on what is the most important thing, and making it central to everything you do, is what makes that a genuine ethos. If the most significant factor is academic learning, then there will always be a percentage of children who fall by the wayside because they don't have the necessary foundations in place – safety, trust, belonging and resilience. If what is most important is well-being, however, then inevitably those foundations will be essential elements of the teaching.

The big question is, do we want a house that looks great but is rushed and built on weak foundations, or do we want a house that might need some furnishing and decorating but is built to last? I think every educator knows the answer to that question, but the system is designed for show homes. The strength and quality of the foundations are less important than how it looks. The current system puts pressure on schools to plaster over the cracks or hang a strategic picture. The problem comes when those fissures start to show and rebuilding the house is too big a task. Children can be taught for the test and to have great grades, but academic grades are a tiny part of what children need to be successful and happy adults. Without the foundations of safety, trust, belonging and resilience, children will find adult life challenging. I want schools to give the children an education that is built to last, not just good for show in the short term.

We can call it compassionate leadership, relational practice or progressive education; it doesn't really matter. It is about putting the well-being of the child first, and knowing that if you do so then the grade will come. It is about the individual being more important than the whole. It is about every child mattering. Making the children's well-being a bigger priority than their academic learning doesn't make learning unimportant; it is about building the house properly with solid foundations before we decorate it.

Many educators will say that the foundations are the job of the parents. I can't argue with that. However, for a multitude of reasons, it is a duty that some parents haven't done. If our task is to meet the needs of our children, then it falls on educators to give that child a chance because, as Marie Gentles (Don't Exclude Me, 2021) observes, 'If we don't do it, who will?'

I will give some examples throughout the book of where rebuilding those foundations has been done with great success, both in my SEMH setting and whilst supporting mainstream schools. Children's names have been changed in these instances to protect their identity.

# Chapter 1

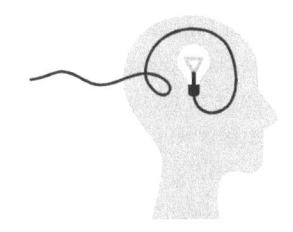

# Relationships

> Relationships are the agents of change and the most powerful therapy is human love.
>
> **Bruce Perry, *The Boy Who Was Raised As a Dog* (2008)**

As great as it would be for every staff member to love every child, I don't think it is possible to love all the children we teach. I often joke that in secondary schools we will settle for like! Love is a word that divides education. The educators I train often feel uncomfortable with the idea of loving their pupils, as it makes a comparison with their own children and they don't feel it is the same. However, for me, it isn't about the word, it is about the feeling. 'Do you love your pupils?' and 'Do you want your pupils to feel loved?' are viewed very differently. How a child is made to feel is what is important.

If, as parents, we go to our own child's parents' evening and get the feeling that the teacher doesn't really know or doesn't like our child, how does that make us feel? We may have spent five minutes with someone and our feelings towards them are negative; we don't want to listen to what they have to say and we are probably quite defensive (or aggressive, depending on how we choose to defend our child). If pupils have the same perception, and as a result feel disliked or unwanted, this is not a good foundation for learning. Children who feel this way will be less likely to reach their potential because they will always hold back.

If we want our children to invest in us and in the lessons we teach, then we must invest in them first. I am not suggesting that we can love (or like) every child equally. Human nature means it is unlikely that we will love every pupil who enters our classroom. Indeed, many children behave in ways that make it very difficult to feel anything positive towards them – they know exactly what buttons to push. But, if we can find a way to convince the child that we are still going to like them, no matter what they do, then amazing things can happen.

# Feelings stick

If you think back to your own time at school, you probably won't remember subjects or lessons, but you will remember individuals. You won't remember the content of classes, but you will remember how you felt in them. The teacher who showed so much enthusiasm for their subject that you couldn't help but get swept away in what they were doing. The teaching assistant who was kind to you when you hurt yourself in the yard and comforted you until your mum arrived.

My outstanding memory of high school was the head teacher who came and sat next to me after I was given out in the school cricket final. I was desperately disappointed and giving myself a really hard time, so I had gone to sit on my own. I have no memory of what the conversation was about, and he didn't attempt to make me feel better or fix what had happened. He just sat with me and talked. Nothing spectacular. No grand gesture or lesson that had taken three weeks to plan. It was a simple connection that helped at the time, and 20 years later I still remember vividly how it made me feel. It was Year 10 and this was the only one-to-one interaction I ever had with Mr Wright, who sadly died the following year, but it makes me wonder how many others he impacted on in the same modest way.

We get so caught up in systems and policies that we forget the most important tool we have. Human connection – how we make the children feel – is what ultimately makes the difference in a school, not what we do. There are no magic strategies to manage behaviour. I was a well-behaved child, but I wasn't a spectacular learner generally. However, I tried harder for some teachers than others, and if Mr Wright had taught me, I would have gone through a wall for him after that day.

# Validate, don't fix

If we can validate feelings of anger, frustration, fear or any other emotion and not dismiss them or try to fix them, if we can show children that it is okay to feel that way but it will pass, and if we share our own experiences, then we can also show them ways to overcome negative feelings. If we expect behavioural mistakes to happen, but teach children how and why to respond to these occurrences, then we empower them.

Nobody wants children to become distressed. Nobody wants children to react with fear or to be fuelled by chemicals like adrenaline or cortisol (stress hormones that prepare the body for fight or flight), but they are part of life, not just school. These hormones regulate a wide range of processes throughout the body, but too much of them over time can cause significant harm.

Teaching children how to deal with fear and stress should be part of what we do in the classroom. If we can use our relationships to support and our connections to replace that cortisol with oxytocin (a bonding hormone that plays a huge role in connection and trust) and increase levels of dopamine (the pleasure hormone), then we reduce fear, drive connections and make young people feel loved. If we have pupils who feel good, and know the power of making others feel good, then behavioural mistakes will decrease naturally without the need for a specific behaviour focus. They will also be in a state that is more conducive to engagement and more effective learning.

Currently, many behaviour systems run the risk of creating an environment where behavioural mistakes are unacceptable and only perfect will do; anything less than this results in punishment, often in a way that has no link to the original behaviour. I will discuss later the dangers of perfectionism and how we can easily compound a child's narrative and shame cycle, especially when there is a reason for the behaviour. If we don't know why they are getting it wrong, how can we teach them to get it right? For example, a child who perceives a psychological or mental threat (and whose body is flooded with stress hormones) is likely to get into trouble because this type of active survival response isn't appropriate. The fight-or-flight response is millions of years old and evolved to keep us alive in dangerous situations. Thankfully, these kinds of threats are much rarer in today's world.

Don't ignore the mistake. Instead, see it as an opportunity to learn, connect, raise self-esteem and teach better responses. If someone has been wronged, a consequence will be necessary, but it must be linked to the behaviour and must give the child an opportunity to repair and redeem themselves. Without this, we feed into the child's narrative that they are bad and should be punished – a narrative that will become harder and harder to change if we don't challenge it.

Without supportive staff guiding the redemption, there is no connection and there is no oxytocin. Without the connection this brings, we are left with mistrust and disconnect. Just being given an unrelated sanction might be a deterrent, but it doesn't teach the child anything. It might give them a message that a behaviour or action is unacceptable, but it doesn't lead to potential repair. It doesn't show the child that something good can come from something bad, and it doesn't offer a satisfactory conclusion to the incident. I will discuss this further in Chapter 7.

Issuing a punishment for a mistake puts a full stop on things and informs the child that it is time to move on. We often say to children, 'Fresh start', and we do it with the best intentions, but this won't work if they don't feel that the situation has been resolved. Resolution gives the child a shot of dopamine that makes them feel good. Throughout the book, I will refer to the bell curve model, which starts at calm and ends at calm, followed by repair. In-between is the escalation to crisis and then recovery. Even in very nurturing schools, the repair often gets missed because having got a child to calm there is a temptation to avoid bringing the incident back up again, as it might trigger the child and take them back into negative feelings. It is a valid concern. Without repair, however, a destructive cycle is created: I am challenged and become dysregulated – I lose control – I am supported and calmed – I go back to class – I am punished – I am challenged and dysregulated – repeat. The adults have the power to interrupt this loop.

The process isn't this simple, and it takes time because we are often trying to change a child's narrative about themselves. When we are attempting to modify beliefs, we are taking the child on a journey through the unfamiliar, and unfamiliarity brings with it fear. Any challenge to the child's learned belief system will be rejected by them and likely sabotaged. However, if we can have faith in the process and stay with it, then we can teach children that although they may feel bad and do bad things, they aren't bad and mistakes can be fixed. We separate guilt and shame. We get them to turn failure into success. In my school, there were many children who were impulsive, who would perceive a threat, storm out of the classroom and rip down the first display they encountered. They were dysregulated and had no interest in the display because they weren't thinking rationally. The priority was to get them calm, and then the behaviour could be discussed.

When the initial response is punishment, the result is a child who believes that they behaved in the way they did because they are bad and therefore they deserve to be punished. They will take the punishment. And then they will make a similar behavioural mistake the next day because they are bad and that is all that can be expected of them. This is a shame loop. Children often find themselves in this position and little has been done by adults to break it. In fact, sometimes inadvertently, they have embedded the children's beliefs even further.

If, instead, the response is to look at the impact of the action rather than the action itself, and if the child understands that their favourite staff member spent hours putting up that display and will be upset about the damage, then the behaviour means something and the child feels guilty. An expectation that the action is repaired becomes not only a logical consequence but of importance to the child. Often, I couldn't give that child a staple gun fast enough to fix the damage. When guilt is used to drive repair, not to feed shame, the child's narrative changes. 'I've done a bad thing, but I'm not a bad child' is a driving force for accountability, and making amends brings with it change. If bad things can be fixed, then so can faulty beliefs.

If the child has experienced how satisfying it feels to do good things, then we can keep reminding them of this feeling. Over time, the positive things win out because the child believes they can do them. Starting with adrenaline and cortisol and finishing with oxytocin and dopamine is a powerful process and journey. Take that path enough times, with enough connection and safety, and the adrenaline and cortisol aren't required and negative behaviour will reduce.

For many of us, there comes a point in our lives when giving the gift becomes more satisfying than receiving it. Getting something nice is great – we get a short-term buzz – but the feeling we get from creating and seeing that in others lasts longer and gives us more. This is what we must teach our children.

Punishment, consequence or sanction without resolution doesn't achieve this. It is why behaviours become cycles and change doesn't happen. Currently, the same children getting the same consequences is a feature in too many of our schools.

## The purpose of this book

When I wrote *Building Positive Behaviour: Returning to Learning Using a Sequential Approach* (2020), it was in response to what I felt was very damaging guidance coming from the Department for Education. The book was about giving schools a scaffold to respond to children who were struggling during the COVID-19 pandemic and what had been an incredibly challenging time. The impact of the pandemic on mental health and well-being was being downplayed in favour of a more authoritarian approach. For example, 'Rebooting Behaviour After Lockdown' by Tom Bennett, the lead behaviour adviser to the Department for Education, published in May 2020, focused on more rules and more adult controls rather than trying to understand and respond to children's losses and experiences. At a time when mental health, well-being and recovery curriculums were being talked about by many, the government's focus was simply managing behaviour.

The sequential approach, which I will share in Chapter 19, will never be more relevant than now. It can be used to guide children back to normality and respond to the fallout of the pandemic, the consequences of which I am seeing up and down the country when I work with schools. As schools come out of survival mode and take a breath, the true impact of the past few years is becoming apparent. I have serious concerns about the rigid behaviour systems on which some schools rely. I hope they will begin to prioritise ethos and whole-school approaches to behaviour rather than more punitive responses, which will result in more children out of education. The numbers of pupils missing from schools is already a big worry. Much of the focus has been on academic catch-up and how resilient children have been – and many have been. However, children are survivors; when they experience a crisis, they are more malleable than resilient. Although children may recover, they may never be the same as they were before.

In *What Happened to You?*, Dr Bruce Perry and Oprah Winfrey (2021) discuss the common misconception that children's brains are like a sponge ball – that when they face adversity, they bounce back to the perfect round shape of the ball because they are resilient. The truth is that they are more like a coat hanger bent out of shape. You can bend it back but it will never be the same, and the point at which it was bent will always be weaker. Resilience is much more complex than it has been portrayed by politicians and the media; it is more than simply bouncing back. (We will explore emotional resilience in Chapter 16.) If and when the crisis finally goes away, the experiences of the pandemic will stick around.

This book is about making sense of future challenging behaviour by digging into the potential causes and responding in the best possible way. I will never suggest, nor expect, teachers to diagnose the causes of challenging behaviour, but equally I don't expect staff to assume that there isn't one. In my experience, the main opposition towards trauma-informed practice is that not all children are traumatised and so we shouldn't treat them as such. I agree, but that isn't what trauma-informed practice is about. It isn't that all children are traumatised; it is that some might be and we wouldn't necessarily know.

Having an understanding and empathetic approach will never cause emotional harm to a pupil, whilst having a zero-tolerance approach to all will definitely harm some pupils. Section 1 of the Children Act 1989 contains the paramountcy principle – that 'the child's welfare shall be … paramount'.[1] This should be front and centre of every school policy and include every child.

Five core beliefs are absolutely central to my perspective on behaviour:

1. Behaviour should not be a reason to fail school. I believe that exclusion rates and children out of education and marginalised are far too high in England, with many pupils being sent to alternative provision, waiting for placements or offered nothing at all. It doesn't have to be like this.

---

[1] See https://www.legislation.gov.uk/ukpga/1989/41/contents/enacted.

2. Teachers' well-being should be prioritised. The provision of quality training to help them better understand children's behaviour is central to this.

3. What happens after an event is just as important as what happens before. If we are teaching behaviour rather than managing it, then we must use mistakes as learning opportunities.

4. A sound awareness of the reasons for poor behaviour is not about asking staff to diagnose. It is about recognising that there is a reason for the behaviour. We may never fully understand it, but that doesn't mean it isn't there. Curiosity, empathy and understanding will never harm a child, but assuming they are simply being naughty potentially will.

5. It takes time to change behaviour. The adult holds much of the power in this process, but only when they have worked on the relationship with the child.

Everything in this book will draw us back to these beliefs. It isn't about quick fixes; it is about long-term change and lasting improvements in behaviour. A characteristic of schools that are failing on behaviour is staff leaving at the end of the day exhausted, frustrated and even angered by the conduct of the children in their classes. They ask: 'Is it me?' 'Are my lessons not good enough?' 'Why don't they like me?' 'Why are they good for … but horrific for me?' 'I can't teach this child!' No teacher should be going home with these misconceptions, and schools shouldn't be allowing it to happen.

Equipping staff to better comprehend the reasons for behaviours and, most importantly, that they aren't personal is the most powerful thing we can do to improve staff well-being. In doing so, we have positive staff, armed with empathy and understanding, who are focused on the solution rather than beaten down by the problem. This sets up a relationship between staff and pupils that will over time transform behaviour. It is too easy for school leaders to claim that if teaching was better, then behaviour would be better, but this removes the context and tries to simplify what can be a very complex issue. The truth is that we don't always know the reasons for a child's behaviour, unless we take the time to find out. This book will show that the same behaviours can have more than a dozen causes. Although they don't need a dozen different responses, they do need to be understood.

My experience, both as a teacher experiencing training sessions and a trainer delivering them, is that educators expect the person who is imparting information about an approach to have employed it in the classroom. However, this is not always possible, and educators are therefore guilty of dismissing ideas or writing them off without giving them a real chance or genuinely trying them out. Asserting that something won't work and evidencing its failure are very different things. Just because something is difficult or different to what we have always been told, doesn't make it wrong.

I am willing to state that many elements of traditional discipline are flawed in that they use consequences as deterrents – that is, the fear of the consequence will get the children to conform. I know the limitations because I used them early on in my career. I don't dispute that traditional discipline works for most children, but the minority who can't control their responses or emotions or who have developed maladaptive long-term survival responses need more than this. Consequence systems tolerate the fact that some children will fail, and they often discriminate against the neurodiverse and those with adverse childhood experiences (ACEs). I don't believe that such a system is justifiable. Too many children are collateral damage and they don't need to be.

If you are like me and want all children to succeed, then we need a different approach. Exploring the use of neuroscience, trauma-informed and restorative practice means that schools can work for all. Developing these approaches in school is certainly challenging; it took my school time and was a difficult mindset shift for some. Yes, it was a change. Yes, it was more work. Yes, it was very difficult at times. But the results are powerful, and so is how it feels as a teacher. Going home believing that we aren't doing everything we can for a child is not a good feeling, and it isn't good for well-being either. However, accepting that things can't always go according to plan, but knowing that we have done everything possible in a situation, makes sleeping at night much easier.

The truth is that it is easy to dismiss an academic non-teacher. It shouldn't be because the work needed to gain a doctorate is more than I will ever achieve, but it is an unfortunate undercurrent in education. It only takes a small amount of time to see this bias in action on social media. The 'It will never work with my class of 30' argument often gets used to shout down and dismiss, but it is only a valid viewpoint if you actually have evidence or experience of using a trauma-informed or restorative approach that has been implemented properly and proved unsuccessful. Without this, it is just an opinion. It is just more of what we have always done.

I have found a way to marry the two elements to a degree. I will always be a teacher first; it runs through my writing, my training and every piece of work I do. This book is therefore filled with practical examples of theory being put into practice. However, I can't possibly claim to know as much as the experts in the field of neuroscience, and I would certainly never claim to do so. I attended a training session on trauma and attachment led by Lisa Wisher in 2017[2] which changed everything for me. It added the missing piece and sent me down a path of professional development that I aim to keep on exploring. It has also led to hundreds, if not thousands, of hours of my own research and learning about every available reason for challenging behaviour. Lisa Wisher is a psychotherapist, not a teacher, and to my knowledge she hadn't taught a class of 30 pupils, but she had worked with exceptionally complex and challenging behaviour day in, day out with adopted children. She had helped them start to overcome the worst of trauma. Her message was a simple one: it always comes back to relationships. Not on their own, not without or as a replacement for boundaries, structure or expectations, but alongside them.

Unconditional positive regard isn't about accepting or ignoring everything a young person does; it is about keeping on coming back and keeping on caring: 'I don't like your behaviour, but it doesn't stop me liking you.' Every child is equally worthy, regardless of their prospective grades or challenging behaviour. Seeking an explanation for a child's actions is not the same as excusing them.

I understand people's reservations. It has taken me years to get my head around the complexities of neuroscience, and much of it will always be beyond me, but it doesn't matter. I am not diagnosing. Any knowledge I do have helps me to signpost. If therapies are needed, then the right professionals will deliver them. Dr Bruce Perry talks about love and how

---

2  See http://www.lisawisher.com.

powerful it is in both *The Boy Who Was Raised As a Dog* (2008) and *What Happened to You?* (2021). Whether it is possible or not, my job isn't necessarily to love or like the children; my job is to make them feel loved when they are in my care (which, incidentally, is much easier if it is genuine).

# How do you love a child who behaves horribly?

For me, learning to love a child who misbehaves comes from understanding the reason for it, and if I don't understand it yet, then by accepting that there is a reason. I didn't always know what it was at the time, but in 20 years I am yet to see a behaviour that didn't have a cause.

The more awareness we can give our staff, the more they can put themselves in the shoes of the child and see things from their perspective. In order to practise empathy effectively, adults need a good understanding of the child's feelings and experiences. *Unconditional* is a very powerful word that is sometimes lacking in schools. Statements like, 'We're hard on our pupils because we love them' are commonplace. If the love children receive is dependent on certain behaviours ('We only love you when you behave in the way we say'), then it is coercive and conditional. We wouldn't accept that kind of love in any other relationship – if a partner behaved that way it would be described as a toxic or abusive – so why is it okay for our children?

Accepting that they can be well behaved and that adults care unconditionally goes against the beliefs of many children. Experience tells them that care is dependent on what they do, not on who they are, so it stands to reason that they will reject that care as a safety measure. Being on the receiving end of a child's self-sabotage is not a pleasant experience, and the natural human response is to take it personally. School leaders who ask staff to keep coming back from repeated rejection without added understanding are failing them because they are likely to believe it is their fault: the lesson wasn't interesting enough, they aren't liked, they aren't a good enough teacher.

But, ask yourself this question: when I am upset, angry, frustrated or scared, who do I tell? To whom do I show my feelings? Who sees me at my worst? The answer for many of us is a parent or partner – the person in our life who cares for us unconditionally and makes us feel safe enough to express our emotions. For some unlucky children that person doesn't exist at home; for some lucky children that person does exist at school. Seeing the worst of a child's behaviour because we make them feel safer than any other adult in their lives is a pretty backhanded compliment, but it is a very powerful reframing of the behaviour we will explore in Chapter 5. It may change how we feel about it.

I have always tried to combine the most important elements of the experiences I have had and the reading I have done in order to take educators to a place of improved understanding, which empowers them to provide unconditional love and care to their pupils. Empathy is about feeling *with*; although many of us will never be able to put ourselves in the shoes of our children, because our experiences are completely different, the more we can feel, the more we can understand. This book will examine what feelings are driving our pupils' behaviours with the aim of helping us to understand what experiences got them there.

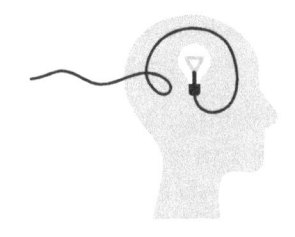

Chapter 2

# How we respond

> When the adults change, everything changes.
> **Paul Dix, *When the Adults Change, Everything Changes* (2017)**

Paul Dix's quotation about change conveys a powerful message. In the current education climate, a great deal of emphasis is placed on systems and policies, but ultimately it is how we respond to situations that matters. We have the power to make things worse or offer a short-term fix, or we can bring about positive, sustainable change.

Children will get it wrong, and we should expect them to do so. We all make mistakes, so where does the idea of zero tolerance come from? Why do we hold children to a higher standard of expectations than we hold for ourselves, and at a stage of development when they should be figuring things out? The simple answer comes back to the adult, and especially the adult's need to control.

It is entirely possible to display the same behaviour for entirely different reasons. I return frequently to the origins of challenging behaviour in this book (see especially Chapter 3). However, if we only see the behaviour, all the complexity and nuance behind the behaviour is ignored. For example:

- Child A might fly out of a classroom in a moment of impulse and smash the first window they see in a fit of rage.

- Child B might rip down displays and tear things to pieces because their stress bucket is overflowing.

- Child C might smash the teacher's laptop to get sent home and avoid the subject they don't want people to know they can't do.

These three children have all damaged property, but by treating them in exactly the same way we miss that child A clearly has difficulties with impulse control, that child B needs support to re-regulate themselves and that child C has adopted a reject-first survival style because they are scared of rejection. It stands to reason that without knowing what needs fixing, things will remain broken. Although the most important factor is still our unconditional care, identifying and targeting interventions early (based on our understanding of what drives the behaviour) is the most proactive response we can have. For example, punishing child A for an impulsive survival response over which they have no control or don't remember ignores the origin and tries to deter them, but how can you discourage a behaviour until the child has control over it?

These types of behaviours from some children are inevitable, partly due to matters beyond our control, like previous experiences or ongoing home difficulties, but also due to things we can control, like the classroom environment and our responses. Often, we don't recognise the importance of changing these details, and so the focus is on the action rather than the contributing causes. It is how we react to their behaviour that determines how we make that child feel. Our reactions can bring fear, anger and resentment or calmness, empathy and understanding. Our aim as educators should always be safe, calm and happy children because then we will have the best chance of engaging them in learning. I will keep reiterating this point throughout the book: happier children engage better, behave better and learn more effectively.

## Scared and angry children can't learn

Empathy is the master key that can unlock the most challenging of pupils. Whatever a child's adverse experiences – whether related to attachment, trauma, additional needs or something else – they will elicit involuntary feelings. If the experiences are negative, then the related feelings will be negative, and negative feelings drive negative behaviours.

If we meet refusal, rudeness and aggression with a punitive reaction, then we get conflict. This cycle of conflict often escalates. However, if we meet the negative behaviour with empathy, understanding and the offer of a resolution, then we contribute towards reducing or avoiding conflict. If we react this way consistently over time, we change the child's experiences, we promote fewer negative feelings and encourage better behavioural choices.

Do we want an approach focused on dealing with a negative surface behaviour, or do we want to change the experiences to result in more positive feelings that drive completely different behaviours? In short, do we want short-term solutions or long-term change?

## How do we practise empathy when we are being abused or facing aggression?

The simple way to cultivate empathy is by looking past the action and understanding where it has come from. As important as de-escalation is, it isn't enough – not if we want long-term change. If we really want to change a child's behaviour, then we have to change their experiences. This requires a relentless consistency of response that changes their beliefs. Schools in which one small team or individual is responsible for behaviour will never have the same impact as all the staff doing it. This is why behaviour systems that rely on pastoral teams end up supporting the same individuals over and over again; whilst some staff are working hard to change the child's experiences, others are compounding them. Having led pastoral teams for many years, I would often find myself being called to escalated situations and very distressed children, but it is too late for prevention work at this point. Being proactive around behaviour means doing early intervention before things escalate, and this can only be done by classroom practitioners.

Whilst being hugely popular, a lot of the backlash that Paul Dix (2017, ch. 4) has received has been about the suggestion that class teachers should 'pick up their own tab' – the idea that adults sending children out of class only undermines their own authority. The message this gives to the child is that the adult doesn't care enough to invest time in changing their behaviour, and therefore that they aren't worthy of that investment. The experience of adults not caring and feelings of low self-worth are unlikely to result in better behaviour. Of course, sometimes children do have to be withdrawn from classrooms, and the adult's intention may not be to pass on the behaviour buck to the pastoral team. However, this is about the child's perception, which may well be mistaken, so it is important to change it.

I don't want to imply that school systems aren't important, but they can be too prescriptive and reactive. I also have a huge amount of empathy for those classroom teachers (especially secondary) who have huge numbers of pupils and the pressures of academic successes. I fully recognise that different people have different roles and wear different hats, but the paramountcy principle applies to all of us. We must question each other as professionals (for example, an assistant head with a pastoral focus might have different ideas to an assistant head with a curriculum/attainment focus or an attendance officer), but when it comes to interactions with challenging pupils, we must agree on and be consistent in our responses. Is it really a surprise when secondary-age children run off from lessons or behave in a way that gets them sent out of the classroom when it means they get picked up by the pastoral team – the people with whom they feel safe, who listen to them and who they feel genuinely care about them? Again, this is not to suggest that class teachers don't care; this is about the child's perception. However, it makes sense that the same children will repeat the same behaviours if it gets them to the people with whom they want to be.

## The conflict spiral

My training background began and, in part, continues as a Team Teach tutor. The theory behind Team Teach has always centred around preventing children getting to the point of crisis or loss of control. Although there is a physical intervention/restraint element to the course, the intention is for that to be an action of last resort.

I have spent a lot of time analysing examples of children going into crisis and restraint gone wrong. The commonality is often an adult who felt out of control; an adult who, when the incident became extreme, didn't feel they had the skills to manage it. This panic is often sensed by the hyper-vigilant child who then escalates the situation, which often prompts the adult to make silly threats of disproportionate consequences. Combine this with a dysregulated child whom you could literally threaten with anything and they wouldn't care, and there really is only one direction for the incident to go.

If, on the other hand, the adult knows they can safely and effectively manage a situation that does reach crisis point, keeping themselves and the child safe, then usually the adult stays calm, staying in the part of the brain that allows for good executive functioning. In doing so, the adult can remember what is in the child's behaviour plan – that is, how to distract, how to regulate and how to calm. The child then responds to and mirrors this composure, and the escalation is averted. By feeling in control ourselves, we can pass that on to the child and the worst-case scenario need not occur.

Let's go back to the very beginning with an infant crying in a cot. An anxious baby's heart rate is around 150 beats per minute and an adult's is 70 beats per minute, but when a baby is picked up their heart rate tends to go down. It is the synchronisation that comforts and calms the child, a co-regulation that is vital during this developmental phase. In situations of potential crisis for young people, we must synchronise and co-regulate if we want to avoid real crisis.

The element of Team Teach theory that had the biggest impact on my practice was the conflict spiral (see Figure 1.1). Such is its importance to understanding and changing behaviour that I built much of my school outreach and other training on it. The simple idea is that children's experiences come from feelings; those feelings drive behaviours; and, depending on adult reactions, those behaviours can result in conflict. Meeting challenge with challenge is commonplace – part of our education system is about the need to show authority and assert discipline – but all too often staff hide behind policies and systems to justify little or no attempt at de-escalation, then blame and punish the child when a serious incident occurs.

Pause for thought: if we refer to the use of restraint in the most extreme circumstances as a last resort, can we still claim it is a last resort if no attempt is made to de-escalate?

Conflict

Reactions

Behaviours

Feelings

Experiences

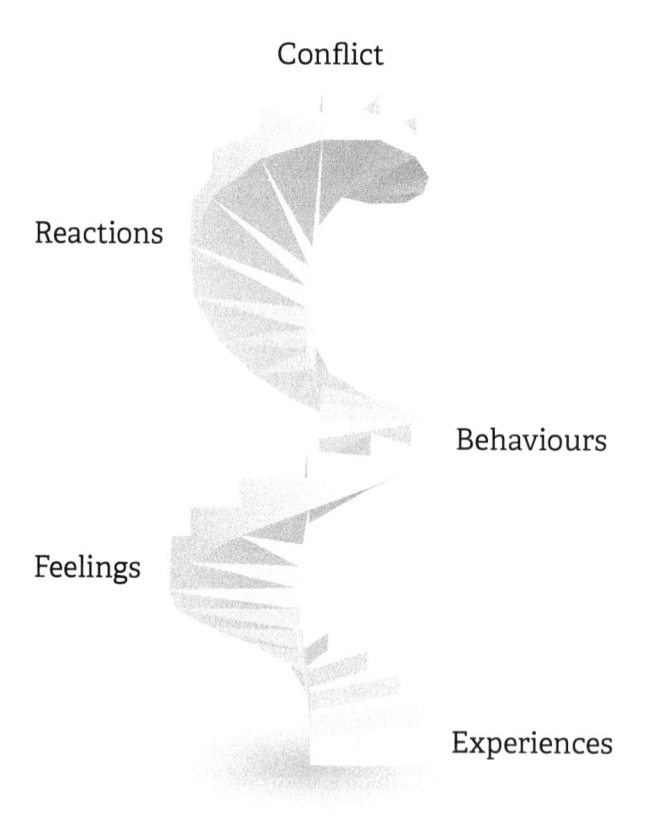

Figure 2.1. The conflict spiral

I often stand in front of a group of people when delivering training and show them a ball. I ask them a simple question: 'Who can catch?' At this point I look around the room. I see lots of confident-looking faces; the PE department are eyeballing me as well as a few who put on their trackies for the INSET day just on the off-chance this might happen.

I will ask a few of those eager individuals how they feel. They are happy to volunteer and confident they could catch the ball, usually because they have previous successful experiences of being in sports teams, of being picked first for teams and of being looked up to by others for their athletic skills. I have no doubt that these people would walk to the front buoyed by their self-confidence and sporting prowess.

Positive experiences = positive feeling = positive behaviour.

Then I try hard to engage with someone who is avoiding me, who has their head down or has shrunk into their chair. I ask them how they feel emotionally. Uncomfortable, anxious, panicked. I ask them how they feel physically. Hot, sweaty palms, nauseous, raised heart rate. Their experiences are of dropping the ball, of being picked last for teams, of being laughed at and humiliated by others. If they came up to the front with their clammy hands and over-arousal, there is a good chance they might drop the ball.

Negative experiences = negative feelings = negative behaviours.

The ball is a metaphor for so many other aspects of school life for our pupils: a certain subject, a teacher they don't like, unstructured time, social situations – the list goes on. Whatever it is, the child has encountered a negative experience, so whenever they are asked to repeat it they will feel anxiety, fear, frustration and other negative emotions. When anxiety and fear are involved and the amygdala perceives danger, children may be hijacked by their brainstem into a survival response; in fact, they may have no say whatsoever in the behaviour choice. This situation is likely to result in poor behaviour, which is when adults have a decision to make.

I would be one of the confident PE teachers in the group, a willing volunteer whose experience of everything sporty would make me feel I have nothing to fear. I might pick out that eager volunteer, throw the ball and let them catch it. Everything is great. Many children start their school experience with confidence, but what if they have a learning need that makes catching that metaphorical ball harder? Dyslexia, attention deficit hyperactivity disorder (ADHD) and auditory or visual processing disorders can all affect their ability to catch the ball.

Next, I might hand some vision-reducing glasses to my athletic volunteer, impeding their coordination. They are now less confident about catching the ball. I might throw it higher or faster or put my flip chart in-between us to reduce their reaction time. With each challenge, their confidence turns to anxiety and they worry that they might drop the ball.

Do they still want to be up there in front of the group being courageous but vulnerable? Probably not, because they are now facing a high probability of failure and humiliation.

I might up the stakes and switch the ball for an egg. It is harder to see and easier to drop. I might hinder them even further by asking them to put one hand behind their back. All of that confidence has now been replaced by self-doubt. I might ask a couple of other course members to come up and whisper in their ear: 'You know you're gonna drop it.' 'Why are you even trying?' 'Everyone is going to laugh when you fail.'

An adult on a training course might be able to cope with all of this, but it won't be pleasant. If we are being honest, how many of our pupils experience this daily? In reality, I would never do this on a course. As powerful as the optics would be, I am not in the practice of humiliating course members, but I will often talk them through it as a perspective-taking exercise.

Equally, we have to change those experiences and our reactions when a child makes a behavioural mistake.

## Firefighting

Many years ago, I had my own training experience delivered by the brilliant Dr Rob Long.[1] His two big mantras that have stuck with me like glue throughout my career are: 'Behavioural mistakes are learning opportunities' and 'Fight fire with water.' They are both simple but powerful, and central to everything I do. The problem, however, is that for whatever reason we don't always bring water. Sometimes, when facing the challenge of a roaring fire, we respond with fire of our own, but the only result will be a bigger fire.

---

1   You can find his blog at https://blog.transformbehaviour.co.uk.

## Escalation

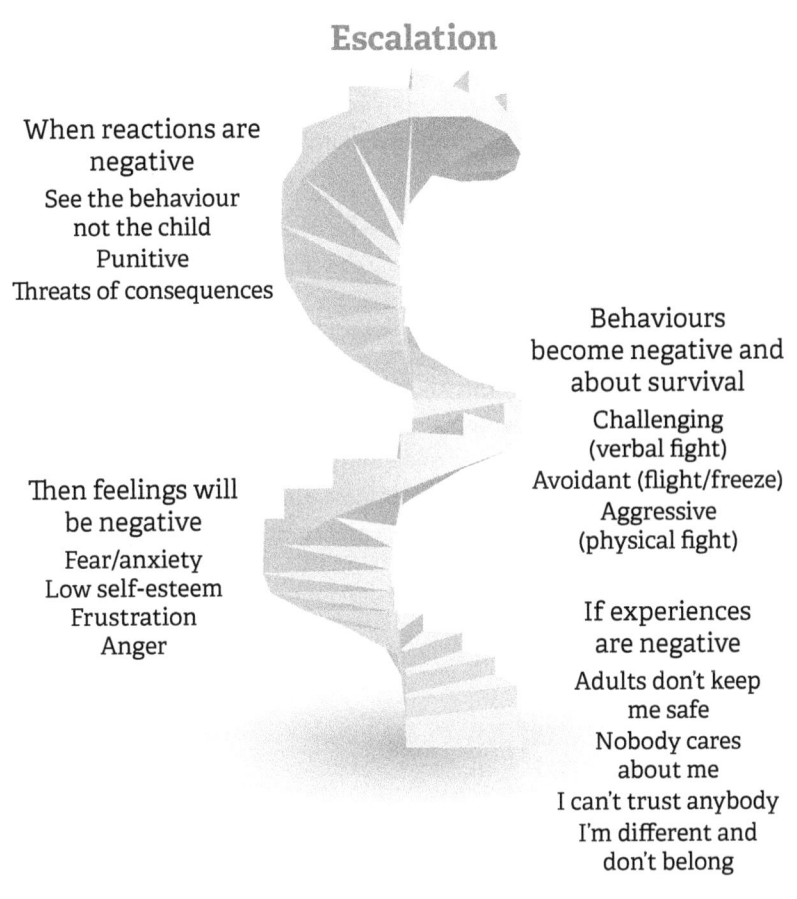

When reactions are negative
See the behaviour not the child
Punitive
Threats of consequences

Behaviours become negative and about survival
Challenging (verbal fight)
Avoidant (flight/freeze)
Aggressive (physical fight)

Then feelings will be negative
Fear/anxiety
Low self-esteem
Frustration
Anger

If experiences are negative
Adults don't keep me safe
Nobody cares about me
I can't trust anybody
I'm different and don't belong

Figure 2.2. Fighting fire with fire = bigger fire

## Putting the fire out

Our first priority should be to put the fire out. We may worry about why we have a fire, but we can investigate how it started later. Right now, at the point when it is out of control, damage limitation takes precedence. It is not always easy to do. Going against your instincts, maintaining self-control in the most challenging environment and making a judgement that might upset colleagues all make focusing on putting out the fire difficult.

However, it is the adults who hold the power. We have the tools to put it out: the water, the fire extinguisher or the wet blanket. The important thing to remember is that *you* are the decision-maker, as hard as this may be when you think people are judging you: 'What will other children think if I don't challenge this behaviour?' 'Will I look weak in front of colleagues?' 'Are parents going to complain that their child isn't being kept safe?' These are all secondary problems that will be dealt with afterwards.

If the best way to put out that fire is to take the child into the gym with a tennis ball, then that is what needs to be done. It isn't about rewarding bad behaviour, it is about re-regulating the child. It doesn't mean you are ignoring the behaviour or letting them get away with it; it just means that now isn't the time for issuing sanctions.

Effective de-escalation is about knowing what is best for the child, knowing what is on their behaviour plan (which should be a prevention tool for that child) and having the trust to deliver it. By identifying the distressed child and putting the fire out with calmness, empathy and understanding, we avoid the conflict altogether, or at least prevent it escalating.

## De-escalation

Positive reactions
Calm
Focused on regulation
Empathetic
Understanding

Negative behaviours
Challenging
Avoidant
Aggressive

Negative feelings
Fear
Low self-esteem
Frustration
Anger

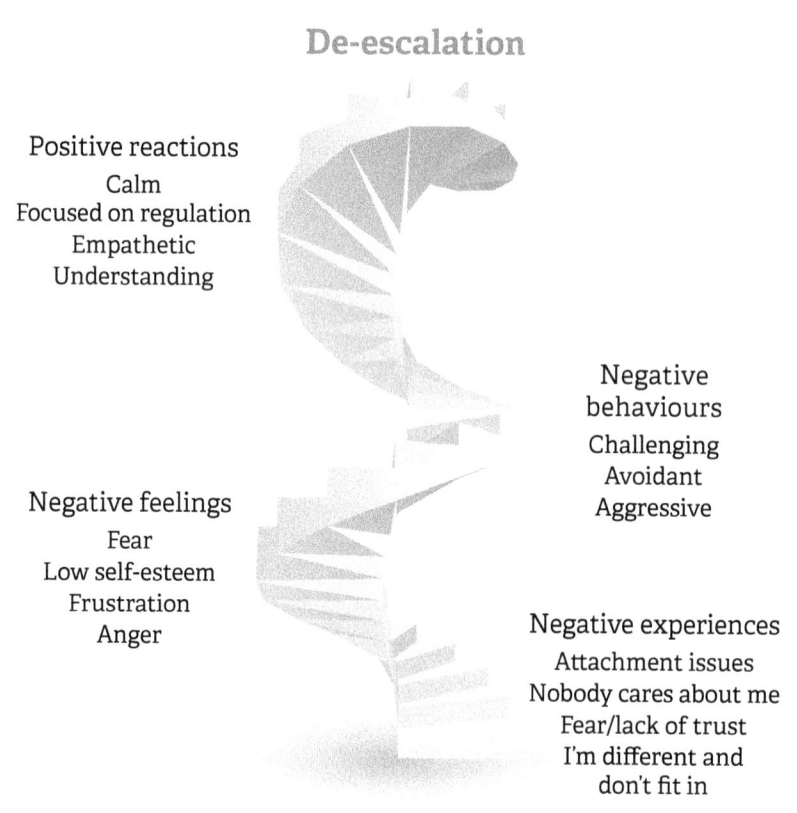

Negative experiences
Attachment issues
Nobody cares about me
Fear/lack of trust
I'm different and don't fit in

Figure 2.3. Fighting fire with water = puts the fire out

# Fire prevention

As important as de-escalation is, we still don't want to be in a position where we are constantly putting out fires. Most of the secondary settings I have worked in have had a brilliant team of firefighters who are doing a fantastic job of extinguishing fires. These are usually pastoral teams working with distressed pupils who have combusted somewhere in the building.

However, the best schools have a culture of fire prevention, which has been achieved by everybody reacting in the same way with a relentless consistency. This actually changes the child's experience: the empathy and understanding come with such regularity that we can re-conceptualise the conflict spiral.

We have the power to change a child's narrative and their perception of adults. If we replace reprimands and the threat of punitive consequences with empathy and understanding, then over time we replace experiences of fear and rejection with safety, trust and acceptance. We replace feelings of low self-esteem, frustration and anger with feelings of security and calmness. We replace defiant, challenging and aggressive behaviours with children who are more able to think, more likely to talk and more likely to remember strategies to manage their own behaviour.

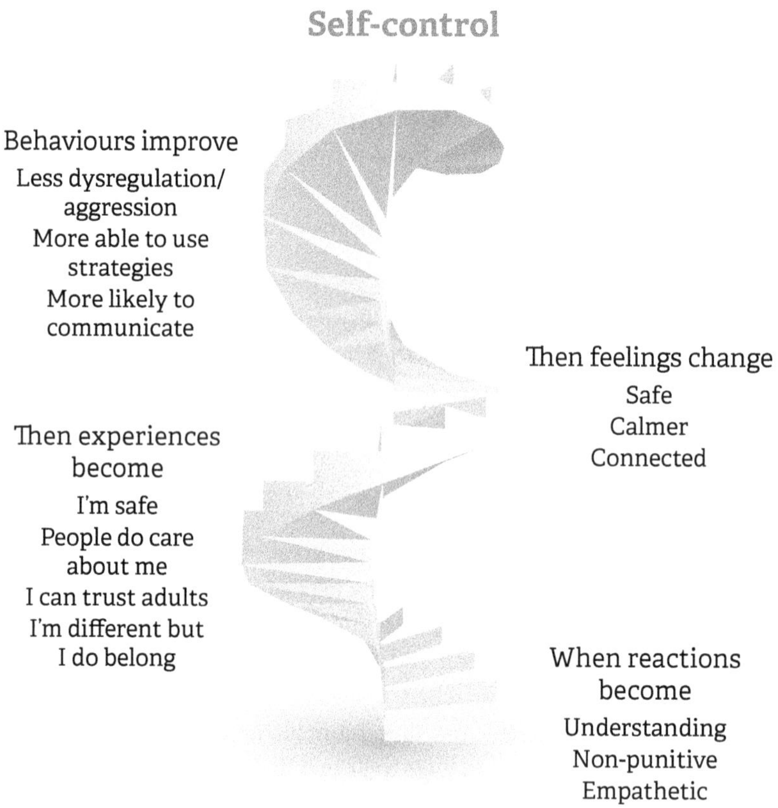

**Self-control**

Behaviours improve
Less dysregulation/
aggression
More able to use
strategies
More likely to
communicate

Then experiences
become
I'm safe
People do care
about me
I can trust adults
I'm different but
I do belong

Then feelings change
Safe
Calmer
Connected

When reactions
become
Understanding
Non-punitive
Empathetic

Figure 2.4. Keeping temperatures cool = fire never starts

Rob Long would walk into a room and ask, 'What do you fight fire with?' and everyone would say, 'Fire!' Then he would pause and ask, 'Why?'

## Recipe for avoiding conflict

Ingredients:

- Water
- Curiosity
- Calm

- Early intervention

Don't:

- Assume children are choosing to be naughty.
- Join their chaos.
- Focus on or wait for the disruptive behaviour.

Do:

- Be curious about the behaviour; not knowing the reason doesn't mean there isn't one.
- Synchronise the child to your body language. Tone, size, volume, tension and eye contact should all be the opposite of the child's in order to bring their chaos to match our calm, not join their chaos.
- Intervene early.
- Work to change experiences.

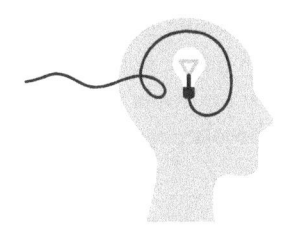

## Chapter 3

# The origins of behaviour

Many factors motivate the behaviour of staff and pupils, and often the elements that shape behaviour cannot be controlled by the school. We need to do our best to understand these factors and the impact they have, but we also need to be cautious about viewing behaviour through the lens of our own experiences. If we are going to have genuine empathy for others, it means putting ourselves into their shoes to the best of our ability.

How we believe other people perceive us plays a huge role in our decision-making because it affects how we feel, whether that is a small child making a decision based on what will best please an adult, a teenager swayed by what their peers will think or an adult trying to please their boss. Before we consider the motives and factors that contribute to children's behaviour, let's first look at adults.

# Adult motives

## Scenario 1

You are at home with your 3-year-old and they want chocolate for breakfast. It isn't Easter or Christmas Day so you say no and explain that they need to eat a proper breakfast. Your child responds with a tantrum. What do you do?

I am guessing that many of us would ignore the behaviour, let them get it out of their system and then have a normal breakfast. We would then talk to them later about how tantrums aren't the way to get what we want and why we don't eat chocolate for breakfast.

## Scenario 2

You are in the supermarket with the same child. They want a toy and you have to say no. They throw a tantrum and start knocking things off the shelves. What do you do this time? Is your response different? You could ignore the behaviour in the same way you do at home, but people are looking at you and expecting you to act (some are even muttering comments under their breath) and the shop staff look really annoyed.

With all this external pressure, you feel as if you have to do something:

- Tell the child off or tell them to stop. You know that more than likely it will make the behaviour worse, but at least other people will see that you are trying to do something.

- Escort the child out of the shop. At least you get away from other people's judgement and protect their dignity. You can then focus on calming the situation when you are outside.

- Give in and buy the toy. It undermines what you are trying to teach your child, but it stops the behaviour and stops the judgemental looks.

You may feel like trying to negotiate with your child, but if you have ever experienced a 3-year-old throwing a tantrum, then you will know that it is best not to negotiate with terrorists. For this approach to be really effective, it has to come *before* the shopping trip when you are in a better position to communicate. This is because rational communication requires rational thought – something you don't usually find in a distressed and emotionally overwhelmed child. When dealing with the parts of the brain responsible for controlling emotions, we are unlikely to be able to communicate verbally. We may be able to communicate non-verbally and use our own calm to synchronise the child to us. However, we would need to be extremely regulated ourselves, which is difficult (but not impossible) if the situation feels out of control and the audience disapproving.

The likelihood is that if the supermarket were empty then you would wait for the tantrum to finish, in the same way you would at home. You do this because you know from experience that it is the best strategy for the child and that achieving calm is your priority. *It is an action taken to support the child.* Without the external judgement, the adult feels in control, is thinking rationally and can keep in mind what the best plan is for the child.

Telling them to stop, shouting or threatening consequences aren't best for the child. These are acts designed to appease onlookers and to make you feel like you are taking action. *It is an action taken to appease others, which is in the best interests of the adult.* Alternatively, the pressure from others may have caused the adult to feel dysregulated, such that they can't remember the best plan for the child. Adults have the same feelings as children, so, likewise, an overwhelmed adult needs to be supported rather than shamed and blamed. (We will explore the dangers of blame culture and parent shaming in Chapter 11.)

Many of us will have had the experience of physically escorting a child out of a shop, such is the pressure to get away from the condemnatory glances. This inconveniences you and doesn't help to change the child's behaviour, but avoidance is better than how you felt in the shop. *It is an action taken to avoid your own feelings of failure and loss of control.* It also gives you an opportunity to protect the dignity of yourself and the child.

Giving in is a short-term solution, but it actually reinforces the negative behaviour. Done regularly, it is likely to lead to similar situations in the future and it is easy to get into a cycle. *It is a quick fix.*

When we find ourselves in a situation like this, it is vital that we accept where we are and respond accordingly. Not challenging the tantrum in the moment does not mean letting the child get away with it. Far from it. It means that we address the behaviour when the child is calm and we have more rational thought. Too often, we try to manage a child's behaviour at a time when they are defensive and we inadvertently escalate it. The influence of others also plays a role.

## Scenario 3

Now switch the 3-year-old having a tantrum for a 13-year-old answering back in class. You know that the best thing to do is ignore it and deal with them individually later, but you worry: 'What if the other children think I'm condoning it? They will all start answering back too.' 'What if those children go home and tell their parents, and then the parents complain that I've got no control?' 'What if a senior leader walks in and witnesses it and I look weak?'

These are valid points, but the child should have a behaviour plan that has been agreed by the senior leadership team, and that plan should say not to challenge publicly and to revisit later when calm. What others think isn't the priority; supporting the child is. All too often, situations deteriorate because we choose a response that benefits others and not the child. If this is the case, we can't blame the child when they react badly to the wrong strategy. This is a very difficult balancing act, but it is a vital element in the equitable classroom. If we want all children to succeed, some children will need more time.

What other teachers, pupils or parents think isn't important because the child is in your care. If you want to explain your actions to staff and parents then do so, but the decision is yours. Children are supportive of different responses to different pupils, but it is important for them to be communicated. Children shouldn't need to see a behaviour being dealt with publicly; they just need to know that it has been. Consistency doesn't have to mean that all behaviours have the same consequence, but it does mean that the children know something will happen.

There may be times when you have no choice but to prioritise other children or staff – for example, if a child is behaving in an aggressive or dangerous manner. You may be hamstrung by policy and have no option but to follow the system. Acting with others in mind is not necessarily the wrong thing to do, but accept that it won't change the behaviour. Exclusion, blanket sanctions and shaming are designed to be a deterrent to the child and a warning to others. They train conformity rather than teaching behaviour and are generic rather than individualised. They are designed to benefit others, not the individual, which is why they are ineffective for many children.

If the behaviour is unforeseen, then we will have to think expeditiously about how the situation is going to be managed. However, if children repeat behaviours, and there isn't an individual plan in place for that child, then there is a failure in the system. Questions will need to be asked of the school about why we are still reacting to behaviour we know is likely, and why we aren't developing a plan to prevent it.

## Child motives

It is easy to see the surface behaviour and focus on it only. When we take this approach to managing behaviour, rather than teaching it, we are dismissing the possibility that there might be an underlying cause. The result is that we are unlikely to change our own approach and instead place blame on the child's choices. If something isn't working, why would we think that continuing to do the same thing would give different results? We change teaching methods when children don't understand something, so why is behaviour any different?

A one-size-fits-all approach to behaviour marginalises and discriminates against certain children; you only have to look at the exclusion figures for proof of that. There seems to be an acceptance that a percentage of children will fail mainstream education. Of course, there are lots of ways to manage these children, including pastoral teams, inclusion areas, designated provision, managed moves and off-site provision. Many of those supporting these children are doing brilliant work, but often it isn't what it is supposed to be, which is inclusive work with a goal of reintegration once they have been supported.

There will always be pupils who need a more specialist setting, but that should be about learning needs, not behaviour. We have to make reasonable adjustments to the school environment for children with special educational needs and disabilities (SEND) who are struggling with learning, yet we don't seem to make reasonable adjustments to our behaviour policies for children struggling with behavioural problems. We don't blame a child with a disability for their difficulties, so why do we blame children with behavioural issues? Why do we assume that a child has behaved negatively for no reason when we haven't attempted to discover the reason?

I often hear staff say that they do make reasonable adjustments once a SEND diagnosis has been made. However, if we bear in mind that many of those conditions take a long time to be diagnosed, we need to consider how much avoidable damage, failure and shame that child experiences during this period. When we are reactive, it is very easy to wait for an education, health and care plan (EHCP) to be told what adjustments to make and to believe that additional funding or staffing are the answer. In this way, we delay making reasonable adjustments, by which point we have likely had lots of failure and fed into the child's sense of shame and low self-esteem.

These preventable negative experiences are only going to make our jobs harder down the line. As skilled educators, we should be attuned to the needs of our pupils. We don't need an external professional to tell us to change an environment. We can be proactive about it. After all, we made the referral in the first place because we identified a difficulty. Of course, most educators won't wait to be told what to do, but they may need help and ideas in order to be proactive.

As we progress through the book, we will look at a multitude of behaviours and their potential causes, but the starting point must be their motive and origin. I believe there are three types of motive for challenging behaviour:

1. Uncontrolled – driven by fear.

2. Overwhelmed – driven by losing control.

3. Masked – driven by long-term survival.

Each is present in every school, and probably in every class.

Taking ourselves out of schools and into the real world for a moment, specifically the judicial system, the idea of not taking motive into account for a wrongdoing would be utterly ludicrous. Giving the same sentence to someone who has assaulted another person in self-defence as someone who has committed a premeditated attack would not happen. The intention outweighs the action, and that motive is heavily sought after by those trying to decide the consequence. Mental capacity also plays a huge part in the outcome. Although some will only have eyes for punishment, many see value in rehabilitation and therapy. Historical experiences are considered and mental health assessments are made.

Why, then, is that intention not given anywhere near the same level of importance in many schools? Why do so many of our school systems ignore what drove the behaviour and assign the same outcome regardless of origin? Is it because of time constraints? Skill sets? Willingness? I understand that investigating every incident takes time, but if the same child keeps making the same behavioural mistakes over and over again, then we spend hours and hours on punitive consequences that aren't working. Surely, it is a better investment to spend an hour investigating rather than an hour punishing? In the long run, once the root cause has been identified and the child given more skills, we potentially save huge amounts of time and reduce disruption in lessons.

If the problem is staff skill sets, then this can be rectified by training. I have already mentioned some of the other positive pay-offs. If it is a lack of willingness, or a determination to live and die by the policy, or a choice to blame the child, then we must accept the fact that the school tolerates a percentage of their pupils failing. That may be acceptable for the Department for Education and even some school leaders, but I know of a great number who don't want to tolerate pupil failure. Those school leaders believe that every child matters, and if every child matters then understanding *why* they struggle to behave matters. To effectively do that we need to understand its origins (see Figure 3.1).

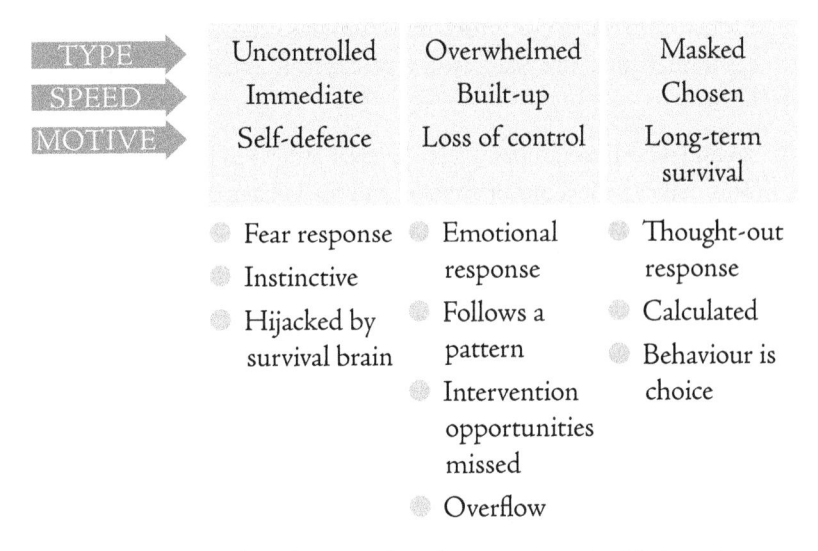

| TYPE | Uncontrolled | Overwhelmed | Masked |
|---|---|---|---|
| SPEED | Immediate | Built-up | Chosen |
| MOTIVE | Self-defence | Loss of control | Long-term survival |

- Fear response
- Instinctive
- Hijacked by survival brain

- Emotional response
- Follows a pattern
- Intervention opportunities missed
- Overflow

- Thought-out response
- Calculated
- Behaviour is choice

If we focus on the *what*, not the *why*, we miss valuable learning opportunities and risk making their behaviour worse

Figure 3.1. Motive – where does behaviour come from?

I believe that when we prioritise motive or origin, we can better understand our pupils. If we understand where the behaviour originates, we can help to change it. How we feel about it also changes – something that even the best classroom actors can't fake and something the hypervigilant child will always pick up on.

When we work with a child afterwards to analyse their behaviour, we are trying to identify whether the root of the child's response was uncontrolled aggression, overwhelmed aggression or a long-term survival strategy/mask.

## Uncontrolled aggression

Uncontrolled aggression is an action decided by the brainstem in a microsecond. It is triggered by fear and is beyond the child's control. What the brain chooses as a response will often result in different adult reactions, even though the pupil in front of us is not the rational child we know.

- A child who freezes or refuses to respond is often deemed to be ignorant, rude or avoidant, so we persistently encourage them to answer.

- A child who hides under a desk is often judged to be disruptive. This makes us feel out of control, and the behaviour is met with an attempt to extricate them from under the table.

- A child who engages in a verbal fight response can be seen as rude or disruptive. It is a natural human response to meet verbal challenge with a verbal challenge of our own, especially when many of us have been trained from our own childhood that talking back is unacceptable and must be challenged.

- A child who responds with physical aggression will often be met with rejection. Physical aggression is the most common reason for permanent exclusion in primary settings and the second most common cause in secondary schools.[1]

---

[1] See https://explore-education-statistics.service.gov.uk/find-statistics/permanent-and-fixed-period-exclusions-in-england.

By working with the child after the event, we can prepare ourselves better for next time and feel differently about their behaviour. If we know there was no intent or control, it isn't right to treat the child as if there was. And, beyond this, it isn't right to make long-term decisions about that child based on their dysregulated actions.

The alternative is to ignore the motive and just respond to the wrongdoing with whatever sanction the school policy prescribes. However, taking any kind of punitive approach in this circumstance is unlikely to change the behaviour if the response is driven by the child's survival instincts. You can't deter a child's brainstem, which isn't interested in good order or learning. It is designed for one purpose, and that is to keep us alive. Threat isn't categorised into high, medium or low. There isn't time to wait and analyse; there is just a survival response. If a fight/flight/freeze response, especially fight, is driving the behaviour, then the only way to prevent it is by making the child feel safe. This is not achieved by being reactive. Just because we, as adults, don't view a situation as life-threatening does not mean we speak for the child.

We also have to be aware that if we challenge any of those limited responses, then we will encourage another one. If we keep asking the child to answer a question when they have frozen, then we take their freeze response from them. If we keep trying to get them out from under the table, then we take their flight from them. If we aren't scared away by their verbal aggression and meet it with our own verbal challenge, then we leave them with only one response, physical fight, which our behaviour policy states must be sanctioned strongly. But we have left the child with no other choice.

For many school staff, the counter-argument for a more punitive approach is that it isn't about deterring one child, it is about the other 29. It is about the victim(s), not the perpetrator. Therefore, the punishment may be designed to dissuade others, to make staff feel supported or even to appease parents. If these factors have motivated the school's response, especially in instances like serious assault where we must prioritise the well-being of those who have been harmed, there may well be an argument for them being necessary.

However, there isn't an argument that punitive responses are effective at changing behaviour. If the action taken by adults isn't to benefit the needs of the young person, then it won't impact on their behaviour. Temporary or even permanent exclusion may be used to protect other pupils, but it won't improve behaviour; in fact, the rejection and shame are likely to make it worse. To change the behaviour, we must keep the individual child in mind – we must make them feel safer and use consequences that teach them about the behaviour. It is important to do both, of course, but if we offer neither, then we can't be surprised when the same behaviour keeps being repeated.

## Overwhelmed aggression

The build-up of negative emotions may eventually overwhelm the child and result in an aggressive act. Opportunities to regulate were missed and the child ends up losing control.

We have all been there. We start the day a little stressed and worried, a few incidents occur that we find frustrating; things that we would normally manage make us angry and we lose our temper over something trivial. Despite leading a pretty stressful existence, I have lost my temper once. I don't even remember the reason, but constructing a flat-pack wardrobe when already edgy clearly doesn't work for me. I became more and more agitated with the door hinges until I finally snapped and launched the door across the room, taking a rather large chunk out of the plaster as it landed. My wife had the choice of having a go about the damage and demanding I fix it or showing concern and checking that I was okay.

If you see something like this happen with a colleague at work, is your instinct to criticise them or to find out if they are alright? I think it would be the latter, but I am not convinced we do the same for the children. Whether it is a pen thrown onto the floor or a chair knocked over, why is our first instinct to challenge the action or make them pick it up? Why does the same scenario elicit empathy when it is an adult, but not when it is a child? I believe it is because with adults we see the distress, but with children we see the behaviour/non-conformity. With adults we have concern for an equal, but with children we want to impose our authority and make them conform. (We will explore this further in Chapter 5.)

For most of us, as adults who have learned to self-regulate, we don't get to the point of losing control. We see the pressure building and take a break or undertake an activity that regulates us and gets us back on track. We do this because we were taught how to do it or we have learned how to do it. Normally, I would have left that wardrobe and gone for a walk. The sooner we regulate, the easier and quicker it is to return to calm. If we hadn't been taught to self-regulate, then we probably would have been much less successful adults. Yet, many children haven't been taught this skill. They don't recognise what is happening to them and their bodies, and they don't know how to change the outcome. It is easy to bemoan this fact – it is a great opportunity for parent-bashing – but it changes little.

The media are big fans of the term 'school ready' (a topic discussed in length in Chapter 11): children can't use a knife and fork, they aren't toilet trained, their reading levels are lower than they should be. Of course, these things are important, but why is there no mention of children who can't self-soothe? Children who don't understand escalating levels of stress and who don't know how to make themselves feel calmer are equally ill-equipped for the school environment. The truth is that we can moan all we want, but the moaning won't take away the need to teach these skills to children and give them a chance at being successful. We don't teach skills by waiting for the outcome; we teach them by looking at the journey. We must identify where the child is on the path to anger and aggression and do something to help them regulate. Recognising when a child is becoming more distressed means we can prevent the overwhelming outburst. If we do this with enough relentless consistency, then we can teach them to do it for themselves.

Some schools in the United States, influenced by Lori Desautels, the author of *Connections Over Compliance* (2020), are not only teaching children how to understand the brain and self-regulation, but they are also making understanding the brain part of the curriculum. Children are taught about what is happening in their amygdala (the brain's centre for stress responses) and also that they have a special personalised toolkit of what is needed to quieten it down. For us, as staff, there is huge benefit in knowing when a situation is escalating and what to use to calm the child. Now imagine a range of short pupil-led interventions which don't require staff involvement: a sensory toy, some colouring in, going for a walk, asking to talk, a quiet space.

If the argument is 'What about the other 29?' then the solution is not to remove the dysregulated child from the classroom; rather, it is to ensure that all the children are regulated and to empower them to do so. Bessel Van Der Kolk, author of *The Body Keeps the Score* (2019), describes the amygdala as the brain's smoke detector. When a smoke detector goes off we can flee the building or calmly check for other signs of fire. If we don't want children fleeing immediately, then we must give them the tools to remain calm and assess whether the fire is real. In this way, we can prevent those overwhelmed responses.

If we ignore the child's feelings, do nothing and wait for the behaviour to unfold, then we fail the child. We will have missed multiple learning opportunities. A punitive action that does not link to the child's feelings is ineffective because the child doesn't recognise the link between the feeling and the behaviour, and the action doesn't teach them how to prevent the same outcome from recurring. I don't know how to play the guitar, for example. You can punish me all you want for not playing it, but nothing will change unless someone teaches me how to play it.

## Long-term survival/mask

An action that results from a long-term survival strategy may appear to be premeditated or chosen. The child has had the opportunity to calm down but still behaves negatively.

There is absolutely no doubt that this behaviour is the hardest one for educators to deal with, and therefore it is no surprise that within secondary schools 'persistent disruptive behaviour' is the most common reason for permanent exclusion.[2]

Seeing a child lose control, as with uncontrolled and overwhelmed aggression, is difficult and often ends in a similar outcome. Frequently, the conclusion is that the school can't meet the need and more specialist support is required. 'It's nobody's fault' is the attitude towards the failure. However, a child who adopts a mask or persona, who avoids or disrupts in order to survive, doesn't get that luxury. It will be their fault for choosing to behave in such a fashion.

---

2   See https://explore-education-statistics.service.gov.uk/find-statistics/permanent-and-fixed-period-exclusions-in-england.

Disrupting lessons, answering back, refusing requests and so on are chosen behaviours, right? Adults regularly decide that the child wasn't in crisis or under threat; they just didn't want to do something. But, as before, how does this compare with how we respond to adults, especially if we care about them and their well-being?

- A friend goes on a string of failed promotion interviews and it is really getting them down. What do we do? Often, we advise that they take a break.

- A family member has a series of really bad dates and it is affecting their mental health. What do we advise? Often, it is to get off Tinder and give dating a break.

- You can't seem to build a good rapport with your personal trainer. What do you do? Often, it would be to change to another trainer or to give the gym a rest for a bit.

These are our adult survival strategies: perfectly acceptable and commonly recommended by others. We change, we avoid or we take a break because we fear failure, because we feel overwhelmed or humiliated or because it is damaging our self-esteem or confidence.

Avoidance for adults is acceptable. Avoidance for adults is a good thing. Avoidance for adults is self-care. So, why is avoidance viewed as unacceptable and a form of defiance for children? Why don't we allow children to have opportunities to protect themselves from the same feelings and make avoidance an option?

As I mentioned, I have never been taught how to play the guitar, but if I am punished for failing at it, I can't see myself wanting to pick up the instrument. Just as with the catching-the-ball scenario described earlier, that guitar could be certain topics, social situations, unstructured time or relationships. It is perfectly logical to want to avoid them, but children aren't allowed to do so. Therefore, finding a strategy to get removed from the classroom is the next best thing.

In my experience, work avoidance has little to do with not wanting to do something and everything to do with the fear of falling short. Getting sent out, and therefore facing a consequence, pales in comparison to feeling like a failure or the fear of failure itself. Our response to the behaviour is very different if we perceive it in this way. If we approach a child in the same way we would approach an adult, we respond differently and are likely to get a different result.

Some of you may be asking, 'What if they are just playing up to their mates?' It is a fair question – it happens. The point in adolescence when what peers think is suddenly more important than what adults think is very real; looking stupid in front of their friends is to be avoided at all costs. So, we can now add to a fear of failure a fear of rejection and humiliation too. Avoidance becomes even more appealing than it was before.

Another issue that comes up is what to do about children who bully. Again, it is a fair question – there are children who target others. There are many reasons for this, none of which are because they are a 'bad kid' – for example:

- Pushing others' buttons may well cause those children to misbehave, thereby triggering the disruption required, whilst also avoiding the consequences for having been the disruptor.
- Believing that you can make yourself and others feel better by making others feel worse is a common belief held by many children.
- Some children have very little control in their lives outside school and look for things they can control within it. In some cases, this may be their own behaviour, but for others it may be other children's behaviour. Manipulation may be the only time they feel any control.
- The fear of rejection has one simple solution: reject first, then sabotage and control the way events unfold.

For me, avoidant, attention-seeking and bullying behaviours are all just survival strategies. They aren't good ones and they shouldn't be ignored. They aren't excuses either, but they are explanations. Blaming the child and implying that they are choosing to be naughty shows a lack of understanding.

If we want to change behaviour, we have to identify its origin first:

- If the origin is in the brainstem and driven by feeling unsafe, then we must prioritise an environment that makes the child feel safe. Feeling safe is very different to being safe. Whilst the environment is well safeguarded and there is no physical threat, the fear of rejection, failure and humiliation may well be present.

- If the origin is in the emotional/limbic brain and driven by feeling overwhelmed and dysregulated, then we must prioritise regulating the young person early so they can manage those feelings.
- If the origin is a long-term survival strategy chosen over time to combat consistent threats or avoiding the negative feelings that result, then we must structure our approaches to focus on safety, trust, regulation and belonging. In that order and with relentless consistency to change that young person's belief systems.

Why would a young person who has only experienced failure ever forecast success? Asking that child to make themselves vulnerable and take risks without believing they can be successful will only persuade them to avoid putting themselves out there, and poor behaviour can be a very effective way to avoid. If we want to improve poor behaviour, we have to build from the bottom up. We can't expect children to run if we have never taught them to walk.

## Recipe for understanding the origins of challenging behaviour

Ingredients:

- Safety
- An open mind
- Curiosity
- Trust
- Calm

Don't:

- Let external factors sway our approach.
- Try to address behaviour whilst a child is dysregulated.

- See a deliberate rule-breaker.
- Take behaviour personally.

Do:
- Focus on regulation first.
- Make a plan for children who repeat behaviours.
- See a distressed child.
- Work to understand the origin.

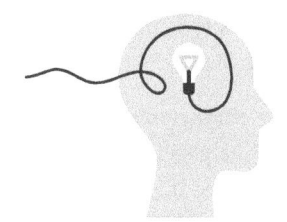

## Chapter 4

# Short-term survival responses

In the previous chapter, we looked at uncontrolled aggression – a short-term, inconsequential and instantaneous response to threat – but we also touched on the fact that those responses don't always result in aggression.

During training sessions, I often put images up on a screen. The first is of a crying child, the second is a child verbally abusing with the assistance of a finger gesture, the third is a child hiding under a desk and the fourth is a child being physically aggressive. The question I put to the group is, what is the difference?

Obviously, the behaviours are dissimilar and how we feel about them probably varies too. The problem is that if we react to the behaviour in front of us based on our instinctive feelings or even the school's behaviour policy, then we will miss a very important point – which is that the difference between the child's experiences and feelings is likely very little. It is what they present on the surface that is different.

Although the behaviours are dissimilar, the experiences and feelings that elicit them are probably similar – primarily fear. And not a gradual feeling like fear of failure or rejection but an instant, debilitating, life-or-death type of fear. The fear that kicks in during survival mode and prompts a fight, flight or freeze response over which the child has no control. It doesn't matter to us, as the adult, whether we think the fear is justified, whether we think it is earth-shattering or whether it is simply frustrating, challenging or disruptive. Our perceptions don't matter.

What we need to understand is that the threat is very real to the child and they are no longer in control.

As discussed in the previous chapter, we should have one aim: to make the child feel safe. We are unlikely to understand their behaviour unless we have had the same experiences. It is very difficult to perception-take in any situation, but it is even harder in situations like these. But empathy isn't about having the same feelings as the child; it is about being willing to be present and learn. Our priority is to help the child regulate themselves back into a state of self-control.

## Feelings versus behaviours

It can be very tempting to ignore the child's feelings in favour of responding to their behaviour, and to respond by punishing that behaviour or to lump the feelings and behaviours together. However, feelings aren't bad and shouldn't be punished; they need to be validated. It is okay to feel a certain way, but it isn't okay to behave poorly as a consequence.

If the feeling and behaviours aren't separated, then we will inevitably end up in a cycle of shame. If poor behaviour has been the result, driven by negative feelings, then it absolutely needs to be repaired, but to punish a child for something that is out of their control is confirmation that they are bad or an encouragement to suppress their feelings. This can be very dangerous, and is something we will come back to in later chapters. If a child thinks that feeling angry, scared or frustrated is bad, then they will believe that they feel angry, scared or frustrated *because* they are bad. I'm bad – I feel bad – I behave badly – I'm punished – repeat. We need to change the child's view of themselves, not perpetuate it through punishment. If the feeling that drives the behaviour is fear, then we must respond with the antidote to fear – safety.

There is little doubt that changing the child's beliefs about themselves is one of the hardest things we will ever do as educators. Not just because it is often in opposition to school behaviour policies, which are usually outcome based, but more importantly because we need to be in complete control (which isn't easy when faced with an aggressive pupil who has lost control) and because we must overcome our own natural instincts.

It is very easy for me to sit here and write about bringing the water, foam or blanket needed to put out a child's fire, but what of our own fight, flight or freeze responses? All I can say is that I have been there on more occasions than I can count; sometimes I have got it right and sometimes I have got it wrong. However, the more I understood about the child's experiences and the better my understanding of what was driving them, the more likely I was to see a child in crisis rather than a child breaking the rules. My natural instinct to get the child to conform or to respond to their behaviour was overtaken by an instinct to create calm. The more we can recognise uncontrolled behaviour, the easier it becomes to bring the water. The more attuned we are to a child's dysregulation, the easier it is to co-regulate – but that dysregulation comes in many forms.

## Crying

The child may not react with a survival-driven response. Instead, it may be an emotional or limbic response: the child may sob. When we are confronted with a child who is upset or overwhelmed, our instinct is to comfort them with an arm around the shoulder and some pastoral support because we perceive no threat to ourselves or our authority. We talk to the child, investigate what has caused their distress and gain context. Our intention is to support. This ought to be our reaction regardless of what the brain chooses in that first millisecond, but often it is not.

## Hiding

It may be that a child freezes on us. They refuse to answer our questions, silently hoping we will go away or they won't be seen. This is a very natural response to fear. As we saw in Chapter 3, we often advise our friends or colleagues to take a break when things become overwhelming. It doesn't matter how it is phrased, as adults, we regularly practise avoidance as self-protection. If it is accepted and even encouraged in our adult lives, then surely it is okay for children too?

In a school environment, however, this common adult behaviour of avoidance is seen as rude, work-avoidant, disrespectful or unacceptable. Children who can't just leave like an adult might have to find another way, and their escape might be to shut down, avoid eye contact or even hide away.

Treating basic survival strategies as disobedient or defiant often means that we perceive a child's freeze/flight as misbehaviour. Again, we can see that our response to poor behaviour is different to that of distressed behaviour. What we must realise, though, is that out of the three Fs, the freeze response is the least disruptive and the safest for us. If we take away this response from the child's already limited tool box, then they are left with only fight or flight.

The child may take their freeze a step further and combine it with flight. When a child hides under a desk, we may see it as defiance or avoidance. Typically, we are frustrated and our instinct is to get them out as soon as possible. When this doesn't happen we feel out of control. The behaviour dysregulates us, and we start to worry about the impression we are making on others. Often, the disruption caused to the rest of the class takes priority over the distressed child.

Children hide when they are scared; for some children, it is the only thing they can do in an unsafe home environment. Coercing them is not going to remove that fear. If we want them to come out, we have to make them feel safe enough to do so. The question we have to ask ourselves at this point is, do we want them to come out because we have told them to or because they have chosen to do so? That is, is the priority conformity or feeling safe? Just because we deem the environment to be physically safe, that doesn't mean it is emotionally safe.

> Creating a safe environment is not the same as making a child feel safe.
>
> **Mark Finnis**, *Teacher Hug Radio* **(2019)**

A lot depends on what we see when a pupil hides under a table. If we see a frightened child, our instinct is likely to help them feel safe. However, we also need to find out why the child felt the need to hide in the first place.

I have often heard adults say things like, 'I only asked them to write the date – what's scary about that?' They are right to a degree. It isn't sufficiently alarming to warrant hiding under a table if you categorise it against other threats that might cause physical harm. This statement is shrouded in assumptions, however, the biggest of which is the false conjecture that the survival brain categorises threat.

The response will be hardwired by the child's experiences. If they have grown up in an aggressive household, for example, not only has hiding become their built-in survival response, but probably it has been encouraged by other family members. If this process has been repeated enough during fundamental developmental stages, then the reaction will be instinctive, whatever the threat. It may seem disproportionate to us, but the pen might mean writing, and writing means potential fear of failure, and fear triggers the go-to survival response – and the next thing you know they are under the table.

Getting the child out from under the table is the opposite of creating safety, so if we aren't going to do that, what are our options?

- **Treat it like a time-out.** Check in with the child and then give them some take-up time to come out. Make them feel safe and seen and then continue with the rest of the class.

- **Get someone to join them.** Obviously, this will depend on whether you have a teaching assistant available, but a lot of safety-building can be done under that table which may prevent the behaviour from recurring in the future.

- **Remove the other children.** If there is someone who can stay with the pupil, you could take the other children elsewhere to protect the child's dignity.

- **Create a safe hiding space.** It takes time to change behaviour, so rather than it taking place in class and in front of an audience, creating a place the child can fly to is a simple and effective way to control the risk. I have seen everything from tents and tables in hallways with blankets over them to sensory rooms.

Obviously, we need find out the reason for the behaviour, but we also need to consider how much disruption is caused by a child hiding under a table compared to taking away their freeze and flight responses. If we provoke fight instead, it will almost certainly cause major disruption, damage to relationships and require more staff resources.

# Verbal abuse

Being on the receiving end of verbal abuse from a child is a challenge. Our perfectly natural emotion is often outrage, and our perfectly natural instinct is to challenge back – to fight fire with fire. If we remain calm, we can avoid worsening the situation, but we still have a child who has been rude and disrespectful and broken the school rules.

We must decide what is more important in the moment: the message we give to the child or what we communicate to the other children? Do we exert our authority to show the class that verbal abuse won't be tolerated, or do we recognise that the child is distressed and prioritise their needs with calmness and co-regulation? Can we do both?

Timing is key. The brain has said fight: the child you know, and any rational thought, is likely no longer present. Any attempt to show authority or threaten them with consequences will be further evidence of danger and will escalate the situation. The priority is therefore to calm the situation and to wait and decide if a consequence is needed afterwards. As mentioned earlier, this often comes in the form of a punitive sanction, in line with the school's behaviour policy, even though the child may have had no control over their response. Children will often accept this when they are calm, and the other children get the deterrent needed to prevent them from behaving in such a way.

However, for the child who presents with a verbal fight response, the punishment will do nothing to reduce the fear that caused their behaviour in the first place, and it will almost certainly add to their feelings of shame. So, if the punishment isn't going to change the behaviour, is it the best course of action? In my experience, a verbally abusive child who is met with composure and support will often feel guilty about their behaviour and will want to make amends. Do we really lose face as adults if we accept an apology or reparation and move on? Must the other children witness a punishment in order to know that this behaviour is unacceptable? The co-regulation that has taken place in this instance will build trust and safety, which will do far more to prevent the behaviour than a sanction.

Once again, it is important to relate this situation to adults. I imagine that most people reading this have had a row with another adult either as victim, instigator or both, and unless one party brings it to a close then the quarrel will continue. I drive my wife bonkers because I won't fuel her anger by yelling back during these disagreements. What might feel better in the moment – when we are driven by fear, adrenaline or anger – doesn't help if it harms relationships. If we can avoid fuelling the fire and saying things we may regret later on, we have much less shame and self-loathing and much less damage has been done to the relationship.

If we see a distressed child who isn't in control, rather than an abusive child, our instinct is to help them. Our instinct to challenge back becomes a wish to help them calm down. Once again, we create a feeling of safety and a learning opportunity rather than more fear and shame.

# Physical aggression

When we are faced with physical aggression, we often get hijacked ourselves. It is very difficult to remain calm under this level of threat and our own defensive responses kick in. We don't feel in control and therefore controlling the situation is difficult. The age, sex and size of the child will temper adult feelings. We will feel more in control when threatened by a small 5-year-old girl than a stocky 6-foot 15-year-old boy. It is very easy to sit here and say that the behaviour is the same, so we should respond in the same way, but the reality is that the bigger the child, the more threatening they are and the more likely we are to feel out of control.

There is no intention of blaming or shaming adults for decisions made in these challenging circumstances. However, recognising after the event that we didn't necessarily feel in control should enable us to see things from the child's perspective. After all, the conflict spiral is the same for us as it is for the child; we have just learned or developed more control over our feelings.

From a de-escalation perspective, the response we want is calm and the goal is creating safety. Prioritising the child's safety when your own is at risk is a very high-level skill, but it is never more important. Once they are calm, this is a vital opportunity to communicate that your care for them is unconditional. Rejecting or excluding the child will tell them that they are unsafe and unwanted, that the care they receive is conditional. This will add to their fear of rejection and make them feel even more unsafe.

Being calm won't always be enough. Timing and levels of distress sometimes lead to a risk of harm. Depending on the danger they represent to themselves or others, we may have to make the decision that de-escalation is insufficient. In extreme circumstances, it comes down to deciding between physical intervention or rejection – that is, stopping the child or sending them out, or sometimes having them taken away. I have been in this position many times and made both decisions.

The outcome will have a powerful and lasting effect on the child. It isn't my place to tell educators what to do in this unenviable position, but I do want to share the impact of the response. Rightly or wrongly, sending them away, having them taken away or excluding them says to the child that you don't want them and can't handle them at their worst. If they can't control their extreme feelings and expect rejection, it is more likely to happen. And, once again, we fail to create a feeling of safety. I would always choose de-escalation if it is an option, but given the choice between physically stopping a child from doing something harmful or allowing them to do it and then punishing or excluding them for it, I am going to stop them.

In the moment, a physical intervention may be met with more aggression, but the message we want to convey during the debrief afterwards is very different: 'I care enough about you to keep you safe no matter what.' Nothing creates safety more for a child than knowing that your care for them is unconditional. I have worked with hundreds of children who have made this journey. Some had experienced many physical interventions, some one or two and many none at all, but whereas previously their fears of rejection had been real – because that was the outcome that had got them to my SEMH school – now that fear of rejection had been reduced. This is the point at which it is possible to start removing their fear of rejection and shame and working on their self-control.

Whether we escalate a situation, or even if we manage it, what happens subsequently is key. Exclusion may be necessary if there is a victim and the situation is very serious, but these instances make up a tiny percentage of incidents. Whether exclusion, either temporary or permanent, is necessary is for individual schools to decide, but I can confidently say one thing: exclusion may send a message, it may make staff feel better and it may appease parents, but it won't help the child in the long term. It may teach them to suppress their feelings, but this will lead to bigger problems down the line. Persistent disruptive behaviour (usually avoidance) and verbal or physical aggression are the cause of nearly all exclusions. How many were actually necessary? I think you know my answer.

I know there will be those who say that exclusion is an important tool in getting young people the support they need, and within the current system there is truth in this. But schools shouldn't be looking externally until we are sure that we have done everything we can internally.

## What do we see?

To return to the images from my training session at the start of this chapter, what is the difference between a crying child, a hiding child, a verbally abusive child and a physically aggressive child? The difference is us. What we see and do matters.

When what we see is poor behaviour, or a child who is breaking the rules, or a child who needs to be stopped, challenged or punished, we make our care conditional. We might feel the need to be an authority figure or our school policy might demand that we are strict, but we are just adding to the behaviour cycle, compounding the shame and increasing the fear. When we claim that we are being tough on children because we care about them, we are telling them that we only care if they conform. As a result, children who don't believe they can conform will be more scared of failure and more likely to dysregulate.

Alternatively, we can approach the situation by seeing a child in crisis: a child who needs our help, who needs us to listen or who needs to feel safe. When this is our mindset, our care is unconditional. We become trusted adults. We make it about the behaviour being bad, not the child, and we start to make them feel safe.

Behaviour is a choice, but often it isn't a conscious one. We have to see it for what it is: self-defence. Our job is to find out what the child is defending against and, more importantly, what they are communicating.

## Recipe for short-term survival responses

Ingredients:

- Safety
- Control of instincts
- Calm

Don't:

- Rely on your authority – it is meaningless to the survival brain.
- Threaten – you can't deter if there is no control.
- Punish – you can't deter if there is no control.
- Try to manage a situation when you are dysregulated; seeking help is a strength not a weakness.
- Shame children, especially publicly. Making them feel bad feeds their internal narrative, making the behaviour more likely to recur.

Do:

- Everything to prioritise safety – it is the only antidote to a fear response.
- Overcome your natural instincts to challenge or get the child to conform.

- Remain calm. If you aren't calm, seek support from a colleague. Being human and showing vulnerability is not a flaw.

- Communicate non-verbally. If the child isn't in a position to process language, we must communicate with what they are using.

- Expect and support children to repair behavioural mistakes when they are calm.

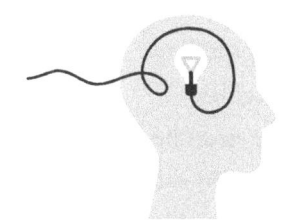

## Chapter 5

# What is the behaviour communicating?

> When we only look at behavior, we stop seeing the child and only look with an intent to judge whether we need to reward or punish. When we look behind the behavior, we see that little struggling human, *our little human*, who needs our help with something.
>
> **Rebecca Eanes**

The intention of this book is to highlight the need to see the behaviour in front of us as being the result of something else, of something more deeply rooted. I am not shy about suggesting that every behaviour is communication. We might not know what it is being communicated, we might not think it is justified or proportionate, and it might not match up with our experiences or perceptions, but it is expressing a need. When we use a lens of understanding, rather than simply dealing with the behaviour, everything changes. If we can change our perspective, maybe we can change theirs too. Figure 5.1 suggests what children may be trying to communicate through challenging behaviour.

- Can't understand/manage feelings
- Can't self-soothe/self-regulate
- High arousal (caused by stress hormones)
- Unpleasant physical symptoms (heart rate/sweating/nausea)
- Systemic dysregulation (can't calm down)
- If children do communicate what they feel, then we have to validate it!

Figure 5.1. Behaviour as communication

> Nine times out of ten, the story behind the behaviour won't make you angry; it will break your heart.
>
> **Annette Breaux and Todd Whitaker,**
> *50 Ways to Improve Student Behavior* **(2009)**

## Adults versus children

If I have a bad night's sleep followed by a disagreement with my head teacher, a frustrating conversation with a social worker, an altercation with a parent and then spend an hour sitting in traffic, I will have a lot going on beneath the surface.

If I am short with my wife when she asks me to put the bins out, my behaviour isn't acceptable, but I haven't just decided to be rude or unpleasant for the sake of it. The rudeness or unpleasantness is the effect of tiredness and frustration turning to anger and resulting in poor behaviour. It might be that I have reached a point where I can't hold it in any longer and my exasperation spills over. Or, it might be that I didn't feel I could express my feelings with my head teacher, the social worker or the parent, but I love and trust my wife enough to let her know how I feel. I know that her care for me is unconditional and won't be taken away.

It still doesn't make the behaviour right, but my wife's response will be key. She could focus on the behaviour, challenge me back and we could have a row. She could recognise my bad mood and leave me to it. Or she could recognise my distress, show concern and comfort or listen to me. Why is it that adults typically get met with the third reaction, whilst children are often on the receiving end of the first?

Another example would be a colleague marking books in the staffroom who suddenly shouts, 'I've had enough of this!', throws their pen to the floor and buries their face in their hands. Our first instinct will be concern and to check they are okay. There is no assumption that they are being defiant and no demand that they pick up the pen. We don't assume that the marking has caused the behaviour; we understand that it is a small part of a bigger picture.

Do we respond with equivalent concern when a pupil behaves in the same way? Do we see their distress and ask them if they are alright? As we saw in Chapter 2, our response is more likely to be, 'You need to pick up that pen!'

Whether it is me snapping at my partner or a colleague hurling a pen, there are ways of communicating that are unacceptable. However, if adults (who generally have better emotional literacy and communication than children) regularly behave in undesirable ways to express their emotions, then why would we assume that it is any different for children?

If my wife chooses to recognise my distress, we aren't prevented from moving forward until I have said sorry. If she accepts that my behaviour was nothing to do with her, is an apology even necessary? She may tell me that I upset her, and I may apologise because it makes me feel better, but it isn't an obstacle to us moving on.

If we focus on the behaviour, we may be preoccupied with the immediate need to correct it. Insisting on an apology or challenging me at that particular moment would have escalated the situation dramatically. Why, therefore, do we respond in this way with children? Is it because we don't see their feelings of distress and instead see their behaviour (see Figure 5.2)?

| This is a child who is breaking rules | This is a child who is in distress |
|---|---|
| • See the behaviour | • See the feelings |
| • Needs to be reminded of rules | • Be calm |
| • Threaten consequences: 'If you don't stop …' | • Have knowledge of experiences, distractions, where to take them and with whom they have relationships |
| • Show you are angry at them | |
| • Give them fuel | • Growth mindset: 'I know how well you can …' |
| | • Don't give them fuel |

Figure 5.2. What information and knowledge of the behaviour are you approaching the situation with?

# Understanding and managing feelings

Expecting young children to understand and manage their feelings is requiring a lot of them. Over time, experience will teach them about different feelings and what to do with them, and so their understanding will increase.

But what if it doesn't? What if experiences from their home life are such that they haven't seen a range of feelings, that feelings are a form of weakness, that showing feelings is dangerous? Inevitably, the child will have communication difficulties. Not knowing how to calm themselves, not knowing how to express themselves and not knowing how to verbalise 'I'm not okay' aren't difficulties confined to younger children. However, they are far less acceptable when the child is older.

Once again, the question we need to ask is whether it is right to respond negatively to a child for not doing something that nobody has taught them to do? Of course, I respect the view that this isn't an educator's job; it is the parents' job. However, if it hasn't been done, it is now down to us.

If a child comes to school upset and we want to cheer them up, we tell them it is going to be fine and not to worry. We distract them with something – an activity, a toy, a joke or a conversation. We minimise and play down the importance of their feelings or we tell them 'It's okay' or 'It doesn't matter.'

We do it with the best of intentions. We want the child to feel better – and we might even be successful in the very short term. However, by not validating their feelings, we lose not only a great teaching opportunity but also an opportunity to build safety and trust with the pupil. If we don't help the child to identify and name their feeling, how do we both learn to recognise it in the future? If neither of us can perceive it, how can we manage it? And, if we don't see it coming, how can we be prepared for it? In *Dare to Lead*, Brené Brown (2018) would describe these as 'empathy fails'; we are choosing comfort over getting into the child's feelings with them.

We can argue that it isn't our job to teach children to manage their feelings: we don't have time, we have a curriculum to teach and we have 29 other children to supervise. But, how much of the time spent managing children's challenging behaviour externally would be saved if we equipped the child to manage it internally?

We can do nothing about the fact that we have in front of us small humans, not robots. Whatever systems we put in place, we can't prevent children from having feelings. By validating those feelings, and teaching the children how to manage them, we don't have to.

I have scoured the internet trying to find a good example of this to include on my course, and I still haven't found one better than the clip from the Disney film *Inside Out* where Bing Bong loses his rocket.[1] I know it is a cartoon, but it is also an incredible example of the power of validation.

---

1  See https://www.youtube.com/watch?v=QT6FdhKriB8.

# Self-soothing and self-regulation

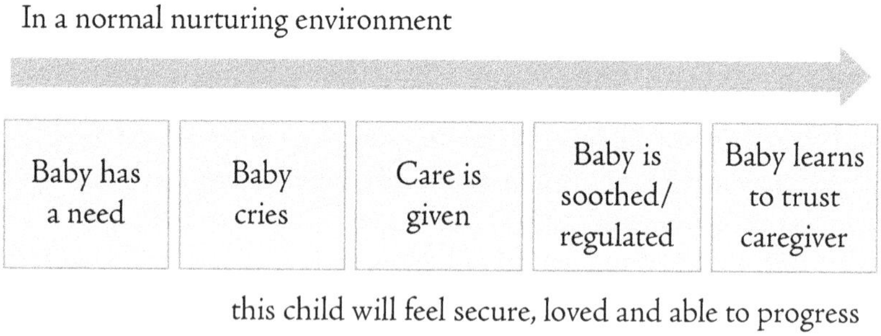

In a normal nurturing environment

| Baby has a need | Baby cries | Care is given | Baby is soothed/ regulated | Baby learns to trust caregiver |

this child will feel secure, loved and able to progress

Figure 5.3. Secure attachment

In normal circumstances, the sequence outlined in Figure 5.3 is what happens to an infant. A need is expressed through crying or distress, and they are picked up by the adult who figures out the need and meets it. The baby learns that they are safe and loved. Having their needs met becomes the expected norm, so they can progress to other forms of learning.

One of the most important elements of this process is being held. As we saw in Chapter 2, a distressed child with a racing heartbeat is pressed against an adult's chest, whose heart is beating much more slowly. As the heart beats start to synchronise, the infant becomes calmer. This is the child's first experience of co-regulation.

Managing feelings, controlling anger and not losing control requires children to have the ability to self-regulate. This can only be achieved if they have been taught how to do this, and the only way to do this is through co-regulation. It is simple enough, then, to teach a baby how to self-regulate, but it is not so easy to teach a teenager who has missed this developmental experience. This doesn't mean that it can't be done, but it has to be done differently. We aren't going to pick up and rock a teenager, but through synchronisation, co-regulation and emotion coaching, we can help them to develop self-regulation.

First, we have to acknowledge that self-regulation is missing. This could be for multiple reasons:

- Neglect: the parents ignored the crying infant and never picked them up. This might have been deliberate or due to substance abuse, post-natal depression or other mental health issues.

- Abuse: the infant's cries were met with aggression, not calm.

- Infant illness: surgery or periods of incubation may have affected the parents' ability to respond to the infant's needs.

Whatever the reason, just like the baby whose needs must be met to create safety and trust initially, we have to do this in school. There is a wide range of strategies to teach self-regulation – such as physical activities, mindfulness, sensory regulation, music or art – but co-regulation from someone they trust is going to be needed at first. The longer we leave it, the harder it will be. I would not like to estimate the number of learning hours lost, of punishments meted out, of exclusions imposed or shame loops reinforced due to a child's inability to self-soothe or self-regulate.

> Children learn how to regulate their own emotions through 'co-regulation'. The better we can soothe them when they are agitated, or support them when they are low, the better they 'absorb' how to do this for themselves.
>
> **Stuart Shanker, *Self-reg* (2016)**

## Recipe for understanding behaviour as communication

Ingredients:

- An open mind
- Understanding
- A willingness to change perception

Don't:

- See the explanation as an excuse.
- Expect children to know how to self-regulate.
- Fuel the child's distress.
- Try to fix or distract children from their feelings.

Do:

- See all behaviour as communication; whether it is acceptable communication is another matter.
- See the child, not the behaviour.
- Focus on co-regulation.
- Validate their feelings.

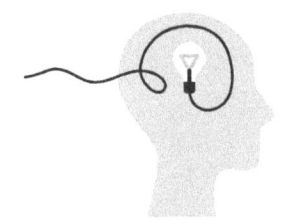

## Chapter 6

# The five responses to threat

If we acknowledge that trauma-informed practice is about having curiosity and an understanding that all might not be as it seems, that the behaviour we see on the surface is a result of fear, overwhelm or a long-term survival strategy, and if we know that parts of our physiology, both brain and body, are more or less active depending on whether we feel safe, I find it difficult to comprehend why we don't prioritise children's safety more. Especially when we know so much more about the way the body responds to threat than we ever have before, and we know that the prefrontal cortex is the part of the brain we need to be working on to maximise learning. Even if we believe that learning is the most important objective, we should still be starting with safety.

Doing the opposite and using fear as a tool for compliance was perhaps forgivable 50 years ago when we didn't know any better and neuroscience was a fledgling science, at best. We can't say the same today, so it is time to change. Whether behaviour is driven by fear, low self-esteem, shame, anger and so on is important in respect of the longer term support given to the child, but seeing that behaviour as a sign of distress rather than challenging it should always be our starting point. It is also the point where everything becomes focused on safety, calm and care. They are the antidotes to fear and can do incredible good without the risk of any harm.

In Chapter 4, we looked at different types of survival response and briefly considered fight, flight or freeze. However, there are five potential responses: *fight, flight, freeze, fawn* and *smile*. In this chapter, we will dig a little deeper into them, their origins and the relationship they have with the whole body, not just the brain.

## Stress – insulate or expose?

It is easy to get drawn into binary ideas when it comes to stress: we are either stressed or not stressed, and all stress is bad. The reality is a lot more nuanced. Stress is part of our lives; we move in and out of stress constantly, and it is near impossible and potentially harmful to insulate ourselves from all stress. Children are no different. Dealing with stress is an important life skill and something they must be taught; therefore, we must give them exposure to stress.

> We tend to think stress is bad, but there is such a thing as good stress. This creates positive stimulation, pushing us to learn new things and be creative, but not so overwhelming that it tips us into panic.
>
> **Philippa Perry, 'Go On, I Dare You' (2022)**

We often feel that we have to protect children from difficult or complicated feelings, so we withdraw them from demanding learning or difficult social situations. However, by taking away the child's stress, we avoid important issues and keep their tool box empty. Instead, we need to control the exposure alongside building resilience. Small amounts of stress for children with some resilience can be motivating – we all need a certain amount of stress to get out of bed in the morning and be alert enough to focus. Athletes often talk of getting into 'the zone' to perform at their best.

What we don't want to see is toxic levels of stress that can overwhelm children and have a catastrophic impact on learning. Toxic stress is the day-to-day engagement of stress systems for prolonged periods.

> [In circumstances of toxic stress], persistent elevations of stress hormones and altered levels of key brain chemicals produce an internal physiological state that disrupts the architecture of the developing brain and can lead to difficulties in learning, memory, and self-regulation.
>
> **National Scientific Council on the Developing Child,**
> *The Science of Early Childhood Development* (2007)

In order to manage stress, we need to understand how the body deals with it and how to create the foundations for resilience. We will explore resilience in Chapter 16, but, in brief, it must be built up from experience. If children don't develop resilience, stress is likely to be met with more primal responses.

## Polyvagal theory

To understand the first three responses we might be met with when a child is distressed, it is worth mentioning polyvagal theory. Developed by Dr Stephen Porges, I have found it to be very relevant for the work I do with children. Like many theories around neuroscience, it is labelled by some as pseudoscience because it can't be tested empirically, and it is not recognised by many neuroscientists. However, it is very popular with those who see extreme nervous responses in their children. All I know is that I have witnessed the states described by Porges on more occasions than I can count.

Having worked with children who are in significant levels of distress for many years, it was clear to me that there was a lot more going on than a child choosing to misbehave. The child's whole body was affected by what was happening to them in that moment.

Polyvagal theory focuses on the nervous system. Porges uses an upside-down triangle to explain the brain, with the brainstem at the base. If the circuits at the bottom are regulated, then it allows us to move up the triangle and experience higher functioning, especially things like learning and self-regulation. If threatened, children stay at the bottom in fight or flight. Porges suggests that, by creating safety, we allow more developed areas of the brain to be utilised, thereby improving social interaction and how we perceive other people. If we aren't feeling safe, we misinterpret facial expressions – for example, neutral faces as aggressive, fearful as angry. In an environment like a school where there are so many faces, this is likely to be very problematic.

The autonomic nervous system is made up of the sympathetic nervous system (arousing) and the parasympathetic nervous system (calming). Porges identified a third state which he calls the social engagement system – a hybrid of either the ventral vagal and sympathetic, which allows us to play, dance and do sports, or the ventral vagal and parasympathetic, which allows for intimacy and quiet moments. It is normal for us to move in and out of different states, although we spend most time in the social engagement system. When we are regulated, the vagus nerve is activated and busy, focusing on muscles, rest and digestion, enabling us to be calm learners who can engage with others socially. The more time we can spend in this social engagement (co-regulation) state, the better for the child's time in school.

Other states that do not involve the ventral vagal system are sympathetic activation (high-stress fight or flight), led by an engaged sympathetic nervous system turning everything on and dispatching or running from the threat. This comes with a cortisol and adrenaline release, which makes it difficult to focus as everything is brighter and louder. A great tool 300 million years ago in a life-or-death situation, but not so useful in the classroom. Even if a child can control the physiological changes in their system, they are unable to interact socially or learn effectively; if they lose control, then we get a more obvious fight-or-flight response.

Alternatively, dorsal vagal shutdown (or freeze response) is led by the parasympathetic nervous system turning everything off. If we can't fight or get away, then the last line of defence might be playing dead. Blood flow slows, focusing on the major organs, and the child will appear pale, apathetic, avoidant and shut down. Again, it is an important response in a life-or-death situation, but not what is needed when a teacher is asking a question.

In Chapter 4, we saw how children who perceive themselves to be threatened experience fight, flight and freeze responses, but the reality is that we need to spend most of our time in a state of social engagement in order for schools to be places of safety and success. However, for children facing toxic stress and other challenges, this is the state that is allocated the least amount of time, which causes a multitude of problems.

Too often, children who suppress these feelings are viewed more positively, despite achieving lower grades, because they cause less disruption. This could also be applied to dorsal vagal shutdown. A child who puts a lid on the jar, trapping all the stress inside, may appear to be in control, but it might not take much to blow that lid off. Equally, if all the child's focus is on not exploding, it isn't on learning.

If we can identify which nervous system state our young people are in, we may be able to help them to spend more time in social engagement. We do this using all the elements of co-regulation discussed throughout this book. If we can help them to process information better and faster, to concentrate more and improve their responses, this will have a huge effect on their learning.

# Fawn

After flight, fight and freeze there is a fourth F: fawn. I think it is a silly name, but we do love our alliteration. Let's move away from nervous system responses for a moment and look at some other long-term survival strategies and learned behaviour that children adopt.

What do you do if you are growing up in a household with aggressive adults and you are too small to fight, have nowhere to run and freezing results in more danger? If your home is a place where bad moods lead to anger and anger leads to violence, the only safety for many children comes from preventing bad moods in the first place. If they can be really helpful and good, then the caregiver will be happy and they will be safe.

If this is the child's reality, then it will be a difficult behaviour to change when they come to school. The child will want to help, to do all the jobs and answer all the questions because that means safety. The 'good child' persona will be their survival mechanism until it becomes viewed as attention-seeking or they perceive dislike or rejection and switch to a different F.

# Laugh/smile

We have already touched on the fact that adult and child expectations differ dramatically, and that is never clearer than in reactions to the smile response. Put an adult in a stressful or anxiety-inducing situation where they feel awkward, uncomfortable or panicky, and the response is usually the same: awkward laughter. Whether we are on a disastrous first date, at a party when someone says something inappropriate or have had a day where everything has gone wrong, we tend to use laughter as a go-to response. It is perfectly acceptable to do so; even in a setting like a funeral when someone can't bottle up their feelings and laughs inappropriately, it would likely be nothing more than frowned upon.

Why, then, is this response unacceptable for children? Why is laughing in a situation where they have done something wrong or are being told off – when they feel awkward, uncomfortable or panicky – deemed to be the height of rudeness and disrespect? Embarrassed laughter has got to be a better alternative than a child shutting down, running away or hitting out.

In order to accept this behaviour, we need to put the smile response in context against the four F responses and to step away from our own learned experiences. Most of us have been the young child who laughed uneasily when we were told off, resulting in a very unhappy adult. We learned falsely that giggling is rude and disrespectful, and it is a belief that many of us carry with us and pass on to the next generation. Better understanding can hopefully stop it being from handed on, but this will only happen if children are given new experiences that stop false messages from taking root. I am not saying that we go as far as to congratulate children on their communication skills when they giggle, but a laughter response is a much better starting point than an F response.

When children learn that laughing is bad when they are being reprimanded, they also learn to suppress it. Now, what do you end up with when you try to stifle a laugh? A smirk. All too often, the smirk is regarded as the most heinous of crimes; I hold up my hands in wanting to throttle my own children when they smirk at me. Even though I know why it is happening, and even though I know the alternatives are much worse, it still pushes a button that makes it very challenging to stay regulated. Remember: if we take this response away from a child without replacing it with something better, then we push them towards high-stakes survival responses.

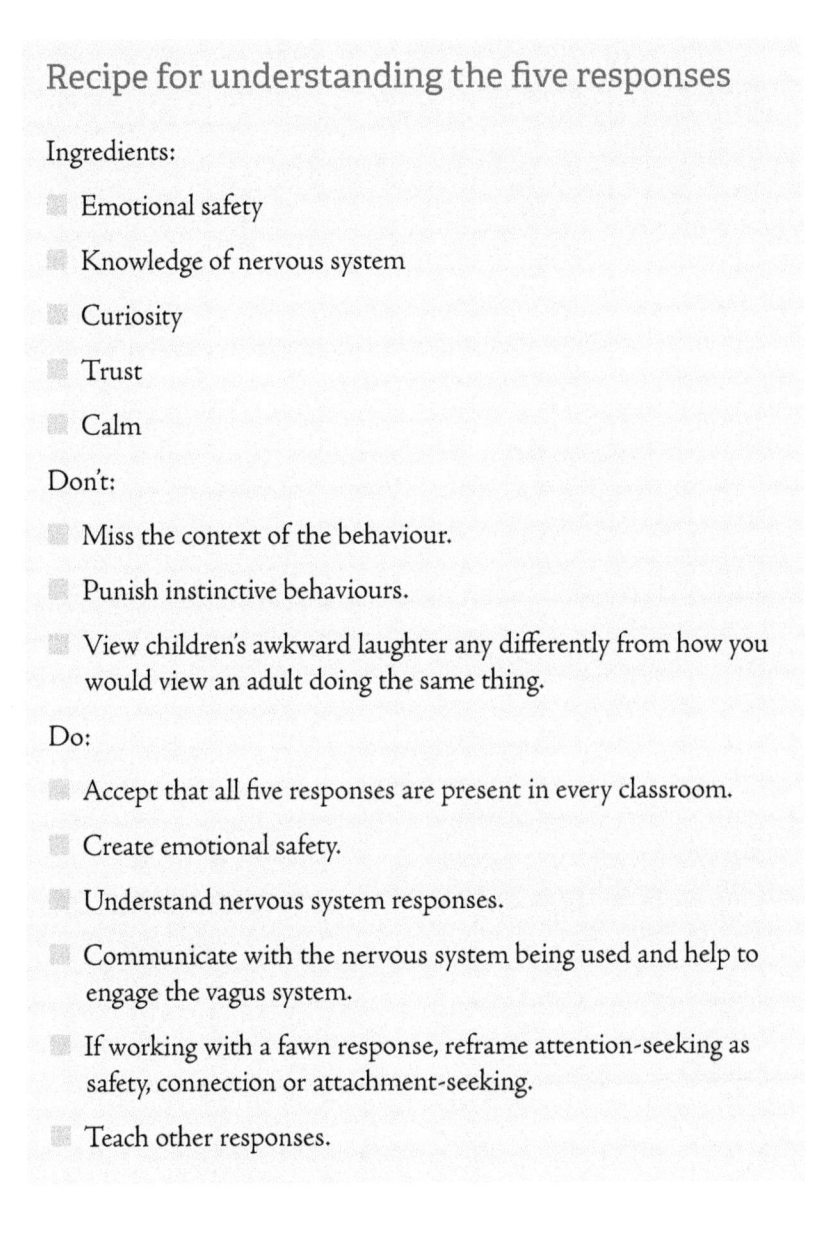

## Recipe for understanding the five responses

Ingredients:

- Emotional safety
- Knowledge of nervous system
- Curiosity
- Trust
- Calm

Don't:

- Miss the context of the behaviour.
- Punish instinctive behaviours.
- View children's awkward laughter any differently from how you would view an adult doing the same thing.

Do:

- Accept that all five responses are present in every classroom.
- Create emotional safety.
- Understand nervous system responses.
- Communicate with the nervous system being used and help to engage the vagus system.
- If working with a fawn response, reframe attention-seeking as safety, connection or attachment-seeking.
- Teach other responses.

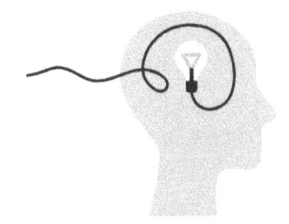

Chapter 7

# Prevention is better than cure

## The window of tolerance

The window of tolerance was developed by Dr Daniel Siegel in *The Developing Mind* (1999), and is a great visual tool for explaining why children struggle to manage their behaviour. Throughout this book, I have emphasised that the way a child demonstrates their distress can vary dramatically from individual to individual. Therefore, when we are considering escalations in behaviour, we are drawing on our attunement and our reactiveness to that young person rather than what we might deem to be generic behaviours, as listed in behaviour policies or incident reports. This might seem as if we are neglecting other children to focus on one child, but focusing on what to look out for and knowing what to do when it happens enables us to prevent escalation, which saves a lot of time and reduces disruption for everyone.

If we have the evidence to suggest that a child is going to escalate, then just hoping they won't isn't a sensible strategy. We undertake risk assessments in every other aspect of school life, so why not in these cases? Of course, we might have to react in a dynamic way to an unexpected situation or emergency, but from that point on we ought to be following a formal plan or set of procedures. Simply hoping that something doesn't happen again would be unacceptable, so this shouldn't be allowed to happen with children with challenging behaviour.

Our formal risk assessment of a child should involve looking out for warning signs before we see the behaviour. Things to watch out for include fidgeting, changes in engagement, facial expressions like tension, gritted teeth and frowning, changes in eye contact or flushed/paler skin. If we are alert to these physiological indicators, then we won't necessarily have to wait for the challenging behaviours to begin.

It is much easier to spot these signs if we have established a baseline for the child and use this as our starting point. We will look at personalised behaviour plans in Chapter 21, but to effectively recognise when things are starting to go wrong, we must know what 'right' looks like for the child. It is all too easy to omit positive aspects of the child in a behaviour plan. However, if we note down what the child is like when they are within their window of tolerance – whether that is calm, settled, happy or chilled – then it becomes easier to recognise when their demeanour changes.

We don't wait for our loved ones to become highly distressed before we do anything. We see changes in their mood, appearance or engagement and we intervene, even though they probably have far superior self-regulation skills than some of our pupils. They may need some encouragement and support, but we can do this because of our attunement to them. We can't possibly be expected to do this with every child in the school, but by changing the way we see our most challenging pupils – and seeing them as our most distressed pupils – we can hopefully attune to them better. After all, they are just a small percentage of the children overall.

In terms of our mindset, it is important to properly weigh the brief amount of time spent preventing poor behaviour in the present with the lengthy amounts of time spent reacting in the future. Waiting for the negative behaviours to start before intervening, rather than supporting at a low level, is counterproductive. It is harder, takes longer and causes more disruption. The truth, as demonstrated by the bell curve (see Figure 7.1), is that the sooner we intervene, the better. And to do that we must understand when a child is exiting their window of tolerance.

First, it is important to recognise that every child's window is a different shape and size. This will be further affected by their experiences, especially trauma. Just as with many other aspects, we can't compare a child's window to our own or of other children because our experiences are different.

When a child is within their window, they are in a calm state, the right parts of the nervous system are engaged and the thinking brain is working. They can think, learn, remember and retain information, love, empathise, play and communicate. They are the best version of themselves. We don't often see certain children in this state because it requires them to feel safe. Just as the hypervigilant child in a threatening physical environment would be looking for an exit and planning an escape, they may be doing the same emotionally.

When a child starts to exit their window of tolerance, this causes a disconnect from their thinking brain. Even at this early point, the effect on learning and executive functioning can be significant. Children who can't think, can't learn. What pushes them out of the window of tolerance is vital information for us to know as educators, and it will be different for each pupil – for example:

- Break times.
- Unstructured time.
- Time of day (especially if the child is medicated).
- Group work.
- Certain children.
- Certain adults.
- Certain rooms.
- Smells and sounds.
- Hungry/tired.
- Being told no.
- Being asked to be a courageous learner.
- Tests/exams.
- Going home.
- Monday mornings/Friday afternoons.
- Contact with birth family (before and after) for children in care.

The list goes on. We have a choice to make: wait for the resulting behaviour when they are out of the window of tolerance or help them to get back in. If we can't prevent the child from leaving the window, the direction they take will vary.

Some children will exit to sympathetic activation: hyperarousal and fight or flight. They will likely adopt one of the many uncontrolled fear responses discussed in Chapter 3. We need to be looking out for those visual signs of distress and work hard to re-regulate the child. The behaviour will appear challenging because it is. However, what might appear to be: 'I'm doing this – what are you gonna do about it?' could easily be: 'I'm starting to lose control – I need you to see me and I need you to help me,' especially if we have missed or ignored low-level signals.

For others it will be dorsal vagal shutdown: hypoarousal and freeze. They will appear apathetic, disinterested, withdrawn and avoidant. The fear is the same as with sympathetic activation, but the heart rate decreases rather than increases, preparing to feign death for survival. It is all too easy to ignore this behaviour because it is not disruptive to the learning of others, but it is very damaging for the child, especially in terms of learning because the thinking brain isn't engaged.

When we co-regulate a child, we are teaching them how to return to their window of tolerance in the hope that they will learn how to do it for themselves. The more consistently we do this, the more chance we have of changing the size and shape of their window. For some children, their experiences have meant that their window is very small; if we can build the resilience of that young person and increase the window size, it will be easier to keep them in it in the future.

# The bell curve

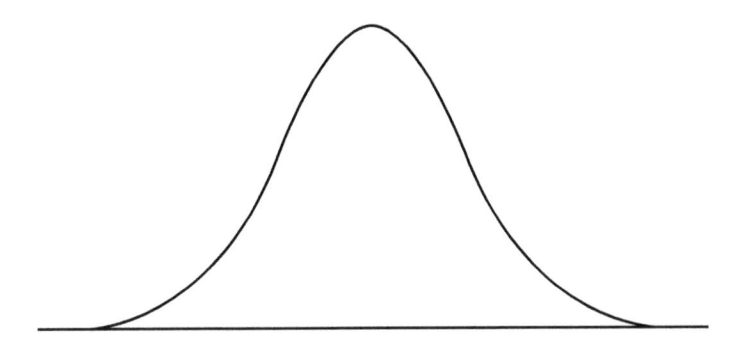

Figure 7.1. The bell curve or normal distribution curve

Many organisations and sectors use the bell curve (Figure 7.1) when talking about behaviour, and rightly so; it has been relevant with all the young people with whom I have worked. It also draws together most of the elements in this book: it is the thread to which everything else is attached and is critical to responses becoming holistic.

This illustration is neat and symmetrical, but there is no doubt that some curves are steeper on one side than the other. Some children may never reach the bottom horizontal line – they will never truly reach calm – and this is an important factor to take into account when working with them.

The reality is that children move in and out of their window of tolerance throughout the day. They flit between vagal states and have multiple bell curves. When we are attuned to a young person, a day may consist of multiple mini bell curves without a high peak. This is a sign of excellent practice, and is as good as it may get for some children who are navigating past or present chaos in their lives outside of school.

It is inevitable that sometimes the curve will be steeply humped and sometimes out of our control, but the power to change this lies with us as adults. How we respond to the child will have an enormous impact; we can speed it up or slow it down depending on whether we bring fire or water. There are no gaps in the bell curve: whilst it may follow a pattern of de-escalation, crisis or recovery, it is a continuous flow. We can avoid the crisis if a child has learned or been taught to manage, supress or even mask their feelings. A child might edge towards the window, dangle a leg out, climb out or even run off. We need different responses to the latter two in order to get those children back inside, but the premise is always the same: keeping the child inside the window in the first place is always going to involve less work, less failure and less shame. This can be achieved more easily if the classroom is a safe place where they want to be.

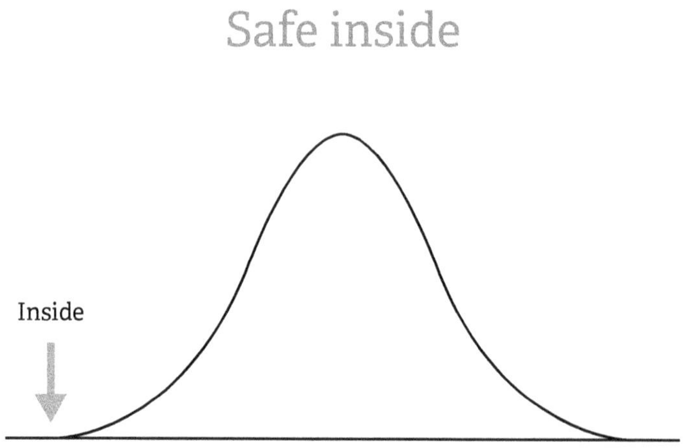

## Safe inside

Figure 7.2. Inside the window of tolerance

When a child is inside their window of tolerance (Figure 7.2) they are socially engaged, equipped for learning and we are liable to see their true character and personality. Whether they are funny, cheeky, loud, quiet, sporty, energetic, kind, helpful or chilled, this is the time when the child is regulated and authentic, and most likely to be the courageous learner we need them to be. It is our opportunity to bank some positive outcomes and build self-esteem.

# Partly outside

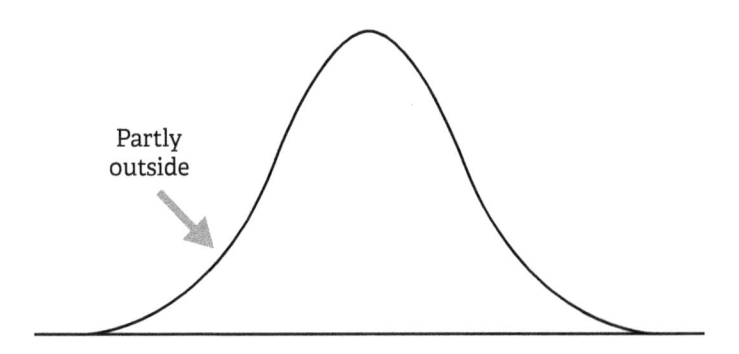

Figure 7.3. Partly outside the window of tolerance

The earlier we can identify the child starting to leave their window, the earlier we can stage an intervention, the more the disruption is minimised and the more tools we have at our disposal.

At this point (Figure 7.3), we are more likely to be looking for a change in the child's appearance rather than a change in behaviour. In training sessions, I often get staff to perform these identifications in reverse. When observing an incident sequentially, it can be difficult to identify when the key changes happen. By going backwards towards an identified baseline, there is a clear space between a calm child and a challenging child on the verge of crisis. We must identify what that gap looks like for our pupils: increased heart rate, probably accompanied by a red face and increased breathing; or the opposite, with slower/quieter breathing, paler complexion, sweating, mention of pain or visible tension, fidgety, agitated, quieter or louder than usual, a funny look in their eyes and so on. In order to identify these signs, we have to know the child and share that knowledge with other staff. The best way to do this is on a simple but detailed behaviour plan.

# Outside

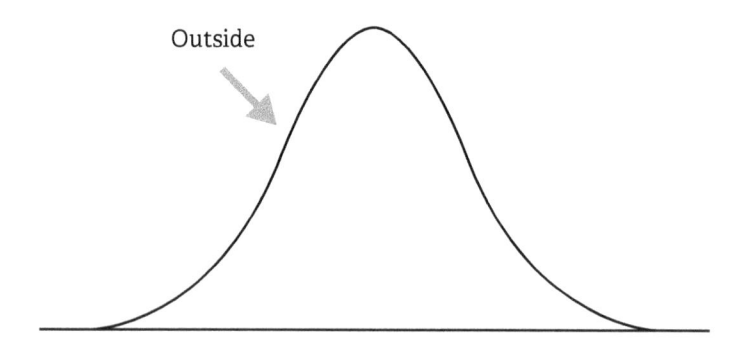

Figure 7.4. Outside the window of tolerance

Even when a child is outside their window of tolerance (Figure 7.4), we still have a chance to persuade them back in. Depending on whether they are hyperaroused or hypoaroused, they are likely to behave in either a challenging or avoidant way. Hyperaroused children may be disruptive: talking over, being out of their seat, messing with equipment, distracting others, swearing and so on. As discussed in Chapter 2, how we respond at this point will dictate whether behaviour de-escalates to calm or escalates to crisis. Are we bringing fire or water? Some children may need to be withdrawn from their peer group if we have reached this point in order to avoid a crisis.

Equally important is our response to a hypoaroused child. If their survival response is avoidance (freeze), but we don't allow it by pressuring them to engage, then we force them to fight or fly. This is the point on the bell curve when cortisol and adrenaline are released. If we have managed to avert a crisis, we must acknowledge and do something about the stress hormones in the body to prevent further harm. The dangers of not doing so will be discussed in Chapter 12.

# Crisis point – fully outside

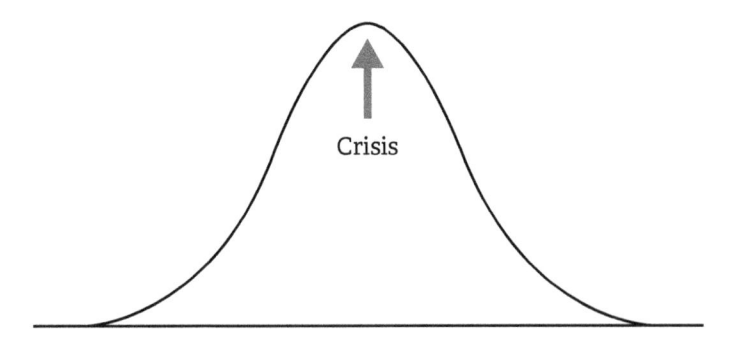

*Figure 7.5. Fully outside the window of tolerance*

At crisis point (Figure 7.5), the window of tolerance is a distant memory: the child is out and in another part of the building. Likewise, verbal communication is likely a thing of the past because the child will be struggling to process language as soon as they leave the window – words may be useless. This is extremely disruptive for all pupils because the lesson can't continue and staff/children may be at risk if physical aggression occurs, so there may be no option but to remove either the child or the other children from the room. It can take a long time to calm the situation, and until the child is separated from the other children, they will not be able to re-regulate.

What we do once the child has been separated is critical to what happens next, both in terms of what happens immediately after the crisis to repair relationships and what we learn for next time. If the crisis isn't managed well, it can be like a fertiliser for shame, creating disconnection and leaving the child feeling unsafe.

## Recovery

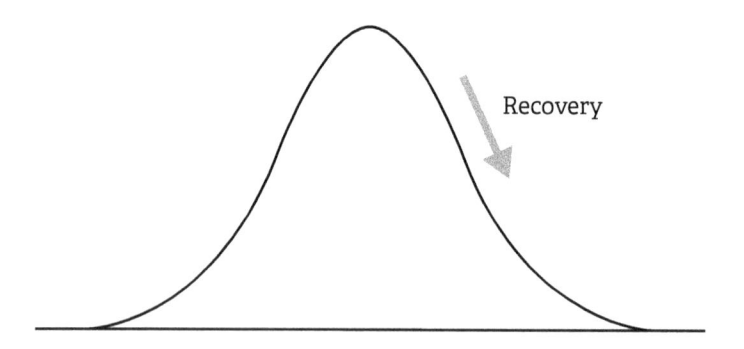

Figure 7.6. Moving back inside the window of tolerance

Supporting a child back to their baseline and getting them back inside their window of tolerance (Figure 7.6) following a significant incident is not an easy task. It will be more straightforward if the crisis point has been well managed.

Although we need to keep it simple, the language we use during a crisis is important. Even though for much of the time when a child is in crisis they aren't listening to what we say, this is our opportunity to build a connection. Team Teach uses the phrase 'I care too much about you to let you be out of control.' When the child believes that we are keeping them safe and that we care, we will enter recovery more quickly. This requires good communication with them afterwards, but most important is how they feel when they are starting to come back down: 'Do the staff care about me?' They may need to be convinced.

## Approach with caution

If a child has gone into crisis, then one positive consequence is that the adrenaline and cortisol in their system have been consumed. It was released for fight and flight and the physical and emotional exertion involved will have been fuelled by it. Now that this has been depleted, we have the opportunity to prompt the release of oxytocin by making the child feel safe and connected. However, we must be careful not to create a cycle in the child's behaviour.

It is logical to assume that the best person to perform the recovery with the child is the adult with whom they have the best relationship, especially as this individual is likely to have played a big part in calming them down. However, if the same adult always does the recovery, then the same adult is always present for the oxytocin release. For children who already have complex attachment needs, this can create an over-reliance on one person. It is better for the child to build trust with lots of different adults because if that adult is not available then we have a problem. We may even find ourselves in a situation where the child will behave poorly to seek out that adult's reassurance, and inadvertently we have created another cycle of negative behaviour.

It is also very common, for various reasons, for the class teacher not to be involved in the recovery process. This means that for an incident that has originated in the classroom, the teacher is present for the cortisol explosion but not for the oxytocin release, for the crisis but not for the recovery, for the fear but not for the safety. Despite teachers and schools being pulled in so many different directions, we have to ensure that the class teacher is involved in the whole process because we need that relationship to be built on safety.

# The fresh start – but approach with care

After recovery, the child may have had a big physical and emotional outpouring that potentially may have sapped their energy, so there is a good chance that they will appear tired and apathetic. They may require a little extra time before they return to normal. We then have a big decision to make. We need to talk to the child about what happened, the presenting behaviour, what they could have done differently and what they will do differently next time, but that means revisiting the incident and eliciting thoughts that might send the child back into crisis. When we have worked hard to recover them, it can be tempting to draw a line and move on, but in doing so, we inadvertently create a loop of shame and normalise the child's behaviour (Figure 7.7).

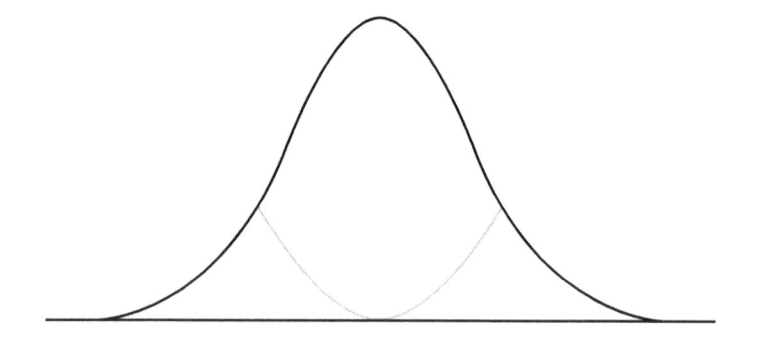

Figure 7.7. The shame loop

When we help the child to return to their window of tolerance, it will bring either guilt and a belief that they have made a mistake but they are still a good child. The adult is going to help them make amends for it. Or it brings with it shame and a belief that they are a bad child who has done another bad thing, which is what is expected of them and out of their control.

Crisis–recovery–return without a learning opportunity means that poor behaviour is likely to be repeated. The child goes back to class – they start to become unsettled – they start to behave poorly because they can't control their feelings and because they are bad – adults care about them so keep them safe and calm – the child goes back to class – they start to become unsettled …

It may be that adults have tried to address the behaviour before the child has returned to their window and this has sent them back into crisis, or it may be that we are under huge time pressures, but we must give the child the opportunity to repair the behavioural mistakes, so they learn to feel guilt and not shame. We must break cycles of shame, not perpetuate them. By failing to revisit, we are doing what is easier in the short term, but we aren't allowing for new teaching and new learning. The learned behaviour therefore becomes learned helplessness.

# Four ways of working with pupils

In his book *Restorative Practice*, Mark Finnis (2020: 51) discusses the four ways model (*to, with, not* and *for*) which builds on the work of Ted Wachtel and Paul McCold (2008). The level of external control and expectations versus how much support we provide is a daily balancing act for schools. Often, we replace one with the other to try to survive as best we can, but things only really work well when both are present (see Figure 7.8).

|  | To | With |
|---|---|---|
|  | Not | For |

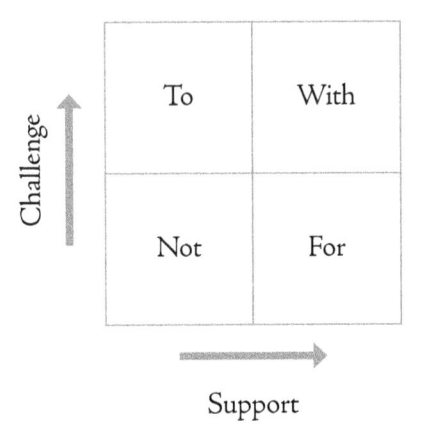

Challenge ↑ → Support

Figure 7.8. Social discipline window
Source: Finnis (2021: 53), adapted from Wachtel and McCold (2008: 124)

Certainly, some children's home-life experiences will consist of little control (boundaries, expectations, discipline) and little support (care, encouragement, belief). This child, based on those experiences, isn't going to have the skills required to be successful. If this is repeated at school, and children end up being allowed to avoid work or are given simple work to occupy them, then they are unlikely to progress. It is fine to do this on rare occasions but it can't become the norm.

Other young people find themselves in settings where expectations and control levels are very high; there are lots of rules to follow but there is little support to back them up. If the child's experiences don't match their environment, then following those rules and meeting those expectations is going to be challenging. The child is highly likely to fail and then be punished with a punitive response. By not giving the child the required support or tools to meet expectations and control measures, they will likely feel done *to* because control is external. For many children with executive functioning difficulties, which can cause them to be disorganised, forgetful or unpunctual, they often fall below expectations and feel done *to* by the consequences.

Sometimes we feel the only option for the child and those around them is to remove the stressors. Whether they are related to work, social difficulties or environmental issues, we don't expect the child to be able to do something, so we take it away or do it for them. Although this might work in the short term, we create a learned helplessness. The problem is that stress is part of life and if we do things *for* them it doesn't help them to manage it in the future.

The most important job for us, therefore, is to have high expectations and boundaries, but to accept that sometimes children will fall short of meeting them – and that is our opportunity to fill their tool box. The solution isn't to punish them until they magically figure it out for themselves or to insulate them from expectations; it is to control their levels of exposure to stress and to pick them up when they fall. By having high expectations and high support, we work *with* them to find solutions, create resilience and fill up their tool boxes.

> Human beings are happier, more cooperative and productive, and more likely to make positive changes in their behavior when those in positions of authority do things *with* them, rather than *to* them or *for* them.
>
> **Ted Wachtel and Paul McCold, 'From Restorative Justice to Restorative Practices' (2004)**

# You broke it, you fix it

If we are going to work with a child, crisis behaviours may still need to be repaired. This is an incredible opportunity to teach them the logical consequences of their actions, even if they weren't deliberate. This is an opportunity to work *with* the child.

Enforcing expectations by putting a punitive consequence on the end will be viewed by many people as the right way to respond. It does put a full stop to the incident, which is better than creating a loop, and I can't argue with that. However, if the conclusion of a negative behaviour is a negative process, then we give the child two more negative experiences, which in turn may result in more behaviour failures, more shame and more damage to their self-esteem and self-belief. How to counteract this negativity and build self-esteem will be discussed in Chapter 16.

I often hear educators say that this is how the real world works, but it isn't. It is how the criminal justice system works – and that should be the last thing on our minds. Real life isn't about punitive consequences when you make a mistake. It is about making up for it, saying sorry, being remorseful, making amends, fixing things that have been broken or giving back time so they can be fixed by someone else. (For example, in my school when children were impulsive and broke things they were not capable of mending, they were asked to help the site supervisor do other jobs like leaf collecting, litter picking or painting, which would save them half an hour that could then be used for the repairs.)

If we do this successfully, then we put a similar full stop on the end of the bell curve but we also cancel out the negative behaviour. Instead of giving the child two new adverse experiences, we don't give them any. If we can teach the child that their behavioural mistakes can be fixed, we can mine a good feeling from the bad. It isn't about having zero consequences. It is about making consequences meaningful, logical and designed to fill the child's tool box together.

## Recipe for prevention

Ingredients:

- The process
- Staff involvement
- Trust

Don't:

- Expect children to feel in straight lines; we wouldn't expect this of adults.
- Rely on the same adult to do the recovery.
- Do fresh starts without repair.

Do:

- Learn from incidents; they are only unexpected once.
- Remember that the real child is the one we see inside the window of tolerance, not the one outside it.
- Quality learning only happens inside the window of tolerance.
- Share the oxytocin around the staff.
- Where possible, include the class teacher in the recovery phase.
- Always complete the repair; it is the learning opportunity.

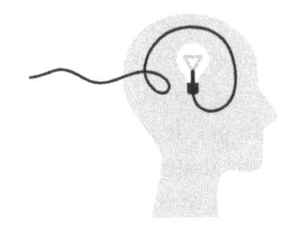

## Chapter 8

# Consequences
## Are they effective?

> Too often we forget that 'discipline' really means 'to teach' – not 'to punish'. A disciple is a student, not a recipient of behavioural consequences.
>
> Daniel J. Siegel and Tina Payne Bryson, *The Whole-Brain Child* (2012)

## Why punitive can be dangerous

If you have the views I do and deliver the training I do, one of the things you are regularly met with is the suggestion that, because you are anti-punitive, you must let children do whatever they want. This is not even close to being the case. I have high behaviour expectations, no different to any other educator, but I understand that threatening punitive consequences in order to get children to meet them is rarely effective. I also understand that many children can be deterred or controlled in this way. However, I am interested in creating a culture of safety and quality learning, and that requires more than just getting children to conform.

There were times early in my career when I did take a more disciplinary approach, but I found that it almost guaranteed that behaviour would deteriorate. Not that I claim to have perfect behaviour now; children aren't robots, and when they express themselves, they will sometimes get it wrong. My job is to help them learn from their mistakes.

If, instead, I see my job as preventing self-expression and forcing children to suppress their feelings because they are bad, then this can be dangerous. Failing to separate the feeling from the behaviour is as far from what we need to be doing as we can get. It is why zero-tolerance approaches are sending many children into shame cycles, and why we are creating young adults who are both scared of their feelings and unable to control them.

If we have never taught children to understand that it is feelings that cause behaviour, then how can they learn to control their feelings? It shouldn't be about the adult controlling the child; we should be teaching the child *self-control*. This means learning from their mistakes, and if a child does something wrong, expecting them to put it right.

I favour logical consequences linked to the behaviour because that is what happens in real life. In the real world, verbally lashing out at your partner and then going and sitting in silence in your bedroom for half an hour doesn't make it all go away. Actions have consequences, but actions also need to be repaired. In many schools, the consequence is more about payback. As we saw in the previous chapter, this is more closely linked to the criminal justice system than it is to everyday life. Punishment without repair doesn't prepare children for life after school, and it compounds the shame children already feel. With enough repetition, 'I have been bad' becomes 'I am bad.' It creates an inevitability for some children about their future that we should be doing everything we can to prevent.

## Reliance on punitive systems

Even with so much in the news about vulnerable pupils, the continuing impact of the pandemic and the widening socio-economic divide, there are those in education who still favour a zero-tolerance approach to behaviour. The language used in these approaches is very often focused on training behaviour, modelling it and copying it rather than learning about it and teaching children how to change. On social media, phrases like 'backing teachers' and 'against pupils' suggest preparation for battle. This 'us and them' is a dated approach to education: 'doing to' rather than 'doing with' will always exclude a minority of pupils who weren't taught to behave in their formative years.

External control may be the easier option in the short term, but what skills are we giving those children in the long term when they leave school and those high levels of control are removed? Many educators continue to believe that as long as we keep telling the children the rules, they will automatically know how to follow them. When did we stop being teachers and become simply tellers?

Systems are important, especially in large schools where they play a vital role in consistency, but the system can't replace the human element in teaching and relationships. In too many cases, the system dictates that when a child doesn't follow the rules – whether it is *won't* or *can't* doesn't matter – they will be met with a punitive response. This will often follow a set pattern, possibly associated with codes like C1, C2 and so on:

- Reminder of expectation.
- Warning.
- Name on the board.
- Tick next to name, probably signifying a sanction.
- Asked to leave the room or removed by a member of staff.

The problem is that each punitive step is unlikely to deter a dysregulated child; therefore, they are going to be withdrawn pretty quickly. Rattling through these consequences leaves them with no place to go.

## What is meant by withdrawal?

Many zero-tolerance settings claim that once a child has been removed from the classroom they are 'supported'. This is often the case, and I have already sung the praises of pastoral teams up and down the land. The pastoral team is likely to get to the bottom of the cause of the behaviour. So, if there was a valid reason, should we still go ahead with the punishment? Might there be a better way to make up for it? We will come to that.

Some schools use isolation as their sanction of choice. The system may dictate straight to isolation without pastoral support. Many people will assume that I am against withdrawal, but that isn't correct. I would always prefer for a child to stay in class, but in an instance where they have been aggressive, violent or very disruptive, withdrawal may be the best option to de-escalate the situation. It may also be the best way to maintain the dignity of a child who is losing or has lost control. However, I have to question how we got to this position and whether everything has been done that could have been done to prevent it. Children failing should be a learning opportunity for the adults as well as the child.

If withdrawal is going to be used as a tool, then how it is managed is very important. Isolation may mean a quiet space to talk through the behaviour, to separate feelings from actions, to address guilt (not shame) and to figure out an appropriate way to repair, move forward and prevent a repeat of the behaviour in the future. This kind of withdrawal and isolation can play a crucial role in teaching children about behaviour.

However, if isolation is about segregation, sitting in silence, not moving and even extending the period of time in isolation for minor behaviours like turning around, then it teaches the child nothing. It encourages shame and instils the idea that feelings are bad. It may appear to be successful as a deterrent, but the long-term effects are damaging. I have been in many schools that claim to be calm: indeed, from the outside they appear quiet and orderly but inside you can feel the tension. Children and staff are wound tight with staff looking out for negative behaviour and children looking over their shoulders.

Emma Condliffe's excellent doctoral thesis '"Out of Sight, Out of Mind": An Interpretative Phenomenological Analysis of Young People's Experience of Isolation Rooms/Booths in UK Mainstream Secondary Schools' (2021) details the use of, and effects of, isolation used as punishment in the UK. It does not reach a positive conclusion.

Conforming-calm is not the same as happy-calm. Not expressing feelings is unnatural, which is why everything feels forced. The child may be sitting in the way we want, making eye contact in the way we want and remaining silent in the way we want, but underneath they are desperately struggling to stay inside their window of tolerance, especially if cortisol is flooding their system. We need to be attuned to all the warning signs discussed in previous chapters.

Not having behavioural episodes does not mean that your school is a place of peaceful learning either. The calmest school I have ever been in was Barrowford Primary led by the brilliant Rachel Tomlinson. A few incidents happened when I was there, and it was how they were dealt with that showed me the school was a genuinely relaxed and joyful place. Children were expressing themselves in every classroom, fully engaged and enjoying their learning. Barrowford has no sanctions policy, but this doesn't mean that the children run wild. It means that restorative approaches are so embedded that the children have learned how to manage their emotions and repair conflict, and do so naturally. I believe that the skills and internal control taught at Barrowford are going to give those children much better skills for adult life than being externally controlled by adults.

# Hidden feelings

Typically, the children who express extreme or uncontrolled emotions, often through a fight-or-flight survival strategy, will eventually get the support they need. Even though they may face exclusion or a managed move, they will eventually end up in a setting where they are loved and supported. I disagree with exclusion, but such is the nature of our broken system that it may be the catalyst for asking the correct questions and getting a child the support they need. This is not to endorse exclusion – in fact, it is a damning indictment of the excluding school – but at least the young person can embark on a more positive journey.

My biggest concern lies with the children who have the same experiences and the same additional needs but don't lose control of their feelings. What have they learned from witnessing the zero-tolerance approach and what happens to others who show their feelings? They have learned that the best way to survive is to blend in and hide. Despite having all the same dangerous feelings as other children who behave inappropriately, their safety comes from suppressing them. For centuries, we have been inculcating boys with the idea that they can't show they are hurt or upset and need to be tough, but look at the difference between male and female suicide rates,[1] the number of men incarcerated[2] or the disparity between genders with respect to who commits domestic abuse.[3] Bottling up emotion means that when it does come out, it is often uncontrolled.

At best, we are failing to notice what is happening to these children and, at worst, we are deliberately ignoring them. They are being forgotten in favour of high-achieving or high-tariff pupils. They have become invisible. Many schools have become compliant with this tactic because they don't cause any bother and don't take up any resources.

Many children with additional needs use masking as a tool to blend in. However, it is not only children with additional needs who mask; any child who feels they can't express their emotions may adopt this strategy. It reveals that they don't feel safe, meaning that the building block that is fundamental to all quality learning is missing.

Masking is hugely detrimental to learning. It is exhausting and often results in extreme behaviour at home. The child simply can't hold their emotions in any more and lets them out in a safe place. If you work in a school and have ever told a parent, 'They are fine in school,' stop and question whether they are masking.

The argument for zero tolerance is that not sending a strong message about poor behaviour implies that it is acceptable. In practice, this doesn't happen. I have been in lots of situations where a child has behaved poorly, and the idea that just because one child throws a chair that everyone throws a chair simply isn't true. It could just as easily be argued that the message understood by the child is that it isn't okay to feel that way – that if I let my feelings get the better of me, I will be rejected; that nobody is interested in how I feel; that what I feel is bad; that I am bad. When we shame children for feeling bad, we are reinforcing a cycle that is never going to allow that child to thrive.

---

1  According to the Samaritans, in 2021 the male suicide rate was 15.8 per 100,000 compared to a female rate of 5.5 per 100,000 – see https://www.samaritans.org/about-samaritans/research-policy/suicide-facts-and-figures/latest-suicide-data.
2  Ministry of Justice data for 2020/2021 state that males made up 96% of the total prison population and females 4% – see https://www.gov.uk/government/statistics/hm-prison-and-probation-service-offender-equalities-annual-report-2020-to-2021.
3  The victim was female in 73% of domestic abuse-related crimes in England and Wales in 2020/2021 – see https://www.ons.gov.uk/peoplepopulationandcommunity/crimeandjustice/articles/domesticabusevictimcharacteristicsenglandandwales/yearendingmarch2021.

# Invisibility

We have all been in a position where, even though we have been scared, outraged or upset, we have had to hide our feelings, whether it is to be strong for someone else, to save face or to avoid inflaming a situation. We also know how tiring and difficult it is. For example, if your boss is totally out of order and having a go at you, you may be outraged and want to tell them how you feel, but you have to suppress it or else you might lose your job. Maintaining self-control and stopping your feelings from overwhelming you requires a huge amount of effort.

Imagine that experience every day and in some schools all day long – every encounter, every lesson. How could you possibly concentrate on your work if all your energy was required to suppress your feelings? Well, you can't. Children in this situation have just enough determination to tick along unnoticed in the background, but they rarely achieve what they are capable of, they rarely thrive and they rarely meet their projected grades. In extreme circumstances, pupils can't access their thinking brain because they are so fixated on survival. For children who are hiding, survival is about accessing just enough learning to stay invisible.

Rather than recognising that this problem is caused by the system, we lay the blame elsewhere. It is because the child isn't trying hard enough, or they don't do enough work at home, or their parents aren't pushing them enough. In fact, schools with a culture of fear create another feeling for the child to suppress, something else to worry about rather than the lesson content.

How do children truly learn? They learn by making themselves vulnerable. They learn by risking failure. They learn by putting themselves out there. When children are focused on surviving, they will be too afraid to put up a hand, engage in discussion or take a lead, particularly in a culture of fear where mistakes lead to punishment and humiliation.

The reason schools without zero tolerance are successful in terms of behaviour is down to safety and trust, but the side effect is a rise in progress. Children feel like they belong, that they can take chances and won't be shamed. Intense feelings might overwhelm some pupils and they may make a behavioural mistake, but it can be fixed. Children in safe environments feel confident enough to be vulnerable. They don't spend all of their time trying to suppress their emotions; instead, they open their minds to learning – academically and behaviourally. Rather than low self-esteem leading to frustration, anger and aggression, it can lead to belonging, self-control and happiness. This is what I witnessed at Barrowford Primary School.

Some schools have the mistaken belief that embracing a trauma-informed or relationship-based approach suggests to children that they can get away with bad behaviour which will cause them to copy it, or that witnessing other children losing control will traumatise them. The truth is that seeing a child losing control at the same time as they are being supported teaches children that it is okay to have strong feelings. In some settings, we are doing the opposite and encouraging children to believe that feelings are unhealthy. We might want to question how big a part zero-tolerance policies have played in the rise in poor mental health amongst young people.

## Fizz

In my work with schools and children, I have been using a fizzy-pop analogy for years. When a child has a negative experience we shake the bottle. Eventually, the bottle is visibly fizzing and will explode if we open it. We then talk about de-escalation and not opening the bottle because we can see the fizz. Too many schools are ignoring the fizz and aren't doing enough to prevent the explosion. Fizz is a tangible warning sign that an intervention is needed.

If everything is about suppressing the fizz, where does it go? It goes inward, along with all the other negative feelings that overwhelm young people – anger, sadness and frustration. Unfortunately, children aren't experienced enough to differentiate between their feelings, so all the hope, joy, optimism and creativity also get swallowed up. When children are grappling with too many big feelings, dissociation can occur: 'I can't feel hurt if I don't feel anything.' (We will explore dissociation in more detail in Chapter 11.)

Alternatively, the fizz is held in and released later: the child can't hurt others so they hurt themselves instead. How many children in zero-tolerance environments survive all day and then self-harm at home? The National Children's Bureau (2020) reports that in 2018/2019, some 28% of 17-year-old females and 20% of males reported self-harming the previous year.

When I ask staff which they would they rather have, the fizzy child or the repressed child, they always want the fizz. Reframing the behaviour as letting the emotions out or bottling them up forces us to think about children's mental health and well-being rather than their conduct.

So, let's teach children that fizz is okay and that it is fine to spill over sometimes. The great thing with spills is that if we clean them up quickly, no harm is done. If we leave them whilst we tell the child off, send them out or punish them, then it will leave a stain. So, let's clean up those spills! Even better, hand the child a cloth and teach them how to clean it up for themselves.

## Actions and consequences

I have made my views clear on the importance of using behavioural mistakes as learning opportunities. Actions and consequences perform a vital role in this process. If they are part of the teaching, they have an important role to play. If the consequences give no repair opportunity, if they are meaningless, if they are designed to appease a system or to be a deterrent to others, then they will have little impact. Therefore, whenever a consequence is issued, we should be asking three questions:

1. Does the consequence match up to the behaviour and take motive into account?

2. Does the consequence teach the child what the behavioural mistake was and help them to understand what to do next time?

3. Does the consequence teach the child how their action has affected others and motivate them to behave differently in the future?

If an honest answer to these three questions is no, then the consequence isn't fit for purpose. A negative answer is likely to be a result of systems that put others first and prioritise conformity and good order over the individual needs of the child.

There is little doubt that we can achieve good order through the use of exclusion. There will always be a large cohort who are driven by the need to please adults and therefore do the right thing. It is easy to point to these children and deem the system as successful, but these pupils would obey the rules under any system. They have the necessary skills and intrinsic motivation and don't require the fear of a deterrent or extrinsic reward to behave well.

A minority of children will never be successful in systems like these because they don't have the necessary skills and because their motivation is directed towards matters like survival. If the child is in a shame cycle or loop (see Figure 8.1), then poor behaviour will be what they know and what people expect. It stands to reason, then, that they will behave poorly.

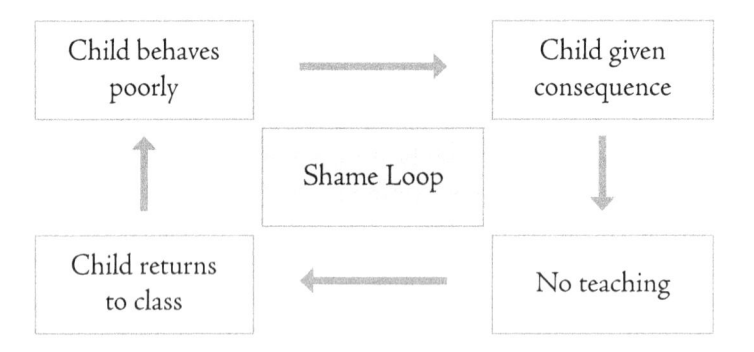

```
┌─────────────────┐              ┌─────────────────┐
│  Child behaves  │ ───────────> │  Child given    │
│     poorly      │              │   consequence   │
└─────────────────┘              └─────────────────┘
         ↑          ┌───────────────┐       ↓
                    │  Shame Loop   │
                    └───────────────┘
┌─────────────────┐              ┌─────────────────┐
│  Child returns  │ <─────────── │   No teaching   │
│    to class     │              │                 │
└─────────────────┘              └─────────────────┘
```

Figure 8.1. The shame cycle

Ignoring the needs of this minority isn't inclusive. Repeating the same process with the same children isn't inclusive. Encouraging children's parents to take them to another school because this school's expectations will be too much for them isn't inclusive. Inclusive means *all* children. It means an approach to consequences by which we teach all children to cope effectively within our school system.

This requires us to look at how we use consequences and to say yes to the three questions on the previous page. Done consistently, we equip children to manage their own behaviour and we don't get stuck in a shame loop.

# Do consequences teach a better way?

Do consequences match up to behaviours? As mentioned at the beginning of this chapter, cause and effect are part of life. Adults have to deal with the fact that their actions have consequences, and very often we have to make amends. Many of these scenarios require the need for repair, but very few require the need for punishment or incarceration. A strong punitive culture might be good for maintaining external control, but being a successful adult requires self-control. That should be the true purpose of consequences.

If I lose my temper or I am physically or verbally abusive to someone, I have to put it right. In order to know how to repair the relationship, I have to know how I made that person feel. If I know what they feel, I can connect to the feeling. We may need to make some adjustments, depending on the age and emotional literacy of the child, but most pupils will be able to connect with sadness, hurt and anger. When a child has acknowledged that their actions have made someone feel a particular way, then we can ask them what would make them feel better if they felt that way. In this way, whether it is saying sorry or being remorseful, rather than the child acting without any purpose other than penance, they are acting to make amends.

We could put a child on detention and make them do extra written work, but they haven't learned anything about their behaviour and nor have they righted their wrong. The adult feels something has been done, the other children have been deterred and the child concerned gets deeper into the shame loop. Alternatively, we could spend the same amount of time talking it through with the child and then putting the onus on them. On the surface it is still an hour's detention, but genuine learning is taking place and the outcome is superior. The child gets a positive feeling from the repair that takes place and develops the belief that mistakes can be fixed. We break the shame loop.

In my experience, restorative practice is one of the most misunderstood elements of education, and is often conflated with restorative justice, which does not work in schools. It is about much more than simply making children say sorry and it should not have a time deadline placed upon it. Restorative practice is the support and expectation that children will repair mistakes and relationships. According to Mark Finnis (2021), it 'describes a way of being, an underpinning ethos, which enables us to build and maintain healthy relationships'. In adult life, time will rarely be taken from you when you make a behavioural mistake, but to be successful you will be expected to give it willingly to benefit others.

## Have we motivated change?

The shame loop doesn't motivate change and it doesn't deter poor behaviour: 'Adults expect me to behave this way so I will.' 'I am bad.' 'This is who I am – I deserve the punishment.' 'It's rubbish, but it's what I know and I'm scared to change because I will fail.'

Instead, we have to break the shame loop by making the child believe that we have faith that they can change their behaviour, by separating guilt from shame and by removing the fear. This then sets them up for repair and shows them they can be accountable for and change their actions, which is what everybody wants. Great behaviour is the goal for everyone; the disagreement comes in how we achieve it.

Changing a child's belief system can't be done overnight and will require relentless consistency. It is important to remember that this has nothing to do with our belief about whether a child will get it right next time; it is about making them believe it. However, our confidence in the child will help them to trust in themselves in the future.

When we have these restorative conversations and make a plan for next time, we have to instil in the child the conviction that they can respond differently and show self-control (even if we don't fully believe it). For example, a child has lashed out at another child at break time:

> Teacher: What happened at break?
> Pupil: Nothing.
> Teacher: What happened with you and Sam?
> Pupil: He wouldn't play with me.
> Teacher: And how did that make you feel?

> Pupil: Angry.
>
> Teacher: Did you hit Sam?
>
> Pupil: Yes.
>
> Teacher: And how did that make you feel?
>
> Pupil: Better.
>
> Teacher: What about afterwards? How do you feel about it now?
>
> Pupil: Bad.
>
> Teacher: How do you think Sam feels?
>
> Pupil: Bad.
>
> Teacher: Shall we figure out a way to make it better?

Discussions on repair can now be pupil led and linked to feeling bad:

> Teacher: So, do you think it was feeling angry that made you hit Sam?
>
> Pupil: Yes.
>
> Teacher: What could you do next time you feel angry with Sam?
>
> Pupil: Hit him harder.
>
> Teacher: But if hitting him made you feel bad, hitting him harder would make you feel worse. It's okay and normal to feel angry but it isn't okay to hit people. I feel angry sometimes, but I take ten deep breaths or I go for a walk, so my anger goes away. What could you do to make your anger go away instead of hitting?
>
> Pupil: I'll walk away and talk to a teacher.

This is a very simple example of a restorative conversation relevant to a primary-age pupil; in secondary, the language would likely be more sophisticated. Now, as an adult, I might not have much faith that the child will walk away in the future, but they have come up with their own plan and I have to make them believe they can put it into practice. It may take a week, a month or a year, but at some point the child won't hit out.

# Separating guilt from shame

Guilt = I did a bad thing.

Shame = I am bad.

In my opinion, the separation of these two five-letter words, guilt and shame, is very important for changing children's behaviour. 'I don't like what you did, but I still like you' is language that should be at the forefront of every conversation about behaviour.

At both ends of the ability range, we are guilty of making what we do more important than who we are, of attaching self-worth to grades, engagement and even effort. Running schools on reward-based systems and sanctions feeds into this problem. At the top end, working for the reward has its flaws for our high achievers in terms of intrinsic motivation and self-esteem, with children constantly chasing the next piece of external approval like an addict chasing a fix. Even though it might be great for the smooth running of the classroom, putting children in a position where how we feel about them is conditional doesn't benefit the child and doesn't prepare them for adulthood.

It is even more damaging at the bottom end, where repeated failure and sanctions can obliterate self-confidence and self-esteem. When a child is repeatedly given the message that it is their actions that sustain their worth, then bad actions equal worthlessness. If they believe that care, love and belonging are conditional on their behaviour, then the narrative becomes: 'Nobody cares about me,' 'Nobody loves me' and 'I don't belong.' We don't give the child a good reason to change that narrative if we are feeding the shame loop by confirming that they will be judged on what they do.

In *Dare to Lead*, Brené Brown (2018) says that the antidote to shame is empathy. That means being there for your pupils, listening despite what is said and being unconditional in your positivity regardless of behaviour. Care, love, safety, trust and belonging aren't earned and they aren't taken away following behavioural mistakes.

If we are successful with our separation, we steer away from shame and are left with guilt. Guilt follows in the wake of poor behaviour. When a child acknowledges that they have done something bad, but we have made them believe the narrative that they are still good, they are motivated to live that narrative. It prompts them to want to repair relationships. Educators shouldn't fear the emotion of guilt; it can be used as a tool to drive positive behaviour. Shame can't take a negative incident and turn it into a positive, but guilt can.

We have to be careful, though, because if we don't recognise and use the child's guilt, it will quickly turn into shame. If we have made them think they are safe and cared about, no matter what, then we have removed much of the fear. It is then a matter of believing they can succeed.

How can we seriously expect children to succeed when all they have experienced is failure? We discuss this in Chapter 16, but the truth is that we can't, and the reality is that if the child doesn't believe they can be successful, then they need other ways to survive school.

## Recipe for logical consequences

Ingredients:

- Safety
- Unconditional care
- Curiosity
- Individual approaches

Don't:

- Use generic consequence systems. If you must, find a way to link it to the behaviour. The system might dictate a detention or missed playtime but you control the content.
- Feed shame by making the child bad.
- Think that tough love will work. A narrative that tells children they only deserve your care if they do what you want is coercive and controlling.
- Use withdrawal to punish.

Do:

- Link the consequence to the behaviour.

- Separate the behaviour and the feeling. The action may be bad but the child isn't.

- Make sure that care isn't conditional on behaviour. The child must be wanted and liked for who they are, not what they do.

- Use withdrawal to teach better behaviour.

- Watch out for quiet children who are masking – they probably aren't okay.

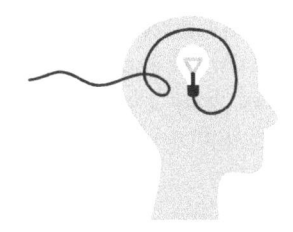

## Chapter 9

# Long-term survival

## Perceptions of behaviour

Why does children's behaviour get under our skin? Why do certain behaviours bother us more than others? Why does a particular behaviour by a pupil have a bigger effect on us than it does on other colleagues?

Sometimes there is a rationality to our feelings, sometimes there isn't. This is the nature of human emotions, and they are hard to change. We might know why something is happening – it could be a perfectly logical behaviour – but that doesn't automatically mean it doesn't bother us. I come across professionals who say that nothing perturbs them, but I find that hard to believe. Not being bothered and not needing to react are not the same thing. We all have experiences that shape us and our feelings, and they can't always be controlled. However, our responses can and should be controlled. With a better understanding of the behaviours we are seeing, it can make it easier to control our responses.

If you asked me what is the one behaviour that pushes my buttons, it would be children's lack of respect for equipment. Being a PE teacher, I had a lot of gear and a very tiny budget. I wanted to purchase a new mini-trampoline, but the £1,000 I needed was a long way off. Each year, I would plan to save some money and buy the trampoline the following year. But, every time, my budget would go on replacing footballs kicked over fences and badminton racquets broken in temper.

It would cause me enormous frustration, even though I couldn't show it. I didn't show my feelings because, as irritating as the behaviour was, it made sense to me. If the children I am teaching go home and smash their Xbox remote in a moment of temper and it is replaced, or if they break their phone and it is replaced, they are causing hundreds of pounds worth of damage without consequence, why would they care about my £5 badminton racquet?

In the previous chapter, we looked at consequences and how they differ from punishments. I want the pupils to know that damaging equipment isn't acceptable. I want them to know how I feel about it. I want them to know that it will require reparation. I don't do that in the moment, though, because it achieves nothing but escalation. I have already lost some equipment; I don't need to lose my lesson as well.

When a calm and logical consequence would be for them to give up some time to help fix other equipment or help with fundraising, I would be happy with a 'sorry' – if it is genuine and unprompted. Detention, isolation or sending home a bill to be paid (or ignored) by parents teaches the child very little. Nobody wins: the child gets two new negative experiences and I am no better off. It is important to acknowledge that although I understand the behaviour and it makes sense to me, that doesn't mean it doesn't make my blood boil! I taught PE for 12 years and never got that mini-trampoline – or, should I say, the children never got their mini-trampoline.

However, there was a phase when I didn't have the same level of understanding, when I would react with exasperation. This was a time when, rather than broaching the behaviour one-to-one after the lesson when the child was regulated and without the aspect of public shaming, I would challenge it there and then during the lesson, thereby bringing into play the child's defensiveness. I will admit to losing my cool and achieving absolutely nothing other than intensifying the situation because, for many of the children with whom I worked, the best form of defence was attack.

This brings us back to one of our earlier questions: what message does allowing poor behaviour send to other children? The key point is whether I am tolerating the behaviour or simply waiting for a more appropriate time to deal with it.

If you mess up at home, do you want your partner to tell you about it in the middle of the supermarket or in front of friends and family? Or would you rather they made you aware of their unhappiness more privately? As an adult, I know that I would feel and respond very differently in those two scenarios. I would argue that doing it behind closed doors is a much faster route to a resolution.

So, why do we often choose to reprimand young people in front of their peers? Why do they have to see bad behaviour being dealt with rather than simply being made aware that it has been? I think the answer has two parts. The first is usually to do with time. Taking the time to deal with a child in the way we would an adult means a certain investment of our time after the event. I fully understand that time is precious for educators, but what is the difference in time spent continually dealing with escalating situations in class versus time spent debriefing afterwards? If we debriefed effectively, how much time might it save us?

The second reason is for the deterrent effect: we must show the other children that it isn't acceptable. But why do we need to show them? Why can't we simply remind them of our expectations and say that we will deal with it in private? If we follow through on what we say we are going to do, consistency and culture is ingrained and the message filters through to all the pupils. Do we really need to make a public show of it?

## Behaviours we find challenging

From my experience of training staff over many years and asking them what behaviours push their buttons, I have compiled a very long list. The behaviours that crop up time and time again include:

- Shouting out/talking over.
- Answering back.
- Refusal.
- Rudeness/bad manners.
- Swearing.
- Spitting.
- Bullying.

- Aggression/intimidation.
- Eye-rolling.
- Lying.
- Telling tales.
- Fidgeting (e.g. swinging on chairs, sticking and unsticking Velcro).

Let's temporarily stick a pin in this list before returning to it later. I will also often ask groups of educators a different question: what do you do that upsets your children? This results in a much shorter list, including:

- Ending an activity.
- Making them wait/spending time with other children.
- Saying no.

What these have in common, according to the adults, is that the young person is perceiving the situation incorrectly. For example:

- Whenever a teacher chooses to end an activity it is going to upset certain pupils – some are only just getting going whilst others have already finished. Therefore, it is only natural that some will perceive the ending as unfair.
- If a class has 30 pupils, the teacher can't possibly give their attention to every child at the exact moment they require it, so it is unavoidable that some children will feel unfairly treated.
- 'My mum never says no, so why should you?' This isn't an uncommon position for a young person to adopt. The fact that there are no boundaries at home doesn't make this misperception the educator's fault.

In one sense, the educators are absolutely right: the child's perception may be faulty. However, our perceptions about their behaviour might be wrong too. Maybe those disruptive behaviours don't mean what we think they do.

At this point, I like to take the role of devil's advocate by offering some alternative reasons for the earlier list of unruly behaviours – reasons that have nothing to do with disliking the teacher, the lesson or the other children. Without attempting to diagnose, but simply to prompt a thoughtful discussion (although perhaps a difficult one), could there be more to those behaviours?

- **Shouting out/talking over/answering back/refusal.** These are all common work-avoidance strategies. As these behaviours are both irritating and a threat to learning, it is easy to see the child as being defiant or having something wrong with them. Alternatively, there is something wrong with the teacher: 'The lessons aren't interesting enough' or 'They don't like me.'

The truth is that it is probably neither. The reason for the child's avoidance might be fear of failure, humiliation or rejection by their peers if they find out they are stupid. Perhaps they can't understand the instruction or the words jump about on the page.

If you were in this position, in front of your peers, wouldn't you want to avoid the work (even more so if you were transported back to adolescence)? Wouldn't being told off or being the 'naughty kid' be preferable to the truth? 'If I can keep people at a distance and focused on my behaviour, they won't find me out' is often a safer option, and getting sent out, being given a detention or even excluded may be preferable to the truth.

Many teaching staff are going home exhausted and upset because they are misperceiving a child's behaviour, believing they hate them or school, when in reality they are just trying to survive.

- **Aggression/intimidation/eye-rolling/spitting/swearing.** These behaviours challenge us on a level that links to our own expectations and values, to our own experiences as children and possibly even to our own parenting. They are also societal: children should be respectful, well-mannered and polite. Whilst there is nothing wrong with having these expectations and values, we must perspective-take the child's experiences. What is their truth when it comes to learned behaviour?

Many of us have been present at a parents' evening at which we would like to challenge a parent on their child's attitude, rudeness or aggression, only to be met with a rude, aggressive or dismissive parent – and suddenly some of their child's behaviours make more sense. Children come to school influenced by what they experience at home. It aggravates us because it challenges the values and behaviours we were taught at home. If the children in your class aren't being taught similar values and behaviours at home, there is bound to be a clash.

For the child who is brought up in a household where they witness intimidation, and whoever is the most aggressive gets what they want, bullying is a learned behaviour. We must accept where it comes from before we try to change it. It might push our buttons, but that shouldn't influence how we see or how we seek to change the behaviour. We shouldn't be surprised by a child who behaves in exactly the way they have been taught to behave; we have to reteach them a better way of behaving in order to meet school expectations.

Similarly, if lying is normalised in the home as a way to avoid getting into trouble – siblings lying to parents, parents lying to each other, parents lying to the police – then we must teach the children about dishonesty, not punish them for it.

It doesn't necessarily have to be home where inappropriate behaviours are learned. We often feel the need to challenge children who are swearing at each other or spitting on the floor. If they are exposed to certain films, TV shows, video games or even football matches, these are all behaviours they will see and perhaps copy.

In the settings where I have worked, I admit that I have become almost completely anaesthetised to swearing. When the children left for the day, the office would often turn blue as we offloaded and decompressed. However, I have the social skills to know when swearing is acceptable and when it isn't. For various reasons, many children don't yet have this ability, so the educators' choice is to be upset by it and take a punitive approach or to teach alternative language (or at least explain about the appropriate time and place for swearing, which is not in school).

- **Rudeness/bad manners.** Whether we are talking table manners or please and thank you, manners are always on the list. If children haven't been taught good manners, then being frustrated at their behaviour is understandable, but it won't help. We can be angry at the parents, but that won't help either. So, let's solve the problem ourselves and teach the child some manners.

- **Telling tales.** This is a personal favourite of mine. When children start school, we tell them, 'If anyone does anything bad to you, you must come and tell a member of staff.' Then, when something happens and the child informs a member of staff, they are told to stop telling tales. The truth is – and I have been guilty of this myself – that even we don't know where the line is between wanting to know about something and not wanting to know about it. And if that line is blurry for us, then children often don't have a clue. (For the record, I am not sure what the solution is to this one.)

- **Bullying.** Obviously, bullying can be linked to intimidation, but the skill of manipulation in terms of control can run much deeper. If you have experienced a life of being treated as much older than your years and forced to grow up too soon because of parental expectations, or of being treated more like a friend than a child by caregivers, or have been a young carer, then this will have an impact. A child in this scenario may well look to try to find some form of control that they don't have at home. In addition, they may have picked up some adult-like skills which may make them more able to manipulate or control others to meet that need. Again, we have a choice: to see the surface bullying behaviour and respond to it, or to understand its purpose and give the child a more positive way to gain control.

Bullying also has strong links with shame. In *Dare to Lead*, Brené Brown (2018) refers to shame as a big dark hole. If children think they are bad, and this can't be changed, they won't believe they can get out of the hole. It doesn't matter how many hands are offered to pull them out, they can't be rescued. If you don't think you can get out of the hole, the next best thing is to pull some other people in with you. I have worked with many children over the course of my career who believed that they could make themselves feel better by making others feel worse. It doesn't work, but it does explain a lot of children's unpleasantness to one another.

So, all might not be as it appears. When we see the behaviour as an outcome rather than a choice, it can change how we feel. Chances are it will still push our buttons, but hopefully in a way that makes us want to support, not challenge.

Children put on masks: it helps them to hide the truth and survive long term. In every class, you are likely to find a devil or monster disrupting with aggressive or challenging behaviour, a clown messing around or a troll doing their best to hide. But what is really going on beneath the surface?

We need to have what Suzanne Zeedyk describes as 'fierce curiosity', in a Teacher Hug Radio interview (see Mahdavi-Gladwell and Chatterley, 2021), to find out the reason behind the reason. We also need to do everything in our power to keep children away from shame, and sometimes that requires us to see shielding behaviours through a different lens. Whilst this is still not acceptable, it is a much better alternative than a child believing they are bad and cannot behave differently.

## Recipe for understanding long-term survival responses

Ingredients:

- Patience
- An open mind
- Fierce curiosity
- Reflection
- Acceptance
- Forgiveness

Don't:

- Try to be superhuman. We all have our limits – it doesn't matter how much patience, knowledge and understanding we have.
- Correct publicly.
- See avoidance as defiance.

- Blame yourself for misperceived behaviour.

Do:

- Correct privately.
- Accept there may be a reason behind the reason for the behaviour.
- See avoidance as long-term survival.
- Reflect on previous behaviour that may have been misperceived.

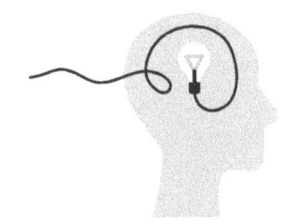

## Chapter 10

# Shielding from shame

## Belief systems

> Shame is the most powerful master emotion. It's the fear that we're not good enough.
>
> **Brené Brown, *Daring Greatly* (2012)**

What we believe matters. It is what gets us out of bed, gives us the resilience to put ourselves out there and makes us believe that we can.

In my opinion, self-belief is the most important thing we can give a child after safety, yet many children arrive at school without it. Repeatedly being told that they are bad and that they can't, especially during the critical early phase of development, shapes the child's narrative. The more failures the child endures, the more toxic the experience, and without the necessary support networks or counter-messages, the child will develop the belief that they are the reason for everything that is wrong in their life, that they are the reason for all those failures.

If nothing has been done to counteract this by the time synaptic pruning takes place, then this narrative will influence the child's beliefs when they walk through those school gates for the first time. Synaptic pruning is a process that occurs in the brain between early childhood and adulthood whereby the brain strips away connections (synapses) that haven't been used or are no longer needed, and keeps the ones that have been used the most.

In very simple terms, it means that during normal childhood development, safety, care and curiosity are retained and mistrust, fear of adults and survival are pruned. For a child who has had toxic experiences, like trauma, abuse or neglect, these structures are reversed. This means that their account of themselves and their life is distorted.

As educators, we can't do much about the first big prune, which is completed by 2 years of age, but the process continues in the brainstem until around the age of 11. Further loss of grey matter will occur and be pruned during adolescence, when we have ample opportunity to alter that narrative and the brain itself, but it requires a desire and determination to do so.[1]

## Changing the narrative

Physical abuse or neglect are not always the reason for high levels of toxic stress; the toxicity can be just as harmful when it is emotional. Blaming and shaming children, telling them they are no good or worthless, or simply the absence of positivity and love can all lead to similar results. Recurrent failure can have a similar although less dramatic effect on a child's narrative. Although the need for short-term survival responses will be less evident, the constant experience of not being good enough will require a long-term protective response.

Many would agree that an absence of love and positivity and an abundance of blame would characterise poor parenting, even a safeguarding concern, yet these faults are the staple of many authoritarian school systems. Zero tolerance and the public shaming of reward and sanction systems are ever present. This is fine if there is the fallback of a home full of love, safety and positivity to buffer and counteract what happens at school, but if home life is more of the same, then the child finds themselves marooned.

Schools often argue that they are hard on the children because they love them. 'Tough love' is an interesting concept, originally coined by Bill Milliken in his book of the same name (Milliken and Meredith, 1968). It

---

[1] If you would like to know more about the synaptic pruning process and neuroplasticity, Norman Doidge's *The Brain That Changes Itself* (2007) contains a wealth of information.

also finds its way into authoritative teaching techniques such as Doug Lemov's Warm/Strict approach (Lemov, 2015). The problem with these approaches is how conditional they are. If love in an adult relationship is withheld depending on whether a partner's actions are deemed desirable or pleasing, we would describe it as coercive and borderline abusive. So, why is it okay in schools?

## Shield against shame

Fortunately, children's experiences are unlikely to be all bad. There will be some adults, both at home and in school, who pick up the pieces and provide a support network. Most of our children won't be stuck in shame. They may have experienced it – whether being told they are bad by parents or moved to the 'dark cloud' on a display board in class – but it doesn't become their internal narrative or belief. Without a way of changing the feeling, they find a different way to defend themselves against feelings of shame.

Shame is a part of life. We have all done things we feel ashamed about, and we are usually driven to apologise. The concept behind this book is teaching behaviour in such a way that children want to make amends and repair their behavioural mistakes. However, this requires them to have the skills to do so. If a child (or adult) doesn't have the necessary skill set, they will develop something else to protect themselves against the feelings of shame – armour.

In *Dare to Lead*, Brené Brown (2018) refers to this process as armouring up, but in 2012, Kim Golding and Dan Hughes gave us the shield against shame model (see Figure 10.1), in which they break down the specific things we can do to avoid shameful feelings because admitting them without repair means we will continue to do bad things. Without positive feelings to counteract the negative, the child has no option but to believe they are bad. Once they have decided on that narrative, they will behave in a way that proves it.

How do we defend against feelings of shame
when we keep getting it wrong?

**Lie/deny**
'I didn't do it'

**Minimise**
'It wasn't so bad'
'I wasn't the only one'

The shield against shame

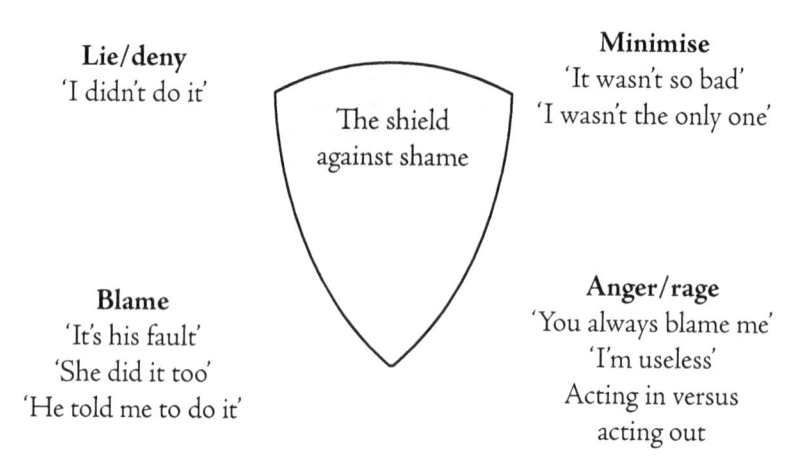

**Blame**
'It's his fault'
'She did it too'
'He told me to do it'

**Anger/rage**
'You always blame me'
'I'm useless'
Acting in versus
acting out

Figure 10.1. The shield against shame
Adapted from Golding and Hughes (2012: 156)

The shield focuses on four responses which we see in schools every day. A shield is a defensive object, but its purpose is often misinterpreted as an attack.

## Lie/deny

If we don't own up to something, we can pretend that it didn't happen and therefore we can't get into trouble for it. Most of us have done something we aren't proud of and then lied about it. The difference is that, as adults, we probably wouldn't tell untruths if someone had caught us in the act.

We have all caught a child red-handed and they still persist in denying their guilt. 'Prove it!' was a popular phrase for many of my pupils. Some children take the stance that if we don't have the behaviour on camera or definitive proof, then denying it is the best approach. There is an element of learned behaviour to this approach, but as a shield it can be very effective.

I am not going to suggest that this never bothered me (it did), but when I look past my initial outrage I can ask myself a question that helps to puts it into perspective. Would I rather have a child lie to me in an attempt to hide their feelings of shame, or a child who has already formed the belief that they are bad and can't be helped? I would rather be fibbed to on any day of the week! Once the need for the armour is replaced with safety, then progress can be brisk.

## Minimise

What could be safer than playing down the mistake we have made? 'It wasn't *that* bad.' 'It was broken anyway.' Or, my personal favourite, 'They did it too!' Another approach often taken by children is to minimise the misdemeanour by claiming it was done collectively.

Admitting the full impact of your misbehaviour can layer on the shame, so keeping it small is a great way to defend yourself. However, as before, if you asked me whether I would prefer a child to avoid admitting to the severity of an action, or a child who ramps up their bad actions because that is who they believe they are, I will take the minimisation.

## Blame

Getting children to take responsibility for their actions can be infuriating. 'They told me to do it' or, even better, 'They dared me to do it' are juvenile justifications for rule-breaking. Our go-to response is generally, 'If they jumped off a cliff/into a fire, would you?' However, if the behaviour was somebody else's idea and they didn't think of it, then that seems to lessen the impact and provide a defence.

## Anger/rage

Many of us will have had the experience of talking to a child about their poor behaviour and found them getting angry at us because they think they are being picked on or treated unfairly. The child is actually disappointed, ashamed and angry at themselves, but instead they direct the rage they feel at us.

For the child, it is often a binary decision – anger in or anger out. Being under pressure or being trapped in a room with an adult means that other alternatives, like taking time out to calm or regulate, aren't an option. However, if it is a choice between the child being furious with me or internalising that rage, I would much rather have it.

If anger is felt, but isn't directed outwards, there is only one place for it to go – inwards. No educator ever likes being abused by a pupil, but if you were given the option of them hurting you or going home and directing that anger at themselves, which would you choose? The overwhelming response in all of the training I have conducted is that outwards is frustrating for the adult but inwards is devastating for the child. The best solution is not to make it binary and give the child time to regulate.

There is one adult example where anger happens most frequently: road rage. Many of us will have had the experience of cutting up (or being cut up by) another driver at a junction. There is only one thing to do in this situation, and that is to speed off, but then we end up sitting side by side at the next set of traffic lights. The majority of people in this situation feel ashamed: they avoid eye contact, try to disappear into their seat and curse the lights for being on red for what feels like 10 minutes.

However, there are others who, despite being the guilty party, get angry with the person they have wronged, especially if that person is perceived to have challenged their behaviour. Sitting in a car means there is nowhere to go and no outlet for the anger we feel at ourselves, and therefore we can't rid ourselves of it in the way we would normally. The feeling of being trapped leads us to the same binary decision as our pupil – anger in or anger out.

If we can better understand the purpose of the shield against shame and see it as an inconvenience that prevents devastation, then what a fabulous mindset shifter that could be. We also have to consider what the toolkit of the child coming into school for the first time consists of and, more importantly, evaluate whether are they are prepared and ready to start their school journey.

## Recipe for understanding the shield against shame

Ingredients:

- Safety
- Unconditional care
- Curiosity
- Trust
- Knowledge of the child

Don't:

- Try to control, minimise or ignore the past. We can't change the past, but it should inform the future.
- Confuse explanations with excuses; challenge staff who do this.
- Make care conditional on behaviour.
- React too negatively to shielding behaviours. They are much easier to work with than shame.

Do:

- Find out as much as possible about a child's experiences and what has shaped their belief systems.
- Focus on safety; children who feel safe don't need shields.
- Set about changing the narrative.
- Work to understand the origin of the shame.

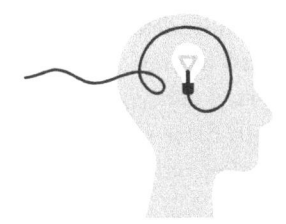

## Chapter 11

# Not school ready

When we look at the starting points of some our youngest pupils, it is important to acknowledge that a perfect storm of factors has been building which has left them with empty tool boxes.

We often hear and talk about equality versus equity, but what does this mean in practice? The idea of giving all children equal opportunities seems fair enough on paper, but it assumes that all children have the same experiences, starting points and the same ability to take advantage of those opportunities. This is not the case. A child who has been played with, interacted with, read to regularly and attended playtimes with other children will not start school from the same place as a child who has been largely ignored, occupied with technology and isolated from others. Those two children have very different experiences, tool boxes and mindsets when starting in reception, so the idea that giving them the same education represents equality is an illusion.

Children are generally ill-equipped for starting school; even for those who have attended nursery or playgroups, it can still be overwhelming. It may be just too much for children without those experiences. As frustrating as this may be, if we are being equitable, we must focus on getting all children to where they need to be. Early years staff are phenomenal at this; it is a skill that often goes unnoticed by those making curriculum decisions based on the experience of educating older children. Plugging these fundamental gaps in the early years provides a secure foundation for all future learning. However, with school resources stretched, we are seeing more and more children struggling in the early years, and it isn't just the children who are overwhelmed.

Before we explore this issue in more detail, we must ask ourselves similar questions to the ones we asked in previous chapters: if a parent hasn't taught their child how to behave, self-regulate or play safely, is it the job of teachers to equip them with those skills? Should we prioritise those skills over learning? If not us, then who?

## Are schools child ready?

According to a recent survey of teachers, half of all children in reception aren't ready to start school (YouGov and Kindred2, 2022). This means that expecting them to fit into existing environments is likely to be problematic. Schools need to be able to adapt to the needs of the children first, before they try to get the children to adapt to school. This is made very difficult by the pressures of an early years curriculum that many specialists in the area believe is not fit for purpose.

The press has taken great glee in pointing out that children aren't toilet trained, can't use a knife and fork, struggle to play or share with others, and lack basic verbal and written skills. It certainly has a huge impact on staff time, increases costs and requires a lot more intervention. It is easy to blame or shame parents for this, but it can be counterproductive when what we need to be doing is working together to best support the children.

What we should really be outraged about are the 7,000 primary-age pupils who are now being educated in alternative provision. The chief inspector of schools in England, Amanda Spielman, told *The Guardian*: 'I'm particularly concerned that the number of primary-age children referred to AP [alternative provision] has risen by 27% since 2017 – there are now over 7,000 under-11s in AP. We're seeing children as young as five attending AP settings, after headteachers have taken what must be an extremely difficult decision to exclude them from primary school' (Weale, 2021).

It is a number that I find difficult to compute. I am furious that this is happening, especially when it is so easily preventable – if early years teachers were allowed to do their jobs and prioritise areas like play and socialisation to replace what is missing. They are more than capable of teaching children what they need to learn, without being over-prescribed a curriculum by people who have never been near an early years classroom.

If we are going to make a big deal about children not being school ready, then let's focus on the real skills gap that many 4- and 5-year-olds have – that is, their ability to feel safe, co-exist and self-regulate – and develop a strategy other than parent blaming. I have encountered many examples of poor parenting during my time in education, but looking down on parents, criticising them or moaning about them (although sometimes satisfying) has never once helped the child.

Isolated parents used to have the support of organisations like Home-Start and Sure Start as well as proactive facilities offered by local authorities, such as parent and child groups, toddler groups and family support. Now, following huge austerity cuts, these services have been depleted and often can't get involved early enough to be properly effective.

Brutal cuts to parental support networks have played a huge part in why parents can't get help, so now we need a comprehensive strategy to support parents who are struggling. If we can support them to do the toilet training, reading, socialisation and so on that is currently lacking, then schools won't need to be bridging the gap for so many children. Unfortunately, that simply doesn't look like it is going to happen any time soon. So, rather than waiting or complaining, we have to do something about it. Whether we like it or not, the support and replacement of missing skills will fall on the shoulders of schools. Just as with the debacle about the provision of free school meals during holidays, requiring the involvement of Marcus Rashford (BBC, 2020), whose fault it is or whose responsibility it is doesn't matter; innocent children need help.

Another major influence on child development is the rise of technology. Although digital devices have their benefits, screens can be detrimental to children's vital early learning experiences. The distraction and captivation offered by these devices can be a barrier when it comes to the delayed gratification that is often required at school. Screens have also been found to shorten children's attention span, inhibit their ability to control impulses and reduce empathy.[1] Add to this parents' own extended

---

1   See https://www.unicef.org/parenting/child-development/babies-screen-time. Alghamdi (2016) is one of the few examples of research in this area.

screen use, which distracts them from their children, and the experience of adult interaction is missing from many children's lives.

Then, on top of all of this, there is the added stress and isolation of COVID-19. I think it is fair to say that in many cases children not being school ready is simply not the child's fault!

It might not be in the job description, but if we don't address children's school readiness in the early years, I dread to think where the exclusion figures may end up. How can we be in a position where a 4-year-old is at risk of exclusion? It shouldn't even be an option. A young child is likely to have significantly limited experiences, very few tools in their tool box and a whole heap of poor learned behaviours. We haven't had the chance to teach this child anything, so it is premature to be showing them the exit.

Before we react to the child's behaviours, we should first look at the position from where they start: what are their experiences (of adults, of other children, of groups)? How do they feel when they enter the reception environment? What strategies do they have to cope with those feelings?

Imagine being in a completely alien place. Everything is unfamiliar and it is full of strange people who keep asking you to do things, taking your stuff and invading your space. I am guessing that it wouldn't feel great at all. (What strategies would you have to deal with this situation? More than a 4-year-old, I would imagine.) Yet, this is exactly what happens to some young children. Through no fault of their own, they are expected to deal with all of this alone and unprepared. Surely, if the child's tool box is empty, the answer is to fill it up, not exclude the child.

## Communication with adults

When a child enters reception, their experience of adults and how to communicate with them, based on their early development, will be critical to how they feel and behave. Their experiences might be:

- Never or rarely hearing the word no.
- Never or rarely being asked or told to wait.

- Immediate attention whenever they require it.

If this is the case, a reception environment of rules, waiting and sharing an adult will go against everything the child knows. The landscape will be very alien. This could prompt a range of feelings, such as:

- Frustration at having to wait – not getting immediate attention and having to share an adult with 29 other children.
- Confusion at new things happening.
- Anger at being told no.
- Fear of the environment, of adults and other children, and of expectations and routines that are unfamiliar and scary.
- Anxiety and/or low self-worth as the teacher is choosing to talk to another pupil and not the child. They might wonder: 'Are they more important than me?' 'Are they more worthy of their attention?' 'Am I not worthy?' 'Am I worthless?'

Faced with this barrage of negative feelings, a child may be prompted to go to their tool box of coping strategies. At age 4, with a narrow range of experiences, it is likely to be almost empty, so many children won't have the ability to regulate themselves. Poor behaviour results from that very limited set of strategies, which might include:

- Throwing a tantrum. It works at home when they need attention or to get their way, so it should work in school, right?
- Aggression or intimidation. It will get people to back off from making requests of the child and might even get people to do what they want. Or they might just be completely overwhelmed and respond in an uncontrolled or dysregulated way.
- Withdrawing or shutting down. When children can't deal with negative feelings, they sometimes believe that the best thing is to avoid them.

Physically avoiding or hiding is difficult for children to do at school, but they can do it mentally. We end up with a child who disconnects from their feelings and locks them away in a box where they don't have to face them; with them shut away the child finds safety in feeling nothing.

In the most extreme and dangerous situations, choosing not to feel might be a useful survival strategy, but a child who is overwhelmed at school is not in an extreme or dangerous situation. Dr Bruce Perry and Oprah Winfrey talk at length about disconnection and dissociation in *What Happened to You?* (2021), including the fact that they are almost always damaging. Small episodes of daydreaming are natural and safe human functions, but excessive daydreaming can be harmful, as elaborated on by Bessel Van Der Kolk in *The Body Keeps Score* (2015).

I have been on the receiving end of plenty of aggressive behaviour. This has often involved teenagers who were still having tantrums and using intimidation as their survival strategy of choice – and were still not school ready. It is never a pleasant experience, but at least I know that the young person still feels. Children who have shut off their feelings are much harder to work with, even if their behaviour is easier to manage. Negative feelings rarely lead to positive behaviours, but negative feelings can be replaced by positive feelings. This means that we can help them to think and feel differently by filling their tool box.

If the antidote to shame is empathy, then the antidote to fear is safety, the antidote to rejection is belonging and the antidote to sadness is joy. If our teaching practice focuses on delivering the antidotes rather than the poison, we make school a place of safety, not survival. We will explore ways to provide these antidotes in Chapter 17.

## Communication with peers

When a young child enters reception, their experiences of other children and how they communicate and interact with them will also be important to how they feel and behave.

Their experiences might be:

- Never shared toys.
- Never took turns.
- Never shared attention or had others in their space.
- Never played imaginatively with others.

Many of you will have been to a toddler group and will know that they are often war zones. There is a lot of snatching, hitting, shouting and sulking (and that is just the parents!). However, what also takes place is a lot of learning. Children are learning to share their environment, in the same way as they would in other face-to-face scenarios, and they can't learn it without having experiences and interactions with others.

Young humans are like any other young animal, with a built-in desire to dominate and mark their territory, which conflicts directly with their need for belonging. Gradually, during these interactions, the dominating becomes less important than the belonging, and children learn that to join in they must share, take turns and play imaginatively. Children who haven't experienced these playful interactions don't know what to do faced with other children, so when they arrive at school they are still working from that primal belief that they need to dominate.

The argument about play-based learning often comes back to the academic model and the idea we must fill children with knowledge. However, it doesn't matter how early or how fast you try to fill a bucket if it is full of holes or, worse still, has a lid on. Until we make school an emotionally safe environment, we are going to end up with that knowledge spilling everywhere rather than being retained.

These experiences will prompt a range of feelings:

- Confusion about new situations and how to manage them.
- Confliction between how to assert their dominance and make friends.
- Fear of being dominated if they allow other children to share their space and belongings.

We will only empower children to overcome their fears by removing the conflict between dominance and belonging. We can't do that for them, although we can support, teach and guide. It is like overcoming any fear, which requires exposure to whatever they are scared of, but it must be their decision. This is the first step to belonging and is essential for a happy child. Without it, they will adopt destructive survival behaviours to manage this alien environment:

- Aggression to assert their dominance, push away or intimidate.
- Withdrawal to box off those feelings ('It's safer on my own').

# Schools are not to blame

Sometimes school systems don't permit the nuance required to replace the missing skills a child needs. It can go wrong if there is a rush to plug knowledge gaps and catch up on learning ages or number bond targets in preference to developing fundamental skills. In my experience, it is the pressure from outside – of trying to balance what is expected and what is needed – that schools are finding increasingly difficult.

It is not the fault of schools that the early years framework is so prescriptive, but punishing young people for not having skills they have never been taught won't help them to learn. We can point fingers of blame and be frustrated, but it doesn't change the fact we can't expect something that isn't there. First, we need to prevent children from becoming overwhelmed and only then we can build them up.

For children to play a game successfully, they must know and understand the rules. When the game is school, children may receive consequences for breaking the rules of the system based on an assumption (sometimes a false one) that they already know and understand the rules. If they don't have that understanding, because they have never been taught it, then it is hardly fair to ask them to play. Telling children the rules is one thing, but teaching them how to play is entirely different and takes a lot longer.

## Recipe for understanding why children aren't deemed school ready

Ingredients:

- Safety
- A new set of tools
- Curiosity
- Understanding
- Patience

Don't:

- See only the surface behaviour.
- Punish children for using the only tools they have.
- View instinctive behaviour as rational chosen behaviour.

Do:

- Acknowledge the combination of experiential factors that affect child development.
- Provide equity before expecting equality.
- Be patient. New skills take time. We aren't going to change a four-year learned behaviour in four weeks.
- Teach belonging – it will always trump dominating.

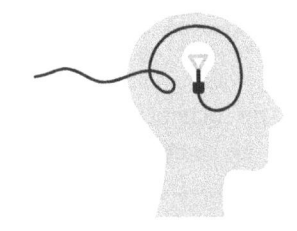

## Chapter 12

# Overwhelm

When considering the origins of behaviour in Chapter 3, we established that one of the primary causes is feeling overwhelmed. You can't go through a social media feed without finding references to well-being and self-care, and advice on how and when to empty your stress bucket or wring out your emotional sponge.

Of course, we have to look after ourselves and manage our feelings. However, when it comes to children, the flaw is in assuming they know how to do it. When an adult feels frustrated, agitated or angry, we might start to get a bit snappy and realise we need to do something. At this point, we might take the dog for a walk, go to the gym or listen to some music. De-stressing, re-regulating and self-soothing are all extremely personal. By adulthood, most people (but certainly not all) have figured out the best way to do this, although many of us fall into the trap of strategies that offer short-term release but long-term harm, such as eating too much, smoking or drinking alcohol.

As discussed throughout this book, children who have not been co-regulated by their caregivers will lack these self-regulation skills, so the co-regulation may fall to schools.

# Emotional literacy

There is little doubt about the benefits of emotional literacy. It is an incredibly powerful skill that can be used by children and adults to make enormous positive change to their lives. However, teaching emotional literacy is complex and may involve many common difficulties:

- Children aren't ready for it. It requires emotional intelligence to identify and name feelings – it is challenging even for adults with good communication skills.
- We feel lots of different things all at once.
- The process isn't child led. Adults trying to tell children how they feel, even with the best of intentions, can be counterproductive.
- Feelings, rather than actions, may be seen as bad. We must validate those feelings.

So, emotional literacy work can have its flaws. Nonetheless, these are skills that we must try to teach, so we must understand and accept our pupils' starting points.

Emotional intelligence was often lacking in my own pupils, so I favoured using the body to help them tell me what they were feeling – for example, fidgety, wound up, dull or tired. This is partly because it is easier to identify physical feelings and they can offer a clue to emotional states – but, more importantly, because it is more difficult to mask bodily sensations. Many children had adopted some of the behaviours discussed in Chapter 8 and had become very experienced at hiding their needs.

When training educators, I get my groups to think of a loved one and write down how they know when they are upset, agitated or angry. I deliberately choose three emotions that look very similar. The first thing we notice is that it is hard to tell which one is which; we can also feel all three at once. These factors make answering the question, 'How do you feel?' or 'How does that make you feel?' very difficult, even for emotionally literate adults, yet we ask children these questions repeatedly. How many times have we suspected that something is wrong with a loved one and asked them to elaborate, only to be told, 'Nothing'? Or, as a married man, the scariest phrase in the English language, 'I'm fine!'? How often does it happen in school?

What comes out of the group activity is that we know there is something wrong with our loved one not because of what they tell us verbally but what their body reveals to us. Physical aspects of their appearance show us that something is amiss: tense body, rapid speech, tone of voice, unusual eye contact, looking in pain, tearful, fidgety, snappy. The fact that this is someone we love and know incredibly well prompts us to see these as warning signs or signals of distress. Even if the behaviours are directly challenging to us, we want to support them and make them feel better. In schools, we need to use the physical appearance of our young people in the same way. This can be done via a bottom-up rather than top-down approach as shown in Figure 12.1.

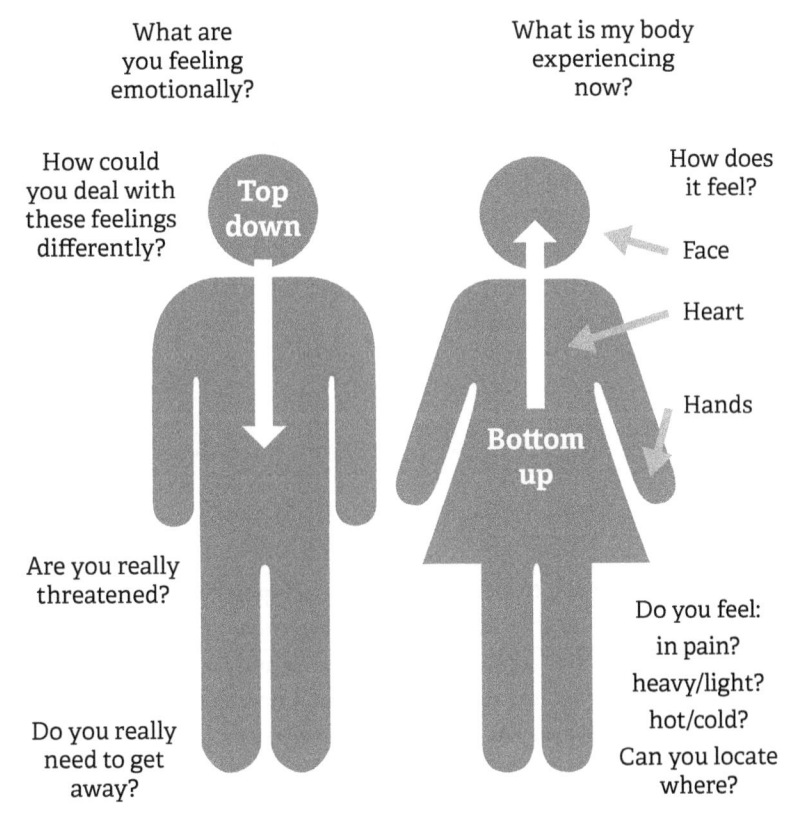

**Top down**
- What are you feeling emotionally?
- How could you deal with these feelings differently?
- Are you really threatened?
- Do you really need to get away?

**Bottom up**
- What is my body experiencing now?
- How does it feel?
- Face
- Heart
- Hands
- Do you feel: in pain? heavy/light? hot/cold? Can you locate where?

Figure 12.1. Top down/bottom up

Identifying an emotion whilst at the same time trying to regulate, is unrealistic for many adults, let alone children. If, instead, we simply observe or ask the child to describe what is happening in their body, we can start to recognise tension, increased heart rate, raised temperature (from a fight-or-flight response), decreased temperature (from a freeze response) or even pain when muscles are affected by high levels of adrenaline. We might then begin to recognise frustration, anger or anxiety rather than just seeing the resulting behaviour.

Physical symptoms are more difficult to hide than feelings, so it is important that we use them. Much of this book has been about looking behind the mask, but there are certain things that can't be concealed. I have always believed that I could tell more from a child's respiration or heartbeat than from half an hour of talking. Obviously, being this close increases the risk of harm to the adult if the child becomes dysregulated and hits out. Practitioners also worry about safeguarding issues, although most schools have a policy on physical contact. Nonetheless, with strong relationships and attunement, positive touch can be a very powerful tool in our tool box.

The brain plays a vital role in the child's responses to threat, but it is very complex and can be deceptive. Children may tell us they are okay even if they aren't. The role played by the nervous system when responding to threat is of equal importance, but its effects are much harder to hide, so if we are attuned to the child and we understand what to look for, we can step in to prevent escalation.

## Children aren't ready to name feelings

For emotional literacy to be successful in changing behaviour, children must first understand their feelings and attach them to a behaviour. This is a tried-and-tested strategy which I have used and trained others in for many years. However, it is reliant on the child having the skills to name the feeling. As with everything in education we need immediate results, so this process is often abandoned when it doesn't work straight away. It is the right plan and it will change behaviour, but only if we accept that it will take time and may falter before it succeeds.

Emotional literacy teaching often fails initially for two reasons. First, many children don't know what anxiety, frustration, jealousy or anger look or feel like. Asking a child to identify what emotion they were feeling when they threw a chair is just too complex, especially when there is a good chance that they won't remember anyway.

Some children may be able to recognise feelings of anger. It is a tangible emotion that they might associate with the colour red, the angry face emoji or the character from the film *Inside Out*. However, if a child has reached anger, then the intervention has come too late. On the other hand, an angry outburst can be a fruitful starting point from which to create a plan together and talk about how to handle those big emotions in the future. For example, a child walking away rather than lashing out is a huge step in the right direction, although it will still require further regulation work, like physical activity or sensory regulation, to use up all the stress hormones in the child's system.

We must be working to identify emotions earlier on in the process. The feelings we need to be detecting are low self-esteem, fear, worry, frustration and so on. When we can recognise these negative feelings, we can avoid anger altogether. Teaching children to recognise these invisible emotional states is incredibly difficult, which is why I prefer to use the bottom-up approach of focusing on physical symptoms.

The second reason emotional literacy teaching can be a struggle is because it requires emotional regulation. We are often asking children to pinpoint how they are feeling at times when they are too dysregulated to think. If they are too distressed to remember the emotional literacy work they have done previously, they won't be able to identify their feelings. If you are rushing because you are going to be late for work, your child is being insolent and you are scared of your boss, and I ask you what you had for dinner the night before, you probably couldn't tell me.

We fall into the same loop with social skills. Retrieving knowledge about body language and facial expressions during an escalating crisis isn't how our brains work; we are likely to misinterpret both. This is why practice and intervening early is vital. We have to build these skills on a solid foundation, so it is essential that this process is led initially by a trusted adult.

# A cocktail of feelings

It is extremely difficult to tell the difference between similar emotions, even with someone we know and love, which demonstrates how hard it can be for children to ascertain how they are feeling. Equally, it could be because they are experiencing many emotions at the same time. In my experience, emotional literacy work usually involves separating emotions neatly so we can identify them, but it doesn't always work like that in real life.

It is all too easy to end up telling children how they feel because we want to label the emotion. This is partly so we can teach the child what to look out for and partly to help teach them a plan for next time they have that feeling. The problem is that we don't know for sure we are right, and telling children they feel something they don't can be harmful. This is a classic case of doing *to* the pupil when we should be working *with* them to explore and name their feelings. Telling a child they are upset, angry or sad when they aren't is unlikely to achieve anything other than making them upset, angry or sad. If we are truly teaching them emotional literacy skills, then this must be a process of discovery done together.

I have stressed the importance of separating feelings and behaviour – as well as validating feelings – throughout this book, but never more so than here. We can't allow children to believe that a feeling is wrong because feelings are involuntary. If we create scenarios where the emotion is the problem, then we are piling shame onto children. The child can't help feeling angry and nor is it wrong to feel angry. Anger is natural and something they will feel thousands of times throughout their life. For the child to respond to the feeling with aggression is wrong, and so the emotion must be validated, not demonised, and then together we can come up with an alternative behaviour or a different outlet for the anger.

## Anger management

One of my big worries is how anger management is approached in schools. It is rarely done well and often causes more problems than it solves. Anger management focuses on our reactions to our emotional feelings and physiological arousal, but the child still requires a channel for those feelings. If we give children an outlet and an opportunity to regulate, then anger management can be effective. Unfortunately, for many children who experience anger management in schools, this isn't what they experience. In too many cases, the child controls their anger, as they have been taught to do, but instead of being given an outlet for their feelings, they have to return to the learning. This does not give them an opportunity to dissipate their emotions, so they may still result in negative behaviour outcomes.

It is even more concerning when teachers misperceive sympathetic activation as anger. Red face, tension, sweating and fidgeting all look a lot like the picture of anger, but they are the physiological signs of cortisol release. Asking a child to manage excess cortisol without an outlet is extremely difficult. It teaches the child to mask or suppress their feelings, it can have a catastrophic impact on learning and it can cause long-term harm. If we think there is even the smallest possibility that the child is experiencing cortisol release, then we must prioritise regulation.

## The aggression train

Despite everything I have said about how hard it is to get right, that didn't stop me from trying to do emotional literacy work with my pupils. Once I had completed my day of training with the speech and language therapy team, I was keen to solve all our school issues. Then, the reality of trying to do this work with children who didn't have the necessary emotional intelligence, as well as the high levels of dysregulation with which we were working, became apparent.

I had to find a method that worked with my pupils and in my setting. All expectations about age and what children *should* know has to go out of the window. For emotional literacy work to be a useful tool for changing behaviour, we must meet the children where they are and build from there, even if that means starting at the bottom. We must also go at their pace and have faith in the process.

One strategy I developed to aid this process was the overwhelmed train line (Figure 12.2). It has been an evolving staple in my work for the last decade.

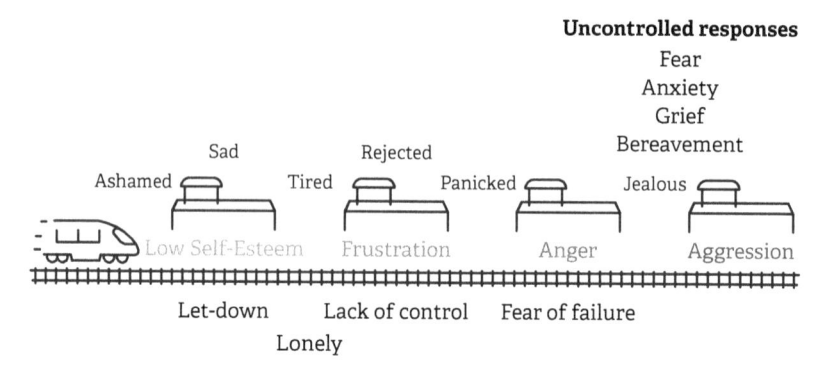

```
                                                      Uncontrolled responses
                                                              Fear
                                                            Anxiety
                                                             Grief
                     Sad            Rejected              Bereavement
         Ashamed              Tired           Panicked              Jealous
              Low Self-Esteem       Frustration         Anger           Aggression
              Let-down     Lack of control   Fear of failure
                          Lonely
```

Figure 12.2. The overwhelmed train line

In Rob Long's *Intervention Toolbox* (2008), and the training session I attended based on it, he says that without intervention low self-esteem leads to frustration and anger. I have added aggression (either verbal or physical) as an end destination. They became stations on a train line, which gave the children a visual image with a clear start and end point. The speed of the train will vary, but it is a journey I have watched hundreds of children take. We could use the diagram in the moment to ask the child where they think they are, or we could use it afterwards to analyse what happened at different points and try to pinpoint the moment when they were no longer in control of their train.

The idea that there are times when someone else is driving the train or that it has become a runaway is important when working with shame and for rebuilding children's self-esteem. Aggression is still not an acceptable outcome, but we can focus on the process rather than the end result. In this way, the child can begin to work out how to maintain control or how to regain it.

# Getting children off the train

From an intervention perspective, our first aim is to get the child off the train. Slowing the momentum is infinitely preferable to the aggression at the end of the line. However, which station we get them off at makes a huge difference to the outcome.

- **Station Anger.** If the child alights at anger, then our interventions are limited. We are probably looking at removal from the class, which may take time, be disruptive to other learners and take even longer to get them back into class. The impact on learning will be significant.

- **Station Frustration.** This is preferable to anger but still disruptive. The process of flooding the body with stress hormones has likely begun and the child may be wrestling to maintain control. We may have more options in relation to interventions (e.g. time-outs, distractions), which will be quicker to implement than with an angry child, but it is still going to have an effect on learning.

- **Station Low Self-Esteem.** At this point, the child is still in control of the train. We have a multitude of fast interventions to get them back on track. Distracting, refocusing, bigging them up or reminding them of past successes might take seconds of investment from us, but it will get them off the train before it picks up speed.

I focused on these three feelings as my stations, but there are many other emotions that pupils might be experiencing (see Figure 12.3). Whatever they are, they will be leading to another station on the track – for example, jealousy might lead to anger, disappointment to frustration or sadness to low self-esteem. Whatever feelings we identify, we need to work out where the child is and what we have to do to get them off the train before they reach crisis point.

```
                    Left out
                         Frustrated
                                          Jealous
          Lost              Loss of
                            control
                                          Angry
   Panicked
                    Feelings
                                            Tired
       Flustered

                                          Different
    Fear of    Anxious      Fear of
    rejection                failure
                                          Hungry
                    Stressed
```

Figure 12.3. So many feelings

The hope is that with teaching and practice they can get themselves off the train. In the future, a hand will go up in class and a pupil will say, 'Miss, I'm feeling angry – please can I go for a walk outside?' 'Sir, I feel very tense – can I have a time-out?' or 'I feel really anxious – can I go and talk to …' Children recognising their own feelings and utilising coping strategies means they are managing those feelings before they reach anger or aggression.

Sometimes, despite everybody's best efforts, we can't get them off the train. How we respond then is paramount. Children are often devastated and disappointed in themselves following an aggressive outburst. It is vital that we separate their guilt and shame. It is reasonable for the child to feel guilty about their actions, but not to feel shame about their feelings. We want them to be motivated to repair the harm done. We want them to analyse what went wrong with us, so we can both learn what to do better next time. Guilt is a driver for change, whereas shame is a handbrake.

> Guilt is just as powerful as shame, but its influence is positive, while shame's is destructive. Shame erodes our courage and fuels our disengagement.
>
> **Brené Brown, *Dare to Lead* (2018)**

What we don't want is for the child to blame themselves and believe that the same things will keep on happening. If aggression becomes inevitable, then getting them off the train becomes much harder.

There are three feelings I always keep separate from the original train line because they are immediate responses rather than built-up ones:

1. *Anxiety* can prompt many reactions. Emotionally it presents as worry, in which case it might begin the route to overwhelm and could be on the train line. However, it could just as easily prompt a physiological and instinctive fight response.

2. *Fear* comes in many forms. Fear of failure, humiliation or rejection could all start the child at the beginning of the train line, but a genuine 'I'm scared' response could cause an instant fight response.

3. *Grief* is an extremely personal and complex emotion. It can cause us to react in unpredictable ways. It is important to differentiate grief from bereavement; bereavement is part of grief but someone/something doesn't have to die in order to feel grief.

## Changing destination

Even better than getting the child off the train and dealing with the fallout is driving it with them or getting them to operate their own train. Without support, the track shown in Figure 12.2 is probably what will happen, but it doesn't have to be a runaway train scenario, as we see Figure 12.4.

In my time as a teacher, I have worked with a huge range of children, from those with autism spectrum disorder (ASD) and ADHD needs to trauma and difficulties with speech, communication, sound and visual processing. Despite being incredibly different in practically every way, all these children had one thing in common: from the day they arrived at school their self-esteem was at rock bottom. They might hide it with disruptive behaviour or mask it with fake confidence, but they each started the same journey. The question for the school was whether we could work together to switch tracks.

When we know the importance of that starting point, often having to look past the defensive bravado and see a child who doesn't believe in themselves, there is only one antidote. We have to rebuild their self-esteem and fill up their bag of experiences with successes (we will find out how to do this in the next chapter). We also have to do it relentlessly because we are going to be challenging that child's belief system, narrative and life experiences. It takes time: sometimes it will be one step forward and two steps back. However, the more often we can lift them up, the more we can change their beliefs.

They will still fail at times, but with the opportunity for repair in place, the damage will be minimised. Building up the child's self-esteem will change their experiences and feelings, and that is how we change behaviour long term.

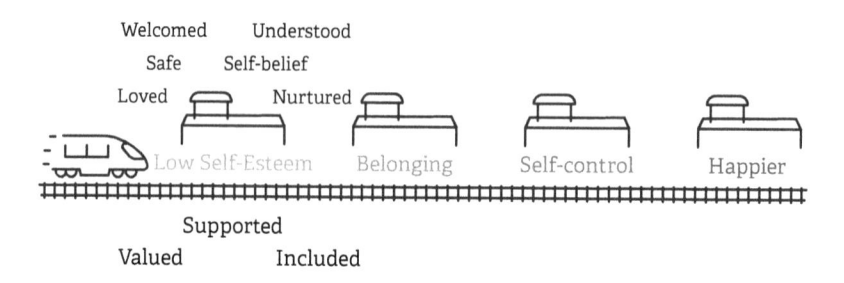

Figure 12.4. A different journey

# How do we boost self-esteem?

We will delve into self-esteem in Chapter 13. For now, there are four easy things we can do to lift up a child:

1. **Talent-spotting.** It is so easy for children to have a negativity bias. They will become very focused on the things they can't do – maths, writing, social situations, sitting still and so on. It is important that we shift this focus onto something they can do well. It doesn't matter what it is or whether it is beneficial to the curriculum – this is about self-esteem. So, whether it is drawing anime characters, performing magic tricks or even rapping, we have to use those interests to help our children feel self-worth.

2. **Catch them doing the right thing.** When a child is constantly making mistakes it is very easy for that to become the focus, so if we want to change the narrative we have to find success. Catching and recognising children doing positive things isn't hard to do. It doesn't have to be academic work either; every act of kindness, every helpful deed, every calm turn-taking or sharing behaviour can go in the bag and be appreciated. It isn't necessarily about big successes either, it can be about lots of little ones too.

3. **The power of 'yet'.** I know there are mixed feelings about Carol Dweck's (2006) growth mindset ideas being utilised in schools, but one element I have always used is the power of 'yet'. Children will often say that they can't do something, but reframing the statement by adding a 'yet' on the end gives them the message that you believe in them and will support them to get there. Even if you know they are capable, simply telling children they can do something, when they don't believe they can, will result in an argument. The journey to achieving what they thought they couldn't do is also the ultimate *with* moment.

4. **Easy wins.** Goal-setting can be a tricky business: too hard and it feels like more failure; too easy and it feels pointless; too long term and children with low self-esteem will give up. We need short-term goals that provide quick successes but aren't too easy to achieve. Linking these targets to the child's talents is a good initial easy win.

If we want to simplify the process even further, we have just one job. Whether we are a teacher, parent or even head teacher, our task is to make sure that, for however long the child is with us, they have more positive experiences than negative ones. That is how self-esteem is built.

## Recipe for reducing overwhelm

Ingredients:

- Knowledge of the pupil, especially what they are feeling and what regulates them
- Adult emotional understanding
- Early intervention

Don't:

- Expect children to have the emotional intelligence to tell you how they are feeling.
- Wait for aggression or focus on anger.
- Mistake anger for systemic activation. Emotions can be managed; stress hormones like adrenaline and cortisol can't.
- Use anger management techniques that don't give the child an opportunity to regulate.
- Encourage children to suppress and mask their feelings.

Do:

- Use a bottom-up rather than top-down approach.
- Have strategies to get children off the train if they don't have self-regulation skills.
- Intervene early.
- Make self-esteem the focus, not anger.
- Build the child up.

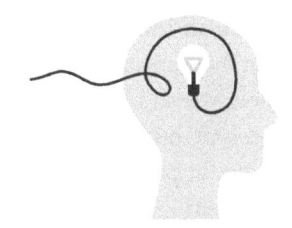

Chapter 13

# Lifting them up

## Back to the bell curve

In Chapter 7, we explored the holistic process that takes place when we treat behavioural mistakes as learning opportunities. We looked at how by not addressing the behavioural mistake we risk repeating a loop in the behaviour, feeding a child's sense of shame and creating a learned helplessness. We make our own lives substantially harder by inadvertently embedding the behaviours we are trying to prevent.

We also investigated how concluding this process with a punishment may provide the child with an end point or full stop that may be a deterrent. However, it doesn't provide any teaching or learning for the children who really need it. It also results in the negative experience of the behavioural mistake *and* the punishment. Both add to the likeliness that behaviours will be repeated. In every school where I have supported children facing isolation, fixed-term exclusion and detentions, the same individuals tend to repeat the same behaviours.

If we are trying to change behaviour, the full stop must be restorative rather than punitive. Teaching the child to repair a negative behaviour by correcting it and making amends is not only a real-life learning experience, but it also prevents them from chalking up two new negative experiences. This allows us to start to building up their self-esteem without it being constantly undone, as well as preventing conflicting messages for a child who is trying to reform their internal narrative.

We might be working our socks off to boost a child's self-worth, but if every bad experience is double the impact of each positive one, we don't stand a chance, and neither does the child. We talk a lot about resilience in children as if it is simply present, but resilience needs to be cultivated (as we see in Chapter 16). One important component of resilience is optimism, but where does that optimism come from if a child's experiences are overwhelmingly of failure?

## The experiences bag

I have always felt that resilience needs to be explained in a visual way, so I developed an activity to demonstrate the baggage and the tools that children bring into school with them. I often use a bag filled with red balls (negative experiences) and yellow balls (positive experiences).

I see it as a bit like a lucky dip. All the child's experiences are in the bag, and when they are faced with a challenging situation they pick out a response. If the bag contains only negative experiences, we will get a negative response – as we so often do with certain children. This behavioural mistake is often met with more negativity and so we add another two red balls to the bag. This process can be repeated multiple times a day and so the bag fills up.

It might be that we have previously managed to put some positive experiences in the bag – perhaps the child resolved a conflict good-naturedly, managed their anger well or was a good friend. Despite this, the red balls in the bag outweigh the yellow ones, so in a moment of potential difficulty or challenge the odds are stacked in favour of the child responding in a negative way.

This was the position of many of the children in my school, who would come to us with a very unbalanced bag. When they were expected to manage complex situations, often in the heat of the moment, it was inevitable that they would make unsuitable choices. It is up to us to help them make better choices.

# Thinking time

What is often missing from difficult situations for both children and adults? Thinking time.

If we ask a child to grab something immediately and at random out of their bag, the probability of them picking a good response is low. Yet, we regularly put them on the spot, often saying things like, 'What have you got to say for yourself?' We create a lucky dip situation when we could be helping more effectively.

Anyone with experience of customer services will tell you that the last thing we need when confronted with an agitated individual is lots of talking or pressure. Instead, long pauses, simple phrases and a supportive manner will calm a distressed adult and get them to a point of rational dialogue and resolution. Likewise, trying to pressurise a child is unlikely to end well.

Rather than rushing children, we need to give them time to think and encourage them to take a minute to look through their bag. Can they think of a situation where this has happened before and the outcome was okay? Many children struggle with the skill of filtering their responses, but we can at least make sure they get the opportunity to stop and consider.

We are our pupils' guides and teachers, so we need to teach them how to search their bag. We can ask questions like, 'Do you remember what we did last time?' or prompt with, 'I know how well you can do this because I saw you do it when …' It's vital to remind children of their successes if we are to change their behaviour. Finding their yellow balls will require skills that some children may not have developed; however, we can exert a powerful influence by remembering for them.

Optimism is about more than saying, 'You can do it' or 'You will succeed.' It is about identifying when the child has done something well before – all the times they have succeeded – and helping to keep those experiences at the top of the bag.

# Fill it up!

There is a fabulous video on YouTube about self-esteem presented by Rick Lavoie.[1] In it, he refers to self-esteem as being like poker chips: some children have massive stacks and some have hardly any. This leads to situations where children with small stacks of self-esteem have to make difficult decisions about whether to take risks, whilst others are free to put themselves out there without any worries. Low self-worth can lead to some children behaving recklessly and engaging in dangerous behaviour, whilst for others it can mean betting only one chip at a time, and being scared to try, to answer questions or to be courageous. Every school has both types of children, but anyone who has ever played poker will know that the most unpredictable player on the table is the one with the fewest chips.

Lavoie says that our job as teachers is to make sure that every child leaves school at the end of the day with more chips than they started with. We do this by taking away only the chips that are necessary in the form of challenge and consequence and always trying to give some back through positivity and restorative outcomes. We challenge any member of staff who does the former without the latter because they make everyone's job harder. But, most importantly, we find as many ways as possible to distribute poker chips. We must notice children engaged in acts of kindness, being a good friend, being helpful, successes in work, special interests and goals scored in the yard. This praise doesn't need to be public and we don't need to hand out certificates; it simply needs to be acknowledged. Lots of smaller positive experiences often have a bigger impact than one big one – for example, something that results in a mention in assembly is often less effective than pointing out a good choice on five occasions and giving a high five as a reward.

The experiences bag works on the same principle. We have to add positive experiences. Every success goes in – and not just academic ones. We need to point out positive interactions and delegate jobs that the children can do well and which will boost their confidence. Of equal importance is how we manage behavioural mistakes. We will still have to

---

1   See https://youtu.be/_BuP5XuMZGA.

add a negative red ball, but that is okay – if we can reach a resolution and balance this by adding a positive yellow ball too.

Over time, we can tip the scales, so that even if a situation is rushed, even if the child is pressurised and it becomes a lucky dip, the odds of them picking out a positive experience, and therefore a positive response, are far higher.

Remember: children know what is in their bag. Many head into school rooting through it for all their previous failures. They play out the upcoming day and forecast the situations where things are going to go wrong. Unless somebody steps in to break this cycle it will repeat, which is where the adults come in.

I had played around with the concept of the experiences bag for a while, but clarity came from working with a particular pupil – Molly.

## Molly

It took me three months to get Molly properly into school. She would come as far as the door, sit in reception and refuse to move. Vicious tongue, too much make-up, too much jewellery, too much phone use – effectively, a flashing beacon above her saying, 'Please challenge me – I'm ready to go!' As far as Molly was concerned, sitting in reception was attending school, and the only reason she did that was to protect her mum from receiving a fine.

I felt genuine concern on her part, yet at previous schools she had been told that her anxiety was feigned and she was just being difficult. The school had threatened her mum (with whom she had a great relationship) with fines for non-attendance, and Molly herself had been met with a multitude of threats and consequences. It had alienated her and obliterated her trust of adults in authority.

Molly would blow up in the most spectacular style, demonising herself so nobody would look too closely. She sat in reception wearing inappropriate uniform or excessive make-up in the hope of being challenged. This would give her the opportunity to 'go off' and be sent home. She had been excluded from everywhere else, so why would this place be any different?

Molly didn't trust adults because they had all rejected her. It was much safer for her to reject from the outset. She hated me at first. Everything about me was what she feared: the guy in authority who says he wants to help and then does the opposite. What gave me the right to demand Molly's respect just because of my position? I had to convince her that when we said that our school was different, that it was somewhere she could feel safe, and this wasn't just words. I didn't feed the hatred because I wouldn't do what she expected – that is, I wouldn't bring any fuel to the fire.

Initially, it didn't matter and she would engineer her own spark. She would insult a member of office staff to get a challenging reaction from them so she could storm out. This usually did the trick. However, as the weeks progressed, despite having no success in getting her into lessons, she was staying longer and being less abusive. Then one day I went to reception to meet her and she wasn't there; she was in the attendance officer's room. She had chosen a person to attempt to trust, not a teacher who was constantly telling her what she needed to do, not a senior leader who was perceived as a figure of high authority, not someone who would immediately give her fire when she asked for it. The attendance officer was someone she didn't feel threatened by and who would listen to her.

She expected to be moved out of there but she wasn't, so it became her place to go on arrival. I would join them in the mornings, and sometimes the attendance officer would 'run errands' and Molly and I would talk. Between us, we identified Molly's interests and gradually got her joining some sessions. There would be blips, but they wouldn't be met with rejection. When she was struggling she could go back to that office for short periods, and she could also touch base during unstructured times.

After a while, the attendance office was replaced with my own office and the need to come out of class waned.

We found out that Molly had a 30-minute walk to school, which gave her lots of time to revisit all her past experiences and past failures, priming her expectations about how the adults would react and what the outcomes would be. It was no wonder that Molly arrived at school prepped for a battle. However, a battle requires two sides. By not giving her one, we changed the narrative, we changed her feelings and we changed her behaviour. From that moment, every walk to school enabled Molly to revisit better experiences, and it was a calmer child who arrived.

## Drip, drip, drip

Building self-esteem isn't about grand gestures. It isn't about reward charts, certificates or stickers. If we make it about external acknowledgement, the children won't believe they can achieve it and may be tempted to give up. This is why recognition is so much more effective than rewards for children with low self-esteem. If they don't believe they can do something, they will find reasons to sabotage it as a safety measure. In contrast, if they are caught having already done something, it can't be taken away. I have listened to so many children tell me they can't, and there is nothing better than pointing out that they already have!

Of course, there will always be children who haven't *yet*, and they will have additional barriers. That is when the poker chips and the experiences bag become even more important.

### Recipe for lifting them up

Ingredients:

- Self-control
- Understanding of the individual
- Patience
- Positive mindset

Don't:

- Put children under pressure to respond.
- Threaten consequences.
- Undo the building of self-esteem by adding negative experiences through punishments.
- Let others (or the system) undo positive progress.

Do:

- Give time and space.
- Look for and remind children of previous successes.
- Prioritise building up self-esteem.
- Use smaller and more private gestures rather than grand public ones.

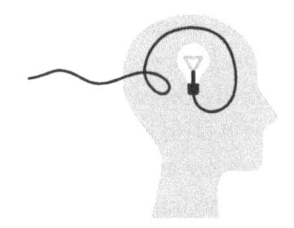

## Chapter 14

# Linking self-esteem and additional needs

If there are parts of this book that I wrote with more than a little trepidation, it is the next two chapters. I have a lot of professional experience in the areas of behaviour and SEMH, but I have had an enormous perspective shift due to my personal experiences. The two have now become so interwoven that it would have been wrong of me to write the next two chapters without declaring a personal perspective. Having preached vulnerability as strength throughout this book, I think it only right that I do the same. In the next chapter, I will share my continuing journey on the autism rollercoaster and how what I learn feeds into the empathy and understanding I have for every pupil and parental interaction.

That vulnerability doesn't take into account the imposter syndrome I feel when discussing children with additional needs when I am not a medical professional, particularly on a subject where it is almost impossible to use language with which every person is happy. So, this chapter comes with a couple of disclaimers. First, I do not intend for anyone reading this book to attempt to diagnose children. My intention throughout has been to raise awareness about the causes of challenging behaviour and understanding the facts around it. If the book helps to aid or direct referrals then great, but it is not an educator's job to diagnose. Second, if any of the language used goes against your personal preference, it was never my intention to offend.

There is a great deal of additional needs training available, both privately and given by specialist settings. However, I knew that I couldn't put a course together or write a book like this without shining a light on unmet needs. The presence of autism, ADHD, pathological demand avoidance and many more additional needs are what often underlie the behavioural difficulties that get children into so much trouble.

The nature of an SEMH school like mine is to do the digging that hasn't been done. The misconception that alternative provision is better equipped to control children's behaviour is a falsehood. It has nothing to do with control or punishment and everything to do with understanding. It is something that Paul Dix (2017: 113) calls the 'punishment contradiction': 'The contradiction at the heart of the behaviour debate is that pupil referral units/alternative provision academies have no need for punishment. Their approach is therapeutic.' We need to have the empathy and willingness to get into the hole with the child, stay there for as long as necessary and help them to climb out when they are ready.

There is still a lot of misunderstanding about trauma-informed practice. Many people still seem to believe that it is about treating all children as if they are traumatised and that, in doing so, we excuse the behaviour. This isn't an accurate description. Trauma-informed practice is about recognising that behaviour is communication – that there is a reason for the behaviour (even if you don't know what it is) – and treating every child in a way that won't cause harm if they have suffered trauma, which comes in many different forms and presents in many different ways. (We will explore trauma in Chapter 17.) Successful alternative provision units have the expertise to deal with the most extreme behaviour, the result of which is that they stop seeing children displaying the most extreme behaviour.

Alternatively, taking an approach that suggests we can't or shouldn't have to understand the behaviour, hoping that children will be fine and favouring systems that respond to behaviour with punitive approaches (with which pupils with trauma are unable to cope) is why we are marginalising these same groups time after time. Sadly, for many children in alternative provision, what caused the trauma was an unmet need not being identified and then being forced to fit into a system without reasonable adjustments.

A new diagnosis that calls for reasonable adjustments to be made by law doesn't mean the needs have only appeared because of the diagnosis. The child will have been in school for a while before this decision was reached, so if support wasn't being provided, the chances are that their self-esteem will have taken a huge hit and their shame intensified, making our job much harder. Inclusive schools see the need before the label is placed on the child, and respond accordingly. If the only reason we provide reasonable adjustments is because a piece of paper tells us to do so, I would question the inclusivity of the school. This takes us back to equity in Chapter 11.

I believe that at least three-quarters of the children in my SEMH setting shouldn't have been there, although I am not able to evidence this. If the need had been identified early on, before it was masked by behaviour, before the failures happened and before self-esteem was damaged, the child would have been successful in mainstream school. By the time we have got to a diagnosis, there is too much failure, too much fear and too much rejection to achieve this in the time we have available.

## Common denominator

The reality in many SEMH settings is that it is a dumping ground for the children who don't fit the mainstream box. However, they don't fit the autism or ADHD box either – or any of the other boxes to get an obvious diagnosis. In the time it takes for schools to get to know the pupil and identify the ingredients of their cocktail of needs, their behaviour has deteriorated or become a mask. They are then labelled as having complex needs and are sent to SEMH provision with a 'See if you can figure them out' request.

This is what alternative provision does, alongside a big dose of empathy, understanding, care, safety-building, trust-building, co-regulation and belonging. The problem is that we are on the back foot: we are trying to repair the damage that has already been done. Listen to the parents of many children with additional needs and they will point the finger at the school environment as being the root of their child's trauma. Whilst this may not always be the case, and certainly not the intention, the accusation is too commonplace not to be taken seriously.

So, what is it that all of these complex individuals suffering from trauma, autism, ADHD, dyslexia, dyspraxia, sound processing and visual processing had in common? Failure and rejection. Failure in their work, in their behaviour and in social situations. Rejection by educators, peers and eventually the school. This meant that the one thing that every child in my care had in common, no matter the need, was low self-esteem. Sure, some hid it better than others. Overconfidence and bravado is phenomenal armour (and is also adopted by many adults) and is rife in alternative provision. It is a simple and effective mask to wear, but when you look past it, the fear and low self-esteem is right there.

I have no intention of discussing additional needs in isolation because there are thousands of trainers and thousands of books and articles that do that. I want to explore how additional needs impact on behaviour and how we can change this. I believe that this is done by understanding the relationship between additional needs and self-esteem. Everything covered in the previous two chapters is entirely relevant to this area, and hopefully, the next two chapters will add an extra layer of understanding.

Despite the range of children's needs I have encountered, the two most common (alongside trauma) are ADHD and autism, very often together. What can sometimes make the more generic training in these two areas problematic is that they try to put children with these needs into boxes, offering strategies that are expected to work for all, but in fact only work for a few. It isn't bad information, but it isn't something to rely on. Just because children have additional needs does not make them the same. If you have met an autistic child, then you have met an autistic child. My home life and work life have certainly taught me that. However, there are some misconceptions that I would like us to consider, and in Chapter 16 we will see why these children aren't as resilient as we would like to believe.

# Attention deficit hyperactivity disorder

One thing that has always baffled me is that we talk about an autism spectrum (I will outline some of the issues with this idea below), but we don't talk about ADHD in the same way. There is understanding and acceptance (although limited) that autistic needs vary and present differently, especially with regard to boys and girls. In my experience, this doesn't seem to be the case with ADHD. The result is a one-size-fits-all approach and a lot of misunderstanding. It is very easy to label ADHD as misbehaviour or to assume that medication will be a quick-fix solution, a problem that is exacerbated by the likely presence of comorbidities and how the physiology of ADHD affects learning.

In the current system, with waiting times for assessment appointments as long as 12 or 18 months, if we suspect ADHD, then we have to make the necessary changes straight away. This has nothing to do with educators attempting to diagnose; it is about making environmental changes to support a child who is struggling. In order to do this effectively, we may need to understand why the problems are occurring in the first place.

As I have explained, one child with ADHD isn't automatically the same as the next, but it is useful to recognise the common characteristics of the main subtypes, even though they may vary by individual:

- ADHD affects one in 20 children, which means there will be at least one child, probably two, in each class.

- A child with ADHD, like other neurodiverse conditions, may be trying to manage up to five things at once, significantly hindering their ability to concentrate and stay on tasks. However, if they can be effectively engaged in something, getting them to stop may be the harder task.

- They are likely to be inattentive and easily distracted, especially by other pupils.

- They may be impulsive and have no thought for the consequences of their actions due to having an underdeveloped or unregulated prefrontal cortex.[1]

On top of the common characteristics come the common misconceptions, according to the ADHD Foundation:

- All children with ADHD are the same.
- They are naughty and ADHD is a conduct disorder. (In fact, ADHD is a neurobiological condition relating to chemical imbalance and abnormality in brain development.)
- ADHD is overdiagnosed and overmedicated. In fact, 5–8% of children would meet the criteria for diagnosis but only 1% are medicated.
- The other 4% should be offered counselling or therapy, but this only happens in 22% of cases, so roughly three out of five children with significant ADHD needs receive no external support from services or professionals.

There is a huge disparity in ADHD diagnosis across the world – for example, it is more prevalent in the United States and almost non-existent in France. This appears to be less to do with the actual existence of ADHD and more to do with its management. In the United States they favour a diagnose and medicate approach, whereas in France they prefer more therapeutic treatment. In the UK, we fall somewhere in-between, but we can see from the statistics above that many children are receiving no external support.

So, yet again, it is over to schools. It is highly likely that there are children in your school with undiagnosed and/or unsupported ADHD. It isn't about treating specific children as if they do have ADHD (although, if we can get the right external support then great). It is about treating all children as if they might, and if they did, then our actions wouldn't cause harm. For example, children who have poor executive functioning will often be late and forget things, so repeatedly punishing these behaviours – and getting nowhere – should prompt a rethink.

---

1  See https://www.adhdfoundation.org.uk.

# Impact on learning

ADHD is likely to create some barriers to learning of which, as professionals, we should be aware. However, as I have said repeatedly, this won't be the case for all children. It may not be the case in different subjects, with different adults or even at different times of day. The bottom line is that traditional school environments are hugely discriminatory for children with ADHD. Long periods of listening, sitting still, large groups, timetables, timings and a plethora of different equipment sets children up to fail repeatedly. How we expect, accept and respond to these failures will have an enormous impact on the success of our ADHD children. Yet again, it is the adult who holds all of the power.

The following characteristics aren't exclusive to ADHD, but they are likely to make mainstream schooling harder for these children.

- **Poor concentration.** Focusing on one thing when you have multiple others to contend with isn't easy for anyone. Try concentrating in a staff twilight following a difficult day. Try not thinking about a bad lesson, or a difficult pupil's behaviour, or a parent you should be phoning, or what you are having for tea. Depending on how engaging the session is, you may be able to refocus or you may struggle. Now imagine doing it for six hours.

- **Poor emotional regulation.** I imagine that most of us have sat across from a critical and unreasonable boss whom we would like to smack or at least verbally challenge. How we respond to outrage usually involves suppressing our anger in order to keep our job. In some cases, an ADHD diagnosis might find us jumping over the table, but for most it is likely to provoke a furious verbal response that will land us in trouble.

    Whichever way we look at it, criticism or challenge is a threat. Some characteristics of ADHD, like hypervigilance, function as a defence mechanism. In hunter-gatherer times, the more vigilant you were, the more chance you had of staying alive. The threats are very different today, and the survival strategies that were once so important have outlived their usefulness (not unlike the polyvagal responses in Chapter 6). The modern world has been transformed but the physiology of our brains has not.

The less developed or weaker functioning prefrontal cortex (thinking brain) associated with ADHD also means that the ability to keep a lid on that outrage or threat response can be diminished.

- **Poor executive functioning.** ADHD is likely to result in difficulties in many areas relating to the 'how' of learning, such as being organised, being on time and having the right equipment. I wish I had a pound for every time I have unpicked a crisis situation that started with a child not having a pen. A lack of foresight or hindsight, difficulty with timelines and an inability to remember and retain information can also affect some children. With that prefrontal cortex being weaker and harder to engage, the brain's priorities may well be lying elsewhere.

  This is in no way the fault of the child and can only be improved by the removal of threats. Therefore, any attempt to exert pressure by talking up the importance of the work, future exams or threats of consequence will be counterproductive. Even if the child manages to avoid a survival response, it is now even more likely that their learning opportunities will have been further reduced because the threat will likely shut down the prefrontal cortex.

Very often, when children had reached my SEMH setting, they were already reluctant learners. However, when I go into mainstream settings this isn't always the case, especially with regard to pupils with ADHD. It is not unusual for them to start highly motivated, eager to please and full of energy, so where does it all go wrong?

If we can place ourselves in the child's shoes, it becomes evident how they are gradually worn down. If you are constantly forgetting information and equipment, getting mixed up and being told off for fidgeting, shouting out or lashing out; if you are constantly being corrected, challenged or punished for things you can't control; if, no matter how hard you try, you keep making the same mistakes, then it is only natural that it will have a devastating impact on your motivation and your self-esteem will take an enormous blow. And with every failure comes an increase in the perceived threat. The antidote is a safe environment, but how do we do that in the current school climate?

# Is variety in the curriculum the prescription ADHD needs?

I will describe my experience of autism in Chapter 15, but, rightly or wrongly, a lot of people link autism with obsessive or compulsive behaviour. This can have a negative impact on the lives of some autistic people. However, I have my reservations about the word 'obsession'; I much prefer 'fascination' or even 'passion'.

I experienced this with my son Max a few years ago when he was learning about the Romans. I have a little knowledge of the Romans from my days as a primary teacher, but a little knowledge wasn't enough for Max. He wanted to know *everything* that happened in the 500 years of the Roman Empire whilst he had me trapped in the car for a short journey across town. Thank goodness for Google and Siri who did have the answers to the barrage of questions he fired at me!

It was brilliant that Max was so interested in the Romans, and he got an excellent report for his work on this topic. The problem was that the rest of the class had now moved on to maths; Max was still thinking about Rome's failed invasion of Gaul!

# Obsession or passion?

For many children, the compulsiveness associated with autism can be even more intense with ADHD. If a child is focused on something, then it is the *only* thing in their world, and refocusing back on a maths lesson can be very difficult. They are blinkered to everything else and have to know *everything* they can about the topic. For Max, simply knowing the information was the driving force, but many children with ADHD also have to know *why*. If there is a problem it has to be solved, if there is a mistake it has to be corrected, if something is incomplete it has to be completed. As a teacher, you might spend hours trying to get a child with ADHD to write something in a literacy lesson, but when they are writing about the Romans you can't get them to stop!

We have a choice as educators: we can fight against this or we can see it for what it is – a huge strength. This desire to finish, fix and solve means that if these children can focus on something that interests them, they will often achieve amazing things. Creating quiet spaces, purchasing ear defenders, devising re-regulation activities and so on are all supportive strategies, but they are designed to fix a problem that our education system creates. Rather than focusing on what children can't do, we should embrace what they can. We need to understand them and their brains; their strengths as well as their weaknesses.

It is easy for me to sit here and say this without having to be challenged by an Ofsted inspector for moving away from the very prescribed curriculum in order to best support a child's learning, but I hope it draws your attention to how the current system discriminates against young people with ADHD. Doing things differently is always going to require bravery, and being inclusive is rarely rewarded externally.

Some neurotypical adults and children may regard this desire to know, solve and develop as obsessive. As a consequence, the child will be made to feel that their fascination is a peculiarity, and therefore that they are different or wrong. The child's self-esteem will take a knock and we will end up with an even more anxious and unhappy child.

In many adults with ADHD, when they finally find the 'right' work field for them, these same traits are seen as a passion. The desire to know is a positive and their problem-solving skills are appreciated and nurtured. Behaviours that were once regarded as unwelcome are now lauded by bosses and recognised as a great attribute. The adult can finally achieve and belong, and their self-esteem gets a well-deserved boost.

Unfortunately, finding your way into desirable employment can be challenging. Many people with ADHD leave school with poor exam results because, despite being intelligent, their organisational abilities were poor or they struggled to focus. All too frequently, they end up in occupations they aren't passionate about, bouncing from job to job and experiencing failure after failure, when in reality they have so much to offer to the right person or organisation. If we can identify that passion early on and see it for what it is, rather than looking down on it as an obsession that must be eliminated, individuals can achieve incredible things.

It is useful to consider what might have become of people like Jamie Oliver if a love of food had been seen as a harmful obsession rather than a passion. But we need more than token pictures on the wall of successful sportsmen and women, actors and business people with ADHD.

## Inclusion is hard

It is in schools where things often go wrong, although I am not blaming schools per se. Schools have to produce children who have learned a balanced curriculum, so we can tick a variety of boxes. Education is a production line of round pegs who are intended to fit into round holes. For many of us this model works fine. However, it holds some children back. It tells them that they are different, that they are doing it wrong, that they are bad. Lots of children arrive at SEMH settings seeing themselves in this way and seeing school as negative. However, every single one could tell me about a subject they enjoyed and every school report contained a mixture of poor behaviour and utter brilliance.

Unfortunately, by the time they get to a specialist setting, the damage is done. There is too much negativity associated with school, so we need an alternative for them. These children are often completely different when they get to college and are engaged in something that enthuses them, like joinery, landscaping and so on. If we are lucky, though, we get to them early enough to find a passion for music, art or sport, and can use that as a vehicle to drive them in school. We know what their outside passions are and we can use them whenever that child is distressed. Whatever it is, we don't make them feel like it is obsessive or wrong because it is our tool to improve their mental health. It is a way to ground them and prevent them from getting into trouble.

If a child is distraught in class when asked to write about something they can't focus on or interest themselves in (despite all their best efforts), can we tweak the lesson and get them to write about something they are passionate about instead? Would that be the end of the world? I know that our system is prescriptive, but is it *so* prescriptive? Or should they be forced to do the same as everyone else? If the argument against personalisation is time, then we need to consider how much time is lost through disruption and negative behaviour. If the argument is about learning, we may want to weigh up the merits of a good piece of work against a more mediocre piece of work, or none at all.

## Curiosity

In our ancient past, hypervigilance would have been the difference between having food and becoming food. Now, it is a disability. In contrast to Spider-Man's 'spidey sense' and Daredevil's heightened sensations, which are seen as superpowers, the child who notices every sound, touch and smell is labelled as hypervigilant or perceived as troublesome because they can't focus. However, skills like these on a sports field or attention to detail in an art class can't be taught.

Lots of schools have become dependent on a prescriptive national curriculum where all children are spoon-fed information. This way of learning has become so normalised that when it comes to being creative or having a debate, many neurotypical children find this very challenging. They feel apprehensive and anxious and don't want to leave their comfort zone. Despite the fact that children with ADHD live with almost constant apprehension and anxiety, given the right topic, the desire to pursue and explore trumps those feelings every time. Their thirst for knowledge and blinkered enthusiasm means that being out of their comfort zone is an adventure and they will be able to stay on task.

## Brainstormers and team leaders

The child with ADHD can also excel in group activities, thinking outside the box and motivating the group. They can take an idea and run with it. Many classes include a child who is difficult to engage, but the other children look up to them. As staff, if we can involve that child, then the rest of the class will follow their lead. All too often, though, we take the easy option and withdraw this pupil.

If a child's confidence hasn't been destroyed by the time they leave school and they are able to enter the right sphere of work, they can become a brilliant brainstormer and an infectious team leader. It is one thing to be able to complete a task well, but it is something else to motivate others with your enthusiasm. What do we actually do with these abilities? We train it out of them and try to make them a round peg.

Surely, we are missing a trick by not teaching these children in such a way that gets the most from them. Imagine if we could combine the skills of our children with autism and ADHD into a research and development team and just allow them to learn in a way that their brain is designed for, rather than trying to stipulate the same stuff every day and setting them up to fail?

A final thought: if the child with autism has a thirst for knowledge which allows them to be an incredible researcher and the child with ADHD has the desire to be an incredible developer, then the child with a combination of both is a one-person research and development team about whom many employers dream!

## Recipe for linking self-esteem and additional needs

Ingredients:

- Understanding of the individual and their needs
- Determination to be inclusive
- Curiosity
- A supportive special educational needs and disabilities coordinator (SENDCO)

Don't:

- Diagnose children, whether as having additional needs or not having them. If we are arguing that we can't diagnose them as neurodiverse, then we can't diagnose them as neurotypical either.
- Only make reasonable adjustments if there is an EHCP.
- Punish children for poor executive functioning.

Do:

- Acknowledge that fake confidence and bravado are excellent armour against low self-esteem.
- Understand that it is statistically likely that at least two of the pupils in your class will have ADHD, whether diagnosed or not.
- See strengths rather than weaknesses, and lift up rather than knock down.

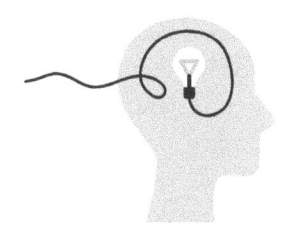

## Chapter 15

# My autism journey

I confessed at the beginning of the previous chapter that I approached it with trepidation; this one takes that apprehension and multiplies it tenfold. Sadly, being neurotypical and talking about autism is a very scary place to be, and I would prefer to avoid the topic altogether. However, it has played such a huge role in my personal and professional life that if I didn't put it into the book it would leave a very large hole. Delegates also say that my lived experience adds a lot to the training I deliver. However, before I come at it from an educational perspective, I think it is important that I share some of my own experiences.

First, I am not autistic. I don't know how it feels to be autistic and, therefore, I can't describe it in the same way that an autistic person can. I can't connect on an experiential level with children or adults in the same way that an autistic person might be able to. However, having experienced it every day for the last 10 years of my life – seeing how it is viewed, the misconceptions and discriminations, the prejudices and stereotypes – puts me in an unusual position.

My life experiences, both personal and professional, help me to communicate effectively with my audience, provide bespoke training determined by the needs of young people and answer their questions. This ranges from delivering trauma and attachment training in severe learning difficulties settings to being able to answer trainees' questions, look behind the behaviour in mainstream schools and discuss the impact of additional needs on self-esteem (as I have in the last two chapters with a behaviour perspective).

This has also helped me to see past the surface to undiagnosed autistic signs in settings like my own SEMH and help with referral paperwork. Most importantly, it has given me a natural empathy with parents — that is, a better understanding of broken systems and why parents often need to be supported using the same de-escalation approaches as their children and using the same bell curve model. For all of this to be effective, we need to work together to provide consistency; in contrast, an 'us and them' school culture towards parents often demonstrates a lack of empathy to parents, meaning that schools and parents are working against each other. If your school has this attitude towards parents, it is worth questioning what it achieves.

## Vulnerability is strength

Having seen the impact that a neurodiverse child can have, both on families and in schools, and having done my best to empathise with the feelings of the parents and children with whom I work, I can do little more than share my own experiences with educators to help them work with these families. I realised the importance of this following an insight I had at a conference.

As with many other conferences I have attended, there was a speaker from outside of education: award-winning comedian Sarah Kendall. Although she could have delivered a crowd-pleasing mini stand-up routine, she chose instead to share her experiences of having an autistic child. It was an extremely heartfelt account of denial, frustration, sadness, despair, hope and joy.

As a talented speaker, she had the attendees feeling everything with her in the most powerful way. All I could do was nod along with everything she was saying because she was pretty much describing the rollercoaster I ride every day. There was a genuine interest in the room, and so I decided to follow her lead and share my own experience.

# Daniel

Sunday 15 January 2012 was the second scariest day of my life. Placental abruption complications, doctors looking panicked and my wife, Eve, being rushed into surgery for an emergency C-section nine weeks before her due date. It all happened so fast I didn't understand how serious it was until afterwards. I knew that something was wrong, but I didn't know how wrong: they had both been seconds from dying.

Ten years on, and I have two vivid memories from that day. One is the helplessness I felt. The other, strangely, was the hospital staff taking my shoes away and making me wear horrible black Crocs whilst I waited in a corridor for what felt like days.

Daniel was born weighing a tiny three pounds and three ounces and with a collapsed lung. We got him home at about six weeks, and he was developing well, hitting his milestones and catching up weight wise. Then at three months everything changed. He hadn't been well all week and my wife was worried. She has taken him to an emergency doctor over the weekend and the GP on the Tuesday, but on both times she was sent away as being 'fussy'. Thursday was to become the worst day of my life; I made a decision that I would live to regret in perpetuity.

I went to football. Eve clearly didn't want me to go, but she kept saying it was fine. I knew I should have stayed at home, but I was stressed out and the doctors said he was okay. So I went. Afterwards, I got into the car, picked up my phone and noticed I had a lot of missed calls. Whilst I had been playing, Daniel had deteriorated and had been taken to hospital in an ambulance. When I got there, a doctor was shaking my baby to get him to breathe, which eventually ended in a seizure and him being resuscitated and blue-lighted to the intensive care unit at Manchester Royal Infirmary. We found out later that he'd had a combination of whooping cough and flu. The flu had made him too weak to cough, so the first two doctors missed it.

He fought through again and came out about a month later, but he wasn't the same child. The little boy who previously had been inquisitive wasn't there. He wasn't making any noise. The first thing he was tested for was blindness because he wouldn't look at us. It was as if a reset button had been pressed. We didn't realise it at the time, but our lives had just changed forever.

## Our relationship

We had three other children at home and both worked with children, so we had a pretty good idea what was wrong but didn't want to say it. The trauma of the birth, the time in intensive care and the added stress of feeling that I should have been there when it happened, followed by the relentless appointments and general overwhelming nature of it all, took its toll, and like the other 80% of marriages involving disabled children, ours fell apart.[1] We both made terrible decisions and hurt each other badly.

I don't know whether grief is the right word to describe my feelings. I described the difference between grief and bereavement in Chapter 12; we can grieve for people and things that haven't died. My child hadn't gone but the idea of the future we planned for him – taking him to football, going to his wedding and sending him off to university – was gone in an instant, and that takes time to process. During that time, anger and resentment fill gaps and decision-making is poor. It didn't mean that I loved my child any less, but I was lost, my wife was lost and we didn't have a map any more. It is entirely possible that there are parents experiencing this in schools up and down the country, so empathy for them is going to be very important.

However, despite the anger we felt towards each other, it was never vented in front of the kids, who I saw every day. They still came first. Love and hate are very close emotions. It takes so much energy to hate someone and anger fades away over time. So, we stopped what we were doing, put our personal lives on hold and became a team again. That was 11 years ago – and they are still on hold!

We made the decision that our personal lives had to be secondary and Daniel had to be the focus – plus, with three other children, we were way down the pecking order. There is definitely more love than hate, and

---

[1] See https://www.children-and-divorce.com/divorce-and-children-with-disabilities.html.

I believe that we could properly reconcile our marriage given the chance, but for now we live separately and have a regimented routine that works for Daniel.

# Help

In the beginning, our parents kept saying things like, 'He'll be fine,' 'It's just been a setback' and 'He'll catch up,' but Daniel continued to miss milestones. Despite pressure from professionals to send him to a mainstream nursery, we resisted. We battled and managed to get a diagnosis before school age. We then battled against sending him to a mainstream school where everyone would be unsafe (especially Daniel) and got him a place at special school for reception. Daniel has to be watched 24/7. He has no concept of risk whatsoever, and when you combine this with amazing problem-solving skills, a lack of fear and above-average speed, strength and gross motor skills, you have a severe flight risk on your hands!

A lot of pressure was put on us to send him to that mainstream nursery – even though every professional knew he wouldn't cope, that we would get called in constantly as his parents, that he would probably hurt someone else (or more likely himself) – but that is how the process works. All children with additional needs, at whatever level, have to be placed in a mainstream setting and fail first before the right support will be given.

It is enough that parents have to come to terms with their child's differences, and possible grief for the child they aren't going to have, without them also having to be the parents of the perceived 'weird', 'aggressive' or 'stupid' kid. Not to mention the damage to the child who understands that this is how they are seen because they are never invited to parties or social occasions and have to sit by and watch other children exclude them.

In a way, we were lucky because I already knew how the system worked and I knew that we were going to have to fight relentlessly to make sure this really hard situation wasn't made any harder. The system thrusts failure on children, feeding shame, damaging self-esteem and making them feel different and alone. Daniel was never going to be able to attend a mainstream setting, but with the right support some children can – but not if they have had to find inappropriate coping strategies in the meantime because of a lack of support.

It angers me when parents who don't know all this get fobbed off by professionals and told they have to follow the advice, go on the courses, put their children's name on waiting lists and adhere to EHCP processes. Meanwhile, they struggle and the child's development is further harmed whilst cheaper options are tried. When we think about some of the more difficult parents we work with, how many have already been through this experience? And, if so, why would they trust any professional? The parent who comes roaring into the office in attack mode has been defending and battling for their child relentlessly. There is no reason for them to expect school to be any different, so it is the school's job to prove it.

We had always worked with all the services involved – doctors, CAMHS, portage, sleep clinics and so on – and managed Daniel's needs well. Despite being offered family support and a social worker on a number of occasions, we held off initially. Part of my job involves training others in positive handling; therefore, I trained Eve so that we could manage Daniel's meltdowns and aggression, keeping him and us safe. But then he got ill.

Daniel is prone to ear infections and he got a bad one, which resulted in five days of non-stop self-harm. When Daniel feels pain in his head, he will headbutt anyone and anything to try to relieve it. I hate having to hold a child who is in crisis at any time, but nothing is quite as bad as restraining your own child who is already in pain and trying to hurt themselves more. After a relentless five days, whilst I was at work, Daniel finally fell asleep, so Eve took the opportunity to nip into the shower. Unfortunately, he woke up and found the hardest floor in the house to headbutt – and did so as hard as he could.

When we got to him to the hospital, we found out that Daniel had fractured his skull. This was a turning point for us. We got a disability social worker, which led us to a helmet, specialist wheelchair and so on, but, most importantly, we had someone else to help fight Daniel's battles so it didn't always fall to us.

# Routine

The 24/7 watching, the aggression, the self-harm, the looks in the street, the constant appointments and the inability to get anyone else to look after your child are all challenging, to say the least, but the biggest barrier to a normal life is the sleep deprivation. There is a good reason why it is a torture technique. A lot of people who read this will have children. They will have experienced sleepless nights with a newborn for periods of time and remember how exhausted they felt. Daniel sleeps on average for three or four hours a night, sometimes less but rarely more. He won't wake us with some gentle cooing either. Sometimes it is a 'friendly' kick to the head to wake us up, and at other times it is a headbutt. Eve has to sleep in the living room with Daniel for fear of him getting up and falling downstairs during the night.

These days, Eve tries to let me sleep as much as possible to allow me to cope with work, but this means that she has to slot in naps where she can, which would be easy during the school day if it weren't for the non-stop appointments with different professionals. Any hope of her returning to work has gone, which only adds to her sense of isolation.

Often, she will call me to come over at about 4 or 5 o'clock in the morning to give her an hour of sleep before getting the kids ready for school and me leaving for work. After work, I go straight to her house, send her up to bed and make tea for everyone else. I will get her back down to eat and then I am dad's taxi service for the other children, if needed. Then Eve goes back to bed whilst I try to get Daniel to sleep after his bath, which on average I manage at about 10 o'clock. Then I go home and go to bed myself.

This is our survival routine. Only people who know me well will know this, and it is only because I have chosen to tell them. Many parents will be guarded about their home life, not because there is something bad going on but because we haven't earned their trust. I have chosen to be open about it because I am not ashamed of our lives, despite the looks we get when we are out shopping or in other public places. If Daniel was in a school that made me feel ashamed at every meltdown, every time he lashed out, every time he failed, there is no way I would share it, never mind write about it in a book.

## Trying for a normal life

Initially, we tried to go out one night a week. One of our older children is responsible enough to look after Daniel and the other is strong enough to manage him if he were to become distressed or needed to be stopped from doing something, but we would barely have sat down before the 'When are you coming back?' texts began, and that, coupled with the fact that we were both constantly exhausted, made it pointless. Even now, with a night of respite every Friday and support from the children's charity Barnardo's, it usually results in a massive headache and an early night.

Both sets of grandparents try to help, but they can't manage Daniel physically. Years ago, we tried to attend a few special occasions together, like birthdays and so on, but we would arrive home just as Daniel was waking up and I would be awake through the onset of my hangover, watching *Rocky IV* (it is always on somewhere in the middle of the night) whilst he bounced around like he was the one who'd had half a dozen Vodka Red Bulls!

Now, we don't go out together any more and we attend special occasions separately. Even if we try to have simple family outings, they often end up feeling like a military operation. From getting all his stuff together, to hoping it won't be too crowded or noisy, to dealing with disapproving looks from others when he shrieks or hits himself or needs to put his helmet on, it all culminates in the feeling that unless it is absolutely necessary, it just isn't worth it.

## Takeaways

I have learned a lot in the last 11 years about living with a child with autism, but here are my main takeaways that are going to affect parents and siblings in your school who live with someone disabled/neurodiverse.

## Acceptance

You have nine months (or seven in Daniel's case) to imagine a future with your child – how clever, how kind, how good at sports and so on they will be. This future has gone and you have a new reality. Take the time to grieve for this, but then accept the new situation. Shift your goals. Perhaps, rather than hoping for them to be head of the school council, you might now aim for your child to not take poo out of his own nappy!

However, little things will become big things. Every interaction is a milestone and every new word is special. We waited seven years to hear 'I love you'. Daniel has no idea what it means, but he knows that it made Mummy happy so he said it. That beats any award in any assembly. I will take him saying 'nappy' rather than painting with his own faeces as a success that far outweighs scoring the winning goal in a football match!

All we ever want for our children is their happiness, and despite Daniel's considerable challenges, I believe he is a happy young man – and that makes everything else irrelevant. However, it can take a considerable amount of time to get to this place.

## Save your armour for the right people

It is human nature to stare when you don't understand something; I get that. As uncomfortable and upsetting as it feels, it is part and parcel of being out with a child who is shrieking because they are overwhelmed by inputs from their surroundings, or hitting themselves because they are distressed, or is wearing ear defenders or a helmet or sitting in a wheelchair.

What is not acceptable is the tutting and muttering that people do under their breath – or even commenting out loud. For families like mine, it has taken a huge effort to decide to venture out with your child. Critical looks is one thing, but being openly judged by someone who has been inconvenienced for a minute, but who knows nothing of your life, is the reason why parents of children with autism and other additional needs become more and more isolated.

Treats are the first thing to go. Soft play centres, for example, are too crowded and another child may get hurt accidentally. Trying to explain yourself to other parents is exhausting, and so are the stares whilst you attempt to do something fun. Shopping is increasingly done online, or someone else has to do it for you, because Tesco has a really high ceiling which makes the perfect amplifier for their whooping, and the lighting in TK Maxx makes a high-pitched sound that only your child can hear and sends them into crisis. You even stop attending family events because you can't bear the fact that nobody really wants your child there, even though they are too polite to say anything.

These are the choppy waters that we need to negotiate. Eve is incredible at putting the negative commenters in their place: she is brave and goes full mama bear on them. She then gets into the car and weeps.

Parents experience stress, loneliness and an emotional toll, which can make it hard to work with them sometimes, but just like empathy and understanding are the master key for unlocking our most challenging pupils, the same can be said for parents. I have absolutely no doubt that having Daniel gave me a natural empathy with parents I wouldn't have had without him, but so much really rests on open-mindedness.

## Support network

Isolation can be a huge problem. You lose touch with friends simply because you can't go out. My best friend of 30 years lives three miles away and I see him once a year, if I am lucky. I go to work to have adult conversations, and as much as she would love it, Eve doesn't have that. Although she has kept in touch with friends, they don't understand what she goes through.

Finding new friends with similar experiences has been a massive help for her. They rarely meet face to face, but they are all likely to be up in the middle of the night and aren't fazed by anything because it is their life too. Social media can be a blessing as well as a curse!

The brilliant Brené Brown talks about empathy, not sympathy, and that is what parents need. When you tell the story of your child smearing poo up the wall, you don't want an 'Oh, poor you, that must be terrible!' response; you want an 'I don't know what to say, but I'm with you!' Having them divulge that 'yesterday, the neighbour knocked on the door because __ was masturbating in the window' isn't entirely necessary, but it can bring a natural empathy to the table! And if the person doesn't have a related experience to share, simply being willing to sit alongside with difficult feelings is important.

Being isolated is an unfortunate inevitability for parents with disabled children, which can be extremely detrimental. You may have to give up on certain people who have been there all your life – and that letting go is hard.

## Pick your battles

Progress *will* be slow and the focus will be on a few things at a time. Choosing what they are is important. Professionals, friends, neighbours and family members will all have an opinion, but the expert on the child is the parent. People telling you how you should be doing things or what your child needs can be frustrating. I am well aware that Daniel should be wearing more clothes and eating a more varied diet, but at the moment I am making sure he doesn't cave his own head in! It can be an exhausting non-stop fight. Parents don't necessarily need advice; they just need someone to listen.

## Find the joy

I don't think I have sugar-coated the fact that parenting an autistic child is damned hard! There will be days when you feel like you are drowning and want to run away. Perhaps you are trying new medication and your child hasn't slept for more than 40 straight minutes for nine weeks, or it is a full moon and they have been relentlessly destroying the house and you are just about to fall off a cliff … Then, suddenly, they will sleep through the night, say a new word or show you affection in a way that melts your heart. These are the moments that make it okay. This is the tiny light at the end of the tunnel. Cherish it!

Will Daniel talk? I don't know.

When will he get out of nappies? I have no idea, but I hope it will happen.

Will I ever be able to let go of him in a shop? I hope so one day.

These are our big targets, and if Daniel achieves them it will be the most joyous of days, but in-between he will keep giving us those little moments.

However, there is one overarching fact that I have learned riding this rollercoaster: Daniel's mum is truly incredible. Eve fights for him every single day, she is patient despite being battered and shattered, and she communicates with him in a language that I am convinced doesn't even exist. It is a bond that you have to see to believe, and Daniel is lucky to have her.

## Daniel's needs

It is best to avoid labels like 'severe', 'low functioning' and 'profound', especially around autistic people and their families, but terms like 'severely mentally impaired' don't just push my buttons, they smash them to pieces! Daniel has huge intelligences that are wrapped up in a different package and with different wiring. That does not make him less. Rightly or wrongly, if I refer to his needs as 'severe', I am referring to his care needs, not his intelligence. The level of care

Daniel requires means that he will always need specialist provision, and he is lucky to attend the school he is in.

I am not attempting to diminish the needs of autistics with lesser care needs, however, of which I have seen the impact first hand. Daniel's older brother received his autism diagnosis in 2021, just as he was starting secondary school. Primary school was a mixed bag and was mostly dependent on whether his class teacher understood him. As he'd had some very positive years, we weren't sure whether he would meet the diagnostic criteria. However, in true system fashion – because of the way his needs present and the fact that he doesn't have any comorbidities – Max ticked every box and sailed through the assessment ready for high school.

Although I am keen to avoid the argument about labels, in Max's case it has led to a very successful transition in the most challenging of circumstances. It made adjustments a necessity rather than a choice, although we chose the school carefully because we believed it had an inclusive ethos and would have made the adjustments required regardless.

Whilst my experience with Daniel has influenced my work with parents, it also helped me immensely in my professional capacity. SEMH settings tend to have a lot of autistic children, many with comorbidities, and the experiences in my personal life have helped me to understand and communicate with these pupils. Many of the difficulties Max has had in education have been mirrored with other children at my school, giving me a good insight into where things can go wrong. The other side of the coin is how it has impacted on my ability to support Max and his school to prevent situations from escalating, which there has been a risk of at times.

## Ethan

Ethan found it incredibly difficult to explain himself and get his voice heard. It had been at the root of many of his difficulties at mainstream school prior to exclusion, where he had been viewed as oppositional and defiant. He was subsequently excluded for verbal aggression and persistent disruptive behaviour, and ended up in my SEMH setting.

On numerous occasions, I found myself having lengthy conversations with Ethan, trying to decode his difficulties and explain the school's position to him. There was very little meeting in the middle with Ethan, initially, and I had to meet him where he was.

School was a tough place for Ethan. He never felt safe, he never felt he belonged and he never felt understood. The school day was littered with misunderstanding and failure, and so it filled him with anxiety and frustration. He would often get things wrong in and out of class, but he didn't understand how he had upset people. He hated anyone thinking badly of him, but he regularly added to this with unconvincing explanations of his behaviour.

I would often spend time unpicking and explaining situations. It was time-consuming, deeply frustrating and at times felt pointless. However, it never was, not only because these conversations showed Ethan that the school was there for him and willing to listen, but also because it gave me the clues I needed about his behaviour that could be cascaded to staff to help them understand and adapt their practice to meet his needs.

My breakthrough with Ethan came when I bumped into him by chance when he was very distressed at having been sent out of PE. My conversation with him went a little like this:

Me: Ethan, you seem very upset about something – can I help?

Ethan: Everybody hates me.

Me: I'm sure that's not the case. Tell me what happened.

Ethan: I didn't get it.

Me: What didn't you get?

Ethan: I didn't get it and he sent me out.

Me: What didn't you get?

Ethan: I didn't get it and when I said I didn't get it, he said I was being silly.

Me: What were you being asked to do?

Ethan: When I said I wasn't being silly and that I didn't get it, he sent me out for answering back.

Me: Ethan, please can you stay here whilst I go and find out. I'm sure it's a misunderstanding.

I knew that if I pursued the matter in this way, I would be going round in circles. When I spoke to the PE teacher, he explained that he was teaching serves in badminton. The method was to practise serving at a target on the other side of the net rather than an opponent, which is a very common way of teaching it in schools. When Ethan had said he didn't understand, the teacher had repeated the instruction. He then judged that Ethan was trying to avoid doing what he was told and, eventually, that he was being disruptive enough to send out. Ethan had had similar experiences on numerous occasions in different schools.

Ethan's eventual explanation connected the dots. Badminton is a game for two people who hit the shuttlecock back and forth, so what was the point of hitting it over the net if there is nobody on the other side to hit it back? Ethan's 'I don't get it' had nothing to do with what he was being asked to do, but everything to do with why he was being asked to do it. Ethan had to know why he was being asked to do something and how it benefited him to learn it.

Knowing the importance of this to Ethan meant that we knew how to approach learning conversations with him. Most importantly, I could share this information with other staff to aid their own explanations of tasks. Hours spent with Ethan became minutes, five times a day became five times a week and then five times a month. The intense support initially given to Ethan wasn't needed because we now had the understanding and empathy to support him better. We had a sequence of support to work through, and he thrived. Staff knew how to work with Ethan and it improved his academic performance. His confidence also increased, and the child who'd had no self-assurance was rapping on corridors at break time, wowing other kids with magic tricks and having the staff in stitches. He was far from perfect and would still have many challenging moments, but he now felt safe and that he belonged. The result was a completely different child.

The following points relate to Max's needs and some of the children with whom I have worked. They are no more than ideas to take away and are certainly not relevant to every autistic child. However, when we talk about communication with children, I don't think being clear is ever going to do anyone any harm.

- **Validate questions.** I have worked with many children who find it incredibly difficult to 'just move on' or 'get on with it' when they don't fully understand what they are being asked to do. For many autistic children, the answer is vital. Until they have an answer, it will become their sole focus and nothing else will matter – not following instructions or threats of consequences. Nothing demonstrates this better than Ethan: once we had validated the question, prioritised his understanding of 'why' and gave him an answer, it made a huge difference. I can say the same for other pupils, and it is something I regularly practise at home.

- **Agree to disagree.** This was also vital with Ethan. At this point in his story (as is the case with many other autistic children), he didn't have the skills to meet me halfway. He couldn't grasp the idea, or didn't care, that we weren't playing a game; that we were practising a skill in preparation for playing the game at a later time. It didn't matter how many ways I explained it, he wasn't going to concede. Therefore, finding a way to accept that you aren't going to agree might be the best chance of a full stop on a discussion in order to move on. Although not fully satisfied, the child will feel heard.

- **Recognise their worry about what people think.** Max is so desperate for adults not to think badly of him that it often gets him into bother. A typical example of this occurred during a practice SAT paper when another pupil asked Max if they could borrow his rubber. Now, the rules of the test are that you can't talk, but the rules of life are that it is rude to ignore people and the rules of friendship are to help your friends if they ask you. Whilst Max deliberated and then made the choice to give his friend the rubber, he had drawn attention to himself and was consequently told off for talking.

Teacher: Stop talking and get on with your test.

Max: But I wasn't talking. They asked me if …

Teacher: I won't tell you again.

Max: But I …

Teacher: Max, you need to stop answering back.

Max: I'm not answering back. I just …

In trying to explain what had happened, in order to prevent his teacher thinking badly of him, he ended up making things far worse than if he had just got on with it. I have seen many children get into this type of situation and I have seen it continue to escalate. Sometimes, it needs an adult to recognise what is happening and put a stop to it.

In my experience, most incidents involving poor behaviour start with something small. If we communicate better when children are inside their window of tolerance, our interventions will be short. The more understanding we have of all the elements, the easier this will be.

# No more spectrum

> Your knowledge of the person is more important than your knowledge of the label.
>
> **Paul Dix, When the Adults Change, Everything Changes (2017)**

We have to move away from the simplistic idea of autism as a spectrum. There are better people than me to explain why treating autism as a spectrum disorder is problematic, but I believe it is much too complex to be regarded as a continuum. I much prefer the wheel representation in Figure 15.1, which allows us to focus on specific areas and paint a clearer picture of children's strengths and challenges.

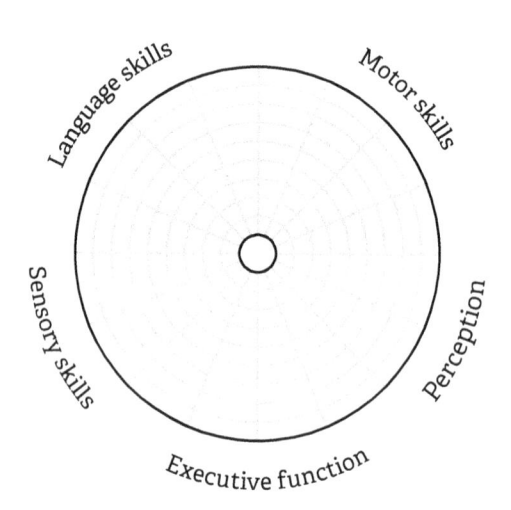

Figure 15.1. Autism as a wheel

The identification of learning difficulties is made even more complicated by comorbidities, but whether it is ADHD, autism, trauma, something else or a cocktail, what brings these children together is the impact on their self-esteem and self-worth and, in turn, their emotional resilience.

## Tentative recipe for working with autism

Ingredients:

- Open mind
- Patience
- Relationship with parents
- A supportive SENDCO

Don't:

- Think you can treat every autistic child in the same way.
- See parents as the enemy. Despite the challenges, avoid the 'us and them' culture fostered in some schools.
- Wait for a diagnosis before making reasonable adjustments.
- Assume that because a child doesn't speak, they don't hear.

Do:

- Work with parents to provide children with consistency.
- Make communication central. We must listen to the child, especially when their words aren't clear or when they are struggling to articulate their thoughts.
- Make every decision based on the interests of the child. Explain this to them and their parents at every opportunity.
- Move away from the idea of autism as a spectrum.
- Expect to get it wrong – a lot!

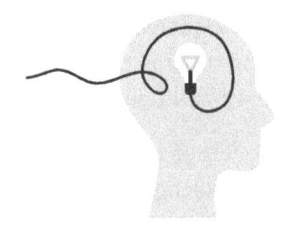

## Chapter 16

# Emotional resilience

The term 'resilience' gets thrown around a lot in education. Following the COVID-19 pandemic, some educators are being positive and focusing on the majority, often proclaiming how resilient children are, whilst others are taking a more pragmatic approach and emphasising that we need to help children to become more resilient.

The suggestion that resilience is about the ability to deal with adversity is overly simplistic. The idea that children are, or should be resilient, is built on certain foundations – similar foundations, in fact, to those that result in good behaviour, like safety, supportive and loving adults, an absence of failure and rejection, and self-esteem. Some children are always going to find it harder to be resilient than others, but if we go about teaching resilience in the same way that we teach behaviour, then we can increase resilience for all, including those for whom it already exists.

However, in order to teach resilience, rather than just demand it or expect it, we must first understand it. We must also recognise the impact of previous experiences and additional needs. We can't teach children to do something correctly unless we identify how or why they are doing it incorrectly. This rings true in every element of a child's education, especially academic learning where building on existing knowledge, learning from mistakes and teaching better ways is a staple of teaching. However, we often ask for resilience from children without appreciating that they have none of the components they need to be resilient and, consequently, they have to overcome enormous barriers.

The previous four chapters have explored barriers to self-esteem and why we need to build it up, but the truth is that self-esteem and emotional resilience go hand in hand. If we build one, then we build the other.

There are several different models of emotional resilience, including the compensatory, protective and challenge models. The best model I have come across identifies seven important components that we need to be happy and bounce back from disappointment: emotional regulation, impulse control, realistic optimism, flexible thinking, empathy, bounce-backability and putting yourself out there.

## Emotional regulation

Getting the balance right between the amount of stress or arousal required to motivate good performance in an activity versus becoming too stressed or over-aroused is very difficult for most young people. However, for certain children, the speed with which the pendulum swings and the effects of outside influences make this infinitely harder.

Children prone to high arousal will be consistently managing stress hormones that make the classroom a very challenging place to be. Being fidgety, uncomfortable and agitated isn't likely to make a child feel at ease. In fact, it is more likely to have a negative impact on learning and will make behaviour management much harder, often resulting in undesirable behaviour.

Equally, managing high levels of stress over long periods of time can have a big impact on the nervous system (which we will explore in Chapter 17). This can also have short- and long-term effects that may lead to behaviour failures.

We have examined the many different factors that can impact on emotional regulation, but one that is sure to is ADHD. The underdevelopment of the prefrontal cortex (which should help the child to calm down effectively once aroused) means that self-regulation will always be an area of difficulty. Teaching regulation can be invaluable in preventing and minimising the impact of stress and high arousal.

## Impulse control

Impulse control is another area that is particularly demanding for children with an underdeveloped prefrontal cortex. They may find it difficult to think before acting, often saying or doing things on instinct that they later regret. As we saw in Chapter 14, our responses to impulse control failures will dictate the impact on self-esteem.

## Realistic optimism

The expectation that children should envisage their own success when they have only experienced failure seems unrealistic (see Chapter 13). Self-belief has to be built on something concrete, so without positive experiences children will revert to what they know. Even if we model optimism and belief, this can challenge their narrative and often results in poor behaviour.

If we really want children to be optimistic, we must remind them of their past successes. If they don't have past successes, we must help them to encounter success in the present in order to build up experiences that we can draw on in the future. Convincing children with adverse experiences that the future can be different has, without doubt, been one of the hardest things I have ever tried to do as an educator.

## Flexible thinking

Flexible thinking is a particular problem for those children with autism needs and those with very low self-esteem. Children develop a belief system about what they are and aren't good at, and don't believe they can change it. When faced with a challenge they will only have plan A; if that doesn't work there isn't a plan B.

The importance of routine for these children can't be underestimated. Any change can be extremely stressful, especially if they are unprepared. The fixed mindset of 'I'm good at this' and 'I'm bad at that' can be difficult to contest, but it can be changed slowly through exposure to new experiences and always pointing to successes. This process is likely to require high levels of support because the child is being taken out of their comfort zone, and that is very scary.

## Empathy

Perspective-taking is a hard skill for all children to acquire, but it is especially hard for adolescents because of the way in which their brains change during this period. Teenagers often get a reputation for being egotistical: their focus is on themselves and so the feelings of others are of little interest. I recommend Sarah-Jayne Blakemore's book *Inventing Ourselves* (2018) for anyone wishing to learn more about the adolescent brain. Having said that, many adults find the skill of seeing things through the eyes of another person problematic, and they have fully developed brains!

Empathy requires us to choose connection even when it is tough, to be with another even when we are uncomfortable. It is a high-level skill which can take a long time to learn, and it can be markedly difficult for some autistic children. However, that doesn't always mean that empathy can't be acquired and it doesn't mean that we shouldn't try very hard to teach it.

One of the hardest things about empathy is trying to connect with someone who has had completely different experiences. Sometimes we feel that we can't relate to them because we haven't had the same life history. It is here that we have to try to connect to the feelings. I can't share the experience of abuse, of having autism or of losing a parent, but I have felt scared, helpless, angry and frustrated, so I can try to relate on an emotional level. Most importantly, empathy is about being present and listening.

## Bouncebackability

Much like optimism, overcoming obstacles and failure is demanding for children who have had few positive experiences. This is what people often think of when they talk about resilience. However, for many young people who have been consistently knocked down, it can be really hard just to get up again. If we want children to overcome obstacles and failures, then we must create a culture that sees mistakes as learning opportunities, not as something to be avoided at all costs. We have to teach children that it is worth getting up and that failure is part of the journey to success.

### Putting yourself out there

None of the best things in our lives would have happened without us putting ourselves out there and risking rejection. Children who fear the rejection of peers and adults find vulnerability terrifying. Why would they put themselves in a position of being humiliated, rejected and failing when they believe these are the only possible outcomes? If we can increase the range of possibilities, then we may be able to encourage the child to become more willing. We can't simply have expectations of vulnerability without the right support and interventions.

## Comorbidities

If emotional resilience is made up of these seven ingredients, then the assertion that children should just become more resilient doesn't stack up. To be resilient means to have a solid foundation of skills and experiences that allow us to get up when we are knocked down, to bounce back from setbacks, to be willing to keep on keeping on. For some children this is simply too difficult, too scary and too exhausting. Therefore, not trying, not believing and not failing is a much safer position to adopt, even if it leaves them unhappy and unfulfilled. At least that is what they know, and familiarity is safety, even if it is actually unsafe.

This is particularly relevant when additional needs such as ADHD and autism are in the mix. Emotional regulation and impulse control require a fully functional and developed prefrontal cortex, and therefore children who have experienced trauma and/or are diagnosed with ADHD are going to find this very difficult. So, the first two components of emotional reliance are missing.

Optimism comes from success, but if you keep getting things wrong, if you don't fit in and if you don't feel you belong, then where does this optimism come from? It becomes unrealistic. Now the first three are missing.

I don't know many people who are unaffected by change, and I regularly come across adults who find it hard to put themselves in someone else's shoes. For many children, particularly those with autism, flexible thinking and empathy are challenging. For children who have both autism and ADHD, then we are missing the first five components.

Getting up and bouncing back is much easier if failure doesn't happen often. The more it transpires, the harder and more exhausting it is to get back up, until finally the child is unwilling to put themselves in situations where they don't believe they can be successful. Children without firm foundations find long-term survival strategies that can be harmful to themselves and others (as discussed in Chapter 9). If we don't want to see these expressed as poor behaviour, we have to give them a groundwork in resilience. I will provide a sequential approach designed to do this in Chapter 19.

When we look at it in this way, expecting children to just become more resilient is nonsensical. Some children will be more resilient than others, but that is because they have fewer barriers and have developed stronger foundations as a result of their experiences; it doesn't happen by magic. Add to this the ADHD Foundation's finding that 40% of autistic children are likely to have difficulties with anxiety and that anxiety will affect 30% of children with ADHD (Foley, 2022), then resilience is complicated even further. If we also add trauma, language difficulties, processing difficulties and other needs, the child is even further disadvantaged.

In the same way that we need to teach behaviour, we also need to teach these seven components of emotional resilience in order to give children a stable base from which to develop. Otherwise, with every expectation of resilience that doesn't happen, we make it harder for them to believe that it can. The big questions we need to ask are, what foundations are you giving your children, and what is happening in their home life that will help or hinder them?

## Recipe for emotional resilience

Ingredients:

- Understanding of resilience
- Knowledge of the individual
- Patience

Don't:

- Assume children are naturally resilient.
- Simplify resilience as simply bouncing back.
- Believe that being hard on children will make them more resilient. This isn't how it works.

Do:

- Recognise that emotional resilience is built and requires strong foundations.
- Set about constructing those foundations if they haven't been already.
- Be empathetic with those children who have had extra barriers to developing their resilience.
- Start from the seven components of emotional resilience and work out what is missing.

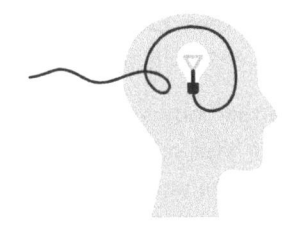

## Chapter 17
# The power of trauma

I expressed a little frustration in Chapter 15 about the fact that autism is often described as a spectrum. The same can't be said for ADHD, which is often assumed to present in a uniform way – an assumption that is equally flawed. This also applies to trauma, which can manifest in many different forms.

Trauma needs to be better defined, especially when it comes to education. Here is the Oxford Languages definition: 'a deeply distressing or disturbing experience'; 'emotional shock following a stressful event or a physical injury, which may lead to long-term neurosis'. There is some mention of the long term but trauma is usually linked to a big experience that causes a big wave.

Significant traumatic events will happen to some children, and they will be managed using the support systems in and around the child both at school and at home. Some schools will be better at this than others, but when a major trauma occurs – such as bereavement, parental break-up or job loss – schools will wrap around the family and specifically the child. They will often give them additional support, understanding and even concessions in terms of their behaviour. This would be known as *tolerable stress*. Although the life-changing event has certainly been part of my experience of trauma in school, it is much more commonly lots of little incidents over a long period of time that have a bigger impact.

The child's ability to recover from trauma is clearly dependent on what assistance is available, but the most significant factor is the stage of the child's development. The earlier the trauma occurs, the greater the impact on the child's narrative of self, especially their relationship with shame.

Trauma is often trapped in the body and stored at an emotional and, more importantly, at a sensory level, causing extreme reactions with little warning and potentially with little understanding by the young person. In order to comprehend a child's trauma responses, we must understand the nervous system responses (see Chapter 6). If children react with great intensity to sights, sounds and smells, this could easily be linked to trauma, even if they don't have a working memory of the event. If a child is storing trauma at a sensory level and showing dysregulation, it is very worthwhile exploring self-regulation with them. Although trauma is often experienced as sights, sounds and especially smells, we found touch to bring great regulatory success, finding textures, objects and deep pressure touch to be hugely impactful.

If we are going to move away from the idea that trauma is simply related to a one-off event, the Adverse Childhood Experiences (ACE) Study comes in very useful, particularly as it takes into account the potential impact of consistent smaller *toxic stresses*.[1] Prolonged exposure to more minor stressful experiences can take much longer to recover from and does more long-term harm: 'This kind of prolonged activation of the stress-response systems can disrupt the development of brain architecture and other organ systems.'[2]

> When our stress system is in good working order, it can help save our lives. When it's out of balance, it can shorten them.
>
> **Louise Bombèr, *Know Me To Teach Me* (2020)**

---

[1] To find out more about the CDC-Kaiser Permanente Adverse Childhood Experiences (ACE) Study visit: https://www.cdc.gov/violenceprevention/aces/about.html.
[2] See https://developingchild.harvard.edu/science/key-concepts/toxic-stress.

# Adverse childhood experiences

The original ACE Study took place from 1995 to 1997 and was led by Dr Vincent Felitti and Dr Robert Anda. The aim was to compare present adult health status with earlier childhood experiences. The researchers focused on 10 potential experiences in a respondent's first 18 years of life:

1. Emotional abuse by a parent, step-parent or adult living in the home.
2. Physical abuse by a parent, step-parent or adult living in the home.
3. Sexual abuse by anyone at least five years older.
4. Domestic violence.
5. An alcohol and/or drug abuser in the household.
6. Someone who is depressed, mentally ill or suicidal in the household.
7. Parental separation or divorce.
8. An incarcerated household member.
9. Emotional neglect.
10. Physical neglect.

The research had some unexpected findings. Few of the experiences are one-off events. Most are ongoing toxic stressors that shape an individual's narrative in relation to shame and require them to adopt survival strategies, many of which can have harmful consequences.

## Facts about adverse childhood experiences[3]

- 67% of people have experienced one ACE.
- One in eight have experienced four or more ACEs and are:
  - Three times more likely to smoke.

---

3   See https://www.wavetrust.org/adverse-childhood-experiences.

- Eleven times more likely to abuse drugs.
- Two times more likely to have liver disease.
- Four times more likely to have underage sex.
- Four-and-a-half times more likely to suffer from depression.
- Fourteen times more likely to attempt suicide.
- Those with six or more ACEs have 20 years less life expectancy.

What this evidence shows us is that if we are unable to support children to manage and recover from toxic stresses, they will look for other potentially damaging coping strategies in the future. If you are overwhelmed by your feelings, then changing them by risk-taking or numbing them with drugs or alcohol may seem like a good alternative.

It isn't just the thrill-seeking behaviour, substance abuse and suicide that leads to the staggering reduction in life expectancy. The more toxic stress is experienced, the more cortisol is released. In the short term the body can manage this, but over the long term too much cortisol has a damaging effect. It weakens bones, damages and shrinks the brain, impairs the immune system, reduces energy levels, contributes to ageing and causes weight gain. All of these conditions increase the chance of stomach ulcers, heart disease and even cancer.

Understanding the long-term effects of ACEs is important and useful, but it doesn't affect the job at hand. We want all children to live long and healthy lives, but as educators we have more pressing concerns in respect of their more immediate responses to toxic stress.

The fact is, though, that none of this is inevitable. The ACE Study doesn't take into account what happens if schools step in, if schools provide children with the skills to change their narrative, if schools teach children how to manage their feelings and remove the shame.

Whatever you think of the ACE Study, it simply can't be ignored. Above all, it should inspire us to change the prospects for children who have experienced high levels of toxic stress using trauma-informed practice.

# How to stop children becoming a statistic

We can never know everything that goes on in a child's life. This is impossible even with the best school–home relationships. Therefore, when we see signs of toxic stress in a child, we have to treat them as if there might be something inappropriate going on at home. Behind the scenes we will need to work really hard to find out if this is the case, but the truth is that we may never find out for sure and we may never be able to influence the child's home life.

This means that we have to support the child as best we can for the time we have them, giving them as much kindness and support in that time and as many skills as we can to help them manage whatever they are facing. If a child doesn't feel safe at home, it is paramount that they feel safe at school. If a child doesn't trust adults, we must show them that some adults can be trusted.

Children tend not to blame the adults who cause their toxic stress, and instead blame themselves. They believe they are undeserving of love or that they deserve to be mistreated because they are bad, and schools can feed into this shame.

> Adults are no more qualified to decide a child has made a fully informed conscious choice that is totally unaffected by circumstance, experience or other unforeseen factors than they are to diagnose trauma.
> 
> **Dan Hallsworth,** *Teacher Hug Radio* **(2021)**

If we view our primary job as academic progress, at best we will fall short of achieving what children are capable of and at worst we will have such dramatic behaviour failures that they won't complete school. Intensifying children's ongoing chronic stress by adding another trauma and another rejection will only make it harder when support finally arrives. Meanwhile, it may push the child further towards perceived escape routes – risk-taking and substance abuse. Underage sex, smoking and drinking were commonplace for the children in my school, some as young as 10. It is very easy to ascribe blame – to the parents, the community, the system, the previous school or the child themselves – but blaming isn't going to bring about change. It is also much harder when the child's way of coping is to use some of the masks discussed in Chapter 9.

> Children who require love the most will ask for it in the most unloving ways.
> Russell Barkley, *Executive Functions: What They Are, How They Work, and Why They Evolved* (2012)

We have discussed how it is easier to support a withdrawn child than a child expressing physical aggression, but children turn to many other survival strategies as a response to toxic stress that are exceptionally difficult to manage. It is all too easy to write off children as a result of their environment and believe that we can't influence their journey – for example, to casually accept that the child of the local drug dealer will follow in their footsteps and there is nothing we can do about it.

I am not for one second suggesting that a child bringing drugs to school is acceptable, but I do believe that excluding them for their actions isn't going to do anything other than fulfil the prophecy. As far as the child is concerned, selling drugs comes highly recommended because it puts food on the table. Simply telling them it is wrong is not enough to stop it, and neither is fear or shame.

It is difficult and it will take time, but the only way to stop that child becoming a drug dealer is to make them believe they can be something else. That is, by giving them self-worth and by believing in them that they might believe in themselves. Many of our young people started at my SEMH school with no plans other than to deal drugs; one of the reasons they were with us was because of either selling or taking drugs at school. If all your life experiences tell you that 'school is worthless,' 'this is all you will ever be' and 'it is all you ever need,' then why bother to try? You can use school for what it is and what you can get out of it until you are kicked out. Yet, the majority left our school with a college place and with the belief that they could improve their life chances. We won't know for sure whether we did enough, but certainly at the time they believed that things could be different.

# What is the antidote?

> Empathy is the most powerful connecting and trust-building tool that we have, and it's the antidote to shame.
> **Brené Brown, *Dare to Lead* (2018)**

Brené Brown's advice about empathy appears to be very focused on the individual, but in fact it is about being solution focused. If we see shame in a child's behaviour or if we see them shielding against shame (as discussed in Chapter 10), then punishing them will only add to the shame loop. To change this we must respond with empathy. We must make the child believe that they aren't bad and that things can change for the better.

Drawing on Chapters 13 and 14, if the goal of educators is to raise the self-esteem of every child and to see the best in every child, then meeting shame with empathy isn't an individualised response aimed at one child, it is part of our whole-school ethos. An individual child's journey might need a little extra help and have a few extra detours, but they have the same destination as every other child in our care. When we give prominence to where we are going, we look for solutions to how we are going to get there.

Chapter 4 showed us that the antidote to fear is safety. Trying to deter a frightened child into behaving is never going to work because nothing we can threaten them with is ever going to be worse than what they are already experiencing. If we respond to fear with safety, we remove fear and fear-driven behaviours.

The antidote to anger is calm. The antidote to mistrust is trust. The antidote to rejection is acceptance. I could go on, but this is about the adult's mindset. When we take a solution-focused approach, we think long term and we are equipping the child to find their own ways forward.

Trauma is too broad a term, which I think makes people apprehensive about embracing it. It is true that trauma comes in many forms and has many outcomes. All that can be asked of educators is to have an open mind to the reasons behind children's behaviours.

# Recipe for understanding the power of trauma

Ingredients:

- Open mind
- Curiosity
- A focus on the antidote rather than the problem
- Patience

Don't:

- Feed the shame narrative.
- Underestimate the harm to the body from prolonged cortisol release.
- See academic progress as more important than well-being; one improves the other.

Do:

- Understand and look out for the effects of toxic stress.
- Recognise that trauma is life-altering and potentially life-shortening.
- See risk-taking as a survival response or escape, not a chosen poor behaviour.
- Provide the right antidote.

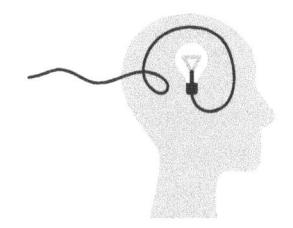

Chapter 18

# Behind the mask

As we saw in the previous chapter, research projects like the ACE Study have enormous value in showing the power and potential impact of trauma and adverse experiences. Now that we know how common trauma is and, more importantly, the impact of toxic stress, it is essential that educators know what signs to look out for in children. One of the big difficulties with the ACE Study is that although participants often ended up using the same coping strategies in late adolescence and into adulthood, there isn't much information about their behaviours during childhood.

The ACE research points us towards potential impact but, as we have seen, the predictions aren't set in stone. If we are determined to change a child's future then we can. As discussed throughout this book (especially Chapter 9), children will adopt a wide range of strategies to mask what is actually going on. This is no different when it comes to trauma.

My determination to find out more, following my enlightenment moment with Lisa Wisher, led me to a book called *Healing Developmental Trauma* by Laurence Heller and Aline LaPierre (2015). Much of the book centres around the NeuroAffective Relational Model (NARM) of therapeutics, which gave me a greater understanding of what might be going on behind the mask.

# NeuroAffective Relational Model

As educators, we often find ourselves in situations where we don't feel we have the full picture. The behaviour of the child just doesn't fit with the information we have been given, and we believe there is more to it than what we are seeing. If we genuinely believe that behaviour is communication, then we must do our best to decipher that behaviour.

Many times, I have found myself in the position of trawling through paperwork looking for information that often wasn't there. However, when I read *Healing Developmental Trauma*, it made me wonder whether NARM was something I could use in school to help me make an educated guess. Remember, my job is never to diagnose, but to treat every child in such a way that if they have experienced trauma I help, not harm. However, in my SEMH setting, many young people did have historical trauma and many were looked after, so improving my understanding would certainly help my own mindset and well-being when I was on the receiving end of difficult behaviours and might also inform some potential interventions to try.

In a similar way to the ACE research, whereby adults used self-destructive behaviours to cope with childhood trauma, NARM takes those behaviours and combines them with personality traits. It then shows how these differ depending on the type of trauma experienced. For example, children who haven't bonded with their parents often become withdrawn and angry adults, and children who have experienced neglect often become caregivers but find themselves in abusive relationships.

The NARM work described in Heller and LaPierre's book took place at the end of the journey – after failure, after long-term survival and after years of cortisol damage. I was encountering those children much earlier in their lives, so I wanted to use the projected behaviours and personality traits as a guide to what underlay the behaviours before the long-term damage was done. What the school found was that the more we used NARM, the more the children's behaviours made sense and the more we could focus our interventions. Also, if we got it wrong, we had lost absolutely nothing and had caused no harm; we just had to try something different.

## Back to shame

What resonated with me about NARM was the way that it emphasised the importance of the type of trauma. Trauma is a big umbrella term that covers a lot of experiences. The range of my pupils' experiences was likewise vast. Masking was commonplace, and so better identification of what masks children wear and when was really beneficial.

Breaking the shame cycle was central to our ethos – and is a major goal of NARM. Similarly, the way it promotes self-acceptance appealed; there is an obvious link to building from self-esteem (as discussed in Chapters 13–14).

When people talk about developmental trauma, they are referring to things that happen *to* a child. However, it can be just as important to take into account the things that don't. It is in the bonding process that co-regulation happens, where attachment needs are met and how trust in adults is developed, and this is often missing in children with behavioural difficulties. Abuse, domestic violence, bereavement, poverty, early surgery and incubation/neonatal issues can all contribute to poor attachment. The NHS reports that 10% of women suffer from some form of postnatal depression,[1] which can sometimes contribute to misattunement with their child, rejection or even neglect.

It is easy to play the blame game again, but many of these problems are nobody's fault and usually can be repaired. However, for some children they won't be and, regardless of context, there is only one person they are likely to blame. Children will rarely point the finger at others, especially parents. Instead, they blame themselves – and this is when the shame begins:

'I was abused because I'm bad and I deserved it.'

'I wasn't cared for because I'm bad and I didn't deserve it.'

Being willing and able to see the child's perception of what has happened to them can explain so many of the behaviours they display, from

---

[1] See https://www.nhs.uk/mental-health/conditions/post-natal-depression/overview.

rejection and aggression to sabotage. Children don't perceive themselves to be a good child in a bad situation; they are a bad child.

The other significant point about NARM is that trauma is viewed as a spectrum. The period of child development in which trauma occurs, the regularity and the intensity of the experience will all impact differently on a child. When we look at the five types of trauma below, many readers will see how their own personality traits have been shaped by their early life experiences, some in a minor way and some even positively.

## Core needs

NARM outlines five core needs that are essential for a child's physical and emotional well-being: connection, attunement, trust, autonomy and love/sexuality. When these core needs are met, children feel safe, trusting of the world and connected to themselves and those around them. Later, as adults, they can address these needs in themselves and others and form appropriate and lasting relationships. As with secure attachment, when these resources are in place, children are equipped to be school ready and to learn and develop.

If these core needs aren't met, particularly over long periods of time, children are forced to resort to survival solutions. They may put their feelings in a box (as described in Chapter 11) or put on a mask that hides their true feelings and/or keeps people away. In the next chapter, we will explore some ways to help us meet any gaps in a child's basic needs.

## Ancient strategies

As we saw in Chapter 6, part of the problem with the approach of the brain and nervous system to survival is that they are hundreds of millions of years old. Today's threats are different – we rarely face the perils of a predator – but the default strategies remain the same: fighting, running and hiding.

If the danger comes from joining in a game, reading aloud, writing the date or walking down a corridor, then these life-saving strategies are often perceived as extreme, unnecessary or naughty. It is not that the threat feels any less real than being chased by a tiger, but there are much better ways to manage them.

The bigger problem for children is that once a survival strategy is engaged, they can't switch it off, so it is easier withdraw socially, to reject first and not put themselves out there. Approaches that evolved for a different time to create safety, now result in real threats like rejection, humiliation and failure. A different world requires different strategies which must be learned. If they haven't been taught in those early developmental years, then it falls to schools.

# Five types of trauma

NARM focuses on five different types of early life experiences: *trauma, physical neglect, overbearing parenting, overprotective parenting* and *rejection/emotional neglect*. How do each of these shape the child as they progress through school? The child's story is complicated depending on the severity of their experiences and whether they have been the victim of more than one type of trauma. However, the biggest factor is the impact of other individuals, which includes educators.

# Trauma

In Chapter 17, we saw how trauma is rarely a one-off event and that repeated exposure to smaller traumas can have just as damaging an effect, if not a more damaging one. We can recover from traumatic events, but just as consistent positive regard can create long-term positive change, so consistent negative regard will do the opposite. We must also acknowledge that this can happen at school: not only can existing trauma be triggered by school but in some cases the school is primarily responsible.

Another factor that plays an enormous role is how early in a child's life trauma occurs. If a child has had some positive experiences beforehand, then they have a base of safety. If their first experiences are of pain, danger and rejection, then they are thrust into a world where survival is all they know.

NARM focuses on five main traumatic experiences:

- **Unwanted pregnancy/thoughts of abortion.** I was stunned when I realised how an infant could be impacted during prenatal development. The worry, doubt, panic and so on felt by many mums-to-be means that babies can be born with higher than normal levels of cortisol. A newborn who is totally dependent on caregivers, but automatically feels stressed and unsafe in what could already be a potentially difficult bonding situation, is likely to be harder to soothe and settle, which only adds to the parents' pressure.

- **Traumatic birth.** The stress and cortisol levels involved during a difficult birth can leave a lasting impact on both parent and child. It can result in trauma for both, making swift bonding even more challenging. Also, babies born with excess cortisol are likely to be fussier and more difficult to settle, resulting in more difficulty.

- **Medical issues/neonatal incubation.** If a child requires a period in an incubator, then the opportunities for physical contact between parent and child are limited. This can be detrimental to bonding. And if, simultaneously, the pain of surgery and illness are an infant's first life experiences, then safety and security will be an alien feeling.

- **Domestic violence.** The emotional harm caused to children from witnessing, hearing or experiencing domestic violence is enormous. It takes away the child's security and creates toxic stress. The earlier and longer a child is exposed, the more damage is done. The child doesn't have to suffer physical abuse directly for there to be a significant psychological impact.

- **Physical/sexual abuse.** Abuse is especially impactful if it comes from a caregiver. For an infant who hasn't been kept safe from others, it can lead to them feeling a lot of anger towards parents who should have been protecting them. It can also result in shame and the child's belief they deserved it.

If we consider trauma as an early life experience that has interrupted bonding and damaged the child's feelings of love and safety, then we are back with the child's tool box of behaviours. A child is unable to fight or flee, so freeze is the only strategy they have. Continually producing high levels of cortisol with nowhere for it to go is very damaging, so the safest thing for the child to do is avoid feelings and relationships altogether. The anger they feel towards the parents they are supposed to love scares them, so they hide it.

A less harmful option for the child is to immerse themselves in fantasy, through stories, books or computer games. They can often appear withdrawn, cold and emotionless and may have poor emotional literacy skills. It is very easy to misperceive these behaviours as autistic traits.

Another long-term survival strategy for the child is to hide behind a mask.

## The rejector mask

| Front (how they present on the outside) | Internal working model (driven by feeling scared) |
| --- | --- |
| Feelings are unimportant. | Adults are scary and will hurt me. |
| Rationality is everything (facts not feelings). | I'm worthless. |
| TV shows, books and computers are more interesting than real people. | It's my fault my parents didn't bond with me. |
| People who show feelings are weak. | I'm bad. |
| I don't need help. | |

If a child's inner working monologue is that they are worthless or bad, that they don't deserve to be loved or deserve to be hurt and that adults are dangerous, then school must be a frightening and overwhelming place.

Children avoid the joy, happiness and love around them by presenting in a way that discourages all of those things. There is safety is not joining in, in not saying how you feel, in not asking for help. The problem comes when we try to offer help or to get them to participate: the more pressure we apply, the more stress we potentially cause. When hiding is the only survival strategy a child has left, encouragement to get involved takes it away. Then there is only fight or flight. If they can't withdraw in school, their only option may be refusal to attend.

If we elicit extreme reactions from children when they are asked to do what should be fun activities, it is likely to be a fear response. If a child is constantly scared, the antidote is safety, and so that is what we must prioritise.

## Portrait of a child who has experienced trauma

Carlos wore a rejector mask. He didn't arrive in my SEMH school until the end of Year 8. His paperwork told me that he was a repeated school refuser and absconder. When I first met him he was a pleasant young man. When I asked him what he liked to do, as I usually did when meeting a new pupil, he said, 'Going out'. His granddad answered many questions for him, explaining that he had done karate, swimming and football, but the truth was he had been taken a couple of times and then quit.

I have taught many pupils over the years, but the only one I could never draw into anything was Carlos. We couldn't find an activity, staff member or pupil he appeared to care about at all. Everything we tried worked for a few days and then was rejected. Every time we pushed, Carlos would refuse, abscond or disrupt. He was capable of significant aggression.

I didn't feel I had all of the information I needed about Carlos, so I went digging. The more I found out, the more his behaviours made sense. I knew Carlos was on a special guardianship order with his grandparents, and I knew that his dad was a drug addict and in prison. What I didn't know was why the guardianship order had been made. I suspected trauma, and we were working with a trauma-informed approach, but I wasn't properly informed.

Eventually, I was given the full story. Carlos' dad had been continuously in and out of prison and generally unavailable. Even when he was present, he took on more of an uncle role and let his own elderly parents look after Carlos and his brother. Before the special guardianship order, Carlos and his younger brother grew up with their mum and stepdad in a house where there was domestic abuse and a lot of drugs and alcohol.

Carlos' brother's personality had always been a bit different. He liked to wear make-up and dress differently. The stepdad didn't like this and wanted him to change. As a result, there was a great deal of verbal and physical aggression in the house, and mum regularly took stepdad's side.

It came to a head one night when Carlos witnessed his mum attempting to smother his brother. The children were immediately removed into care. In due course, Carlos and his brother went to live with their grandparents, but he didn't really interact with them or show them any love. There was nothing to suggest a difficulty in understanding and he communicated well enough with people, but he had no meaningful relationships with any adults or his peers. Carlos would consistently move friendship groups and be on the periphery. The children would talk about him in a positive way because of the things he would do 'for a laugh', but nobody actually knew him.

Carlos could not stay within safe boundaries and would often put himself in significant danger. He was drawn to risk-taking behaviour, and showed no remorse or empathy for how it made his grandparents feel.

At the point Carlos arrived with us, too much time had already passed. Too many negative experiences of adults in his early life – compounded by rejections from previous schools and frequently changing professionals – meant Carlos' fear of adults was ever-present. He had low self-worth because of the belief that he was bad, that it was his fault his parents behaved the way they did and that he couldn't keep his brother safe. Carlos would act out because he was bad, and then be told he was bad for his poor behaviour. Any attempt to change this narrative was rejected.

In the end, we got Carlos some qualifications and a place at college. I hope he succeeded. However, I wish we could have been involved earlier and changed his narrative. We wouldn't have done anything differently to what we tried – we would have focused everything on creating an environment where adults weren't to be feared and boosted his self-esteem – but we would have done it before the rejector mask was so entrenched. In addition, we could have supported Carlos in getting some therapeutic help, which had come too late and been refused.

Case study examples often represent extremes – thankfully, few children are going to have an experience as traumatic as Carlos'. However, it does demonstrate the logic behind a survival strategy. Seeing only the behaviour and imagining that a child like Carlos could be deterred by the fear of a consequence is a nonsense. Nothing negative we do can compare to what has already happened. The only way is to provide an antidote and hope we have delivered it early enough.

## Physical neglect

We looked at the powerful impact of attachment in Chapter 5. When children are helpless to meet their own needs, and adults respond inappropriately, the child must find a way to survive. This will often come in the form of suppressing their own needs. A child who isn't receiving the required nurturing will learn to limit their emotional and physical needs in line with the nurturing available. When they are no longer reliant on their caregiver, they will often become very capable people. They may even go one step further and become a carer to others by seeking out a caregiver role. However, underlying all of this is the fact they are likely to be resentful that their own needs were never met, that adults can't be trusted, that they weren't loved and therefore that they aren't worthy of love.

## The Atlas mask

Atlas was a Greek Titan who carried the world on his back. This is a survival strategy that a child with the experience of physical neglect may adopt; it is something I have seen very often.

| Front (how they present on the outside) | Internal working model (driven by wanting to belong) |
|---|---|
| I'm the shoulder everyone cries on. | My needs are bad/wrong. |
| I don't need anything. | My needs don't matter. |
| I can take care of everyone around me. | I'm not entitled to have my needs fulfilled. |
| I can take it. | I'm jealous. |

It is all too common for a child to believe that they don't deserve to have their needs met and that those needs don't matter. However, they are often jealous of other children whose needs are met. One way to fill the hole might be to take care of everyone else.

Children who have been neglected are often very attuned to the needs of others, offering them care and attention. The problem is the underlying shame that goes alongside it. Providing care for others that they lack themselves is rarely a satisfactory substitute. It doesn't make them happy and it doesn't remove the shame. Remember that children don't blame the adults who neglected them, they blame themselves.

Those nurturing moments of connection, safety, joy and happiness haven't been experienced and are therefore unfamiliar – and the unfamiliar is scary. Instead, these children become stuck in sadness, shame and low self-esteem. We have to take away their fear and help them to belong, and also show them that their own needs are important and can be met.

It is important to recognise that caring for others but not about yourself – believing that you don't deserve to be loved, cared for or respected – can open up the door to toxic relationships and abusive partners. When individuals tolerate more than they should and try to help others who take advantage, it can be a bad mix. It may seem that we have no control over these adult choices or that it isn't our job. However, if we can change the journey, then we can change the destination. By enhancing children's self-worth, we can stop them from accepting less than they deserve in the future.

## Portrait of child who has suffered neglect

A fine example of the Atlas mask was Leah. She arrived at my SEMH school in Year 7. She was sullen and cagey but very kind to others, especially younger children. She was lovely on a one-to-one basis, but she could become volatile and extreme when challenged. There were obvious difficulties with Leah's mood. She was well known to CAMHS and had identified difficulties with eating disorders and self-harm.

Leah was the daughter of a young mother – herself a survivor of abuse. As a child, she received minimal nurturing due to her mum's poor mental health and drug taking. Leah consistently tried to care for her mother and made regular excuses for her and her grandmother, despite how they treated her. When her mum had another child, Leah took on a caring role for her half-brother when her mum and his dad were unavailable.

We were making good progress in school when her mum's partner took his own life. As her mum was in and out of mental health units, Leah was placed with her grandmother, who continued the emotional abuse. It was strongly suspected that the grandmother had contributed to Leah's mum's abuse many years earlier. We were able to support her through this trauma because we had built good trust and relationships, but the specialist work with CAMHS continued.

Then Leah's brother was taken into care and adopted without her being allowed any contact. This was remarkably hard for Leah and nearly undid everything. She was angry that she had no legal rights over a child who, rightly or wrongly, she had raised. She lost control of her behaviour for a short period. However, supported by certain staff members, she channelled her anger and pain into one of the finest art projects I have ever seen. It is the only time I have ever witnessed an exam moderator break down when viewing a display.

Haunted by the fact that she could not care for her brother and keep him out of the care system, even though she was only 14 years old when it happened, Leah planned to work in the law and become a passionate advocate for individuals with mental health issues and children in care. She achieved the grades she needed and went to college. Sadly, her own mental health meant that she didn't manage to complete the law course, but was working successfully as a nursery nurse the last time she visited the school.

I am confident that it was the work done by the school with Leah on belonging that gave her the resilience to overcome some huge setbacks in her life. Leah is another extreme example, but she demonstrates the impact we can have. Her trust in us to guide her was vital. I will never forget the conversation between Leah and her art teacher about that project. Initially, she didn't want to do it, and really let us know about it, but she changed her mind and the value was enormous. The A* wasn't bad either.

## Overbearing parenting

Trauma and neglect are reasonably familiar and the effects fairly well understood by most schools. What is less well known is how extremes in parenting style can impact on children. This includes overbearing caregiving, which can come in two forms:

1. Caregivers who try to live through their children and put pressure on them to be someone they are not. Stereotypical examples might be pushy football or dance parents, but this can involve any

circumstance where the child doesn't get to enjoy their own passions because they are dictated by the caregiver.

2. The caregiver who treats the child more like a friend and the relationship becomes blurred.

I experienced the latter much more commonly amongst our pupils, but both occur with some frequency, although to different degrees and levels of impact.

## The manipulator mask

When you have had little influence over your early life experiences and are looking for things that you can control, one of the things children will often choose is how they behave. However, a child who has been forced to grow up too quickly will have a set of adult skills that may be used to manipulate the behaviours of others.

| Front (how they present on the outside) | Internal working model (driven by wanting to belong) |
|---|---|
| Strong and in control. | I feel small and helpless. |
| Larger than life. | Nobody cares about me. |
| Put others down to make themselves feel better. | I have to be grown-up. |
| No loyalty to anyone. | |

When a child who has always believed they are small and helpless because of a lack of autonomy suddenly realises otherwise, it can be the start of a very negative path without the right intervention. Many children who have had experiences like this are often popular with their peers and looked up to as leaders. However, the reality is that because they don't feel like anyone really cares about their feelings, they seldom worry about anybody else's. For some children, wanting to belong and knowing how to achieve it are very different things.

When a child has been manipulated, they may in turn wear the manipulator mask. By appearing strong, in control and larger than life, others will look up to them. By portraying themselves as superior, they are in a position to put others down – and the short-term fix can be addictive. Many children – and adults – believe they can make themselves feel bigger by making others feel smaller, or make themselves feel better by making others feel worse. These are learned behaviours from their early life experiences that they mirror and project onto others. Unfortunately, if we only look at the behaviour in isolation, it appears a lot like bullying.

It might not only be other children who are on the receiving end of the manipulation. The child has spent their formative years faking enthusiasm in things they don't want to do. They may well repeat this in school for extrinsic rewards, if they perceive there is something in it for them. However, when the extrinsic reward is removed, so is the enthusiasm.

It isn't that these skills are all negative; being skilful at making an impression, selling yourself and motivating or manipulating others can make you very successful in the adult world. Equally, it can also lead to abusive relationships.

With this child, the challenge for us as educators is first to look past the behaviours and understand where they come from. It is all too easy to label a child as a bully and try to tackle their behaviour from that perspective. However, shaming a child who displays bullying behaviour is likely to have the opposite effect.

We can look at the behaviour as being manipulating or influencing. We can choose to give children power and control in positive ways rather than taking it negatively. If we can view the behaviour as trying to find a way to belong, then we can teach the intrinsic benefit of helping or leading others rather than manipulating or bullying them. As we discussed in Chapter 13, catching the children being good is the perfect antidote to low self-esteem and shame.

## Portrait of a child with overbearing caregivers

A good example of the manipulator mask is Rishi, who was in Year 8. He was small in stature but in nothing else: big ego and big bravado. He could be very verbally abusive.

Rishi now lived with his granddad due to his mum's alcohol and drug problems, but during his early life he had lived with his mum and older brother. He was very scared of his brother, who had been in and out of prison for violence-related offences, although he would never admit that in front of anyone. His mum had been isolated and lonely and had encouraged Rishi to take the place of his older brother. As a consequence, from a very young age, he had been having adult conversation and drinking and smoking. Rishi had been forced to find a place in a grown-up environment without experiencing childhood.

Rishi would share his passions and be open about his home circumstances with trusted adults. When he was calm and regulated he could be very articulate about how he felt. However, he didn't have any peers with whom he could share this information, partly because he didn't trust them but mainly because he believed his vulnerability would be seen as a weakness.

Rishi was a very skilled athlete. He was handsome and appeared popular and intelligent. His voice could often be heard front and centre of an entourage. He presented as egocentric, confident and cocky whenever he was around others. If he found work challenging, he would often refuse and encourage others to follow his lead. This persistent disruptive behaviour had led to his exclusion from a previous setting.

Over time, it became clear that the dynamic of the relationship with the other pupils was not one of friendship. Other children often referred to Rishi as 'cool' or 'sound', but they were also intimidated by him. Rishi had learned a lot of intimidation skills from his older brother, which he used on his peer group. Since he was clever, he could manipulate others and use them for his own entertainment. He admitted that he did this for a 'buzz', but it wasn't satisfying.

What was important to Rishi was the persona he had developed: it made him feel safe to have control over others. He also believed that if he showed any weakness, then others would treat him in the way his brother did. He would occasionally admit to being physically tired of pretending, but he was too scared to change.

The one place where Rishi dropped the performance was playing football at break times. A big range of age groups would often play together, which changed the social dynamic. He was such a good player that he didn't need an act: the older children had respect for his ability and the younger ones were in awe of him. He would get fouled regularly, but understood that it was because he was skilful and fast, so he didn't react angrily or aggressively.

Coaching the younger children became part of Rishi's personalised plan. He didn't feel threatened by them, so he didn't need to use intimidation to get their respect. He thrived. Rishi and some of his peer group went on to take a qualification in sports leadership. What he wanted to achieve outweighed the fear. The group thrived too. He became a very strong team captain using encouragement rather than bullying to get the best out of the players. The role of mentor for younger children crossed over from football and he became a house captain. Now, the children looked up to him not because he was tough but because they cared what he thought.

The manipulator mask would still return in times of crisis around children of his own age, and I would be lying if I said he stopped the intimidation tactics altogether, but Rishi went to college to complete a sports leadership course and hopefully he will go on to be a football coach.

Together with Rishi we found a place where he could be himself and channel the need for control and influence in a positive way, but his journey could have been very different. It is important to look at where the mask slips; for Rishi it was sport. If we are going to use something as a driver for positive influence and change, we must be looking to identify it.

# Overprotective parenting

The polar opposite of treating your child like an adult is not letting them grow up. Anyone who is familiar with child development knows the importance of play and discovery. The transition from adult-led to healthy independent play is an important milestone. For some children this has not occurred.

One of the reasons could be due to a caregiver not allowing a child to experience self-determined play. Instead of encouraging independence, everything continues to be prescriptive and about pleasing the adult. Even love itself can become associated with bondage to the caregiver. When the child becomes aware of this, and they realise that they aren't like their peers, it can result in resentment and the development of survival strategies.

## The angel mask

When everything you have ever known has been about gaining adult approval and doing the things they have predefined, then the school environment and expectations of independence can be daunting. Safety is in familiarity, which adult approval can provide. However, as discussed in Chapter 11, these children lack the skills to manage their environment or interactions with other children.

When you have never been asked the question, 'What do you want?' it can be a shock to realise that your needs are important too. This new revelation can be scary. It is also hard to suddenly be asked to think for yourself when your only experience is of conforming and being told what to do.

| Front (how they present on the outside) | Internal working model (driven by fear of rejection) |
|---|---|
| Nice/sweet. | I'm not allowed to think for myself. |
| Compliant. | I must do what others want. |
| Good boy/girl. | What I want isn't important. |
| Proud of how much help they can be. | Jealous of others who get to play and explore. |

To avoid this shift, many children will adopt the angel mask. Being a good boy or girl won their parents love, so surely it will do the same for them at school. Consequently, these children present as well behaved and compliant. They want to be monitor for everything and are always on hand to help.

There will no doubt be some reading this who are thinking, that sounds great! What could be wrong with that? The problem comes when the approval doesn't materialise or something goes wrong and they receive disapproval. With their only survival strategy now failing, how does the child manage the situation? The answer is likely to be very badly. Tantrums may be an acceptable response for a 2-year-old, but if there is nothing else in the child's tool box then this kind of extreme and disproportionate reaction can be commonplace.

So, what appears to be positive is built on very shaky foundations. Although it is tempting to feed this child's need for extrinsic praise (for example, through behaviour charts), it is actually the worst thing we can do. We must teach them that there are other ways to gain approval and that self-approval is equally important. Exposure to independent play is key in changing their narrative, and the use of PACE (playful, acceptance, curiosity and empathy) is a great way to do this. If behaviour is driven by the fear of rejection, then teaching the child to belong (with a reliance on self-approval) is critical.

## Portrait of a child with overprotective caregivers

Kante wore the angel mask. He arrived at my school in Year 7, reeling from a failed transition to high school. In primary school, he had been made responsible for every job and had praise heaped on him daily. This had fed into the narrative from home that he was a good little boy. At home, he had been treated as far younger than his age – for example, despite his near teenage years he was still being given toddler toys. When Kante had gone into a secondary environment – where suddenly he was without the extra responsibilities and received less overt approval and praise (and even some disapproval) – his response could be extreme. He appeared very pleasant and polite until he was challenged or sensed disapproval.

We knew that we had to aim somewhere in the middle and gradually wean Kante off praise rather than quitting cold turkey. It wasn't something we were always able to get right. Kante saw himself as more of an adult assistant than a pupil, so he would want to be involved in everything, especially other people's business, often to the detriment of his school work. He was often late to lessons because he was caught up in things that didn't concern him. He would also be very resentful of boundaries or consequences imposed by authority figures.

Eventually, we found a mentoring role for Kante with some of the younger pupils. In fact, he was learning to play independently at the age of 13. In time, he was able to share spaces and adult attention and went on to take a vocational course in woodwork.

Kante's maturity levels were nowhere near the level of his peers, but he now has the ability to manage himself when things don't go the way he wants or expects. We also persuaded his mum to give the toddler toys to his nephew when Kante was in Year 10. We had to undo an awful lot with Kante; if the intervention had been made at primary age, he may have coped much better with high school.

# Rejection/emotional neglect

We have already explored physical neglect in this chapter. Emotional neglect is no less significant, although it does present differently.

Even if it happens unknowingly, the impact on a child can be devastating when an adult is present physically but they are neglected emotionally because the carer is unable to bond with them. At other times, it may appear to be a choice – for example, when a parent chooses to give the child money rather than time, or to occupy them rather than interact with them.

## The performer mask

Not being 'seen' by your primary caregiver can have a catastrophic effect on young people. One of the most important gifts we can give our children is time; without it, we run the risk of them feeling unwanted and unloved, thereby feeding their shame and damaging their trust in adults. Socio-economic trends are making it harder for families to spend time together, with many children living with single working parents or in families where both parents have to work.

| Front (how they present on the outside) | Internal working model (driven by mistrust of adults and wanting to belong) |
|---|---|
| Perfect/overconfident. | I wasn't wanted. |
| Everything is about looking good. | People can't be trusted. |
| Unable to acknowledge mistakes or show imperfections. | I'm not loved and unlovable. |
| Reject first. | |

What is the most effective mask when you are unseen and don't trust anyone? You make yourself as visible as possible. What is the most effective mask when you feel shame and low self-confidence? Fake confidence and bravado. Acting the class clown, risk-taking behaviour or wearing the coolest clothes are all good covers for being seen without really being seen. As soon as anyone sees through the act or tries to connect on anything more than a superficial level, the relationship must be abandoned or sabotaged.

## Portrait of a child who has suffered from emotional neglect

Den wore the performer mask when he came to our school. He had been in a residential setting where he had been thriving, but his mum wanted him back home. She had him put into care because she said he was unmanageable and blamed him for everything. She'd had him when she was very young, almost had an abortion and once said in a meeting in front of him that she wished she had.

Den had been a very challenging baby and there had been some bonding difficulties. Things settled down until his mum met a new partner and had Den's brother. All the things that Den had never experienced were now being given to the new baby: care, love, time. Den was included even less and he didn't feel part of his mum's new family. His behaviour became more problematic and he was put into residential care. Things started to turn around for Den. After a few good visits, his mum wanted him back home, where he feared it would break down and he would have to start all over again.

His mum blamed everything on Den's behaviour: 'See what he's doing – if you do that you're choosing to go back into care!' 'Why can't you just be like your brother?' Den was diagnosed as autistic and showed a lot of ADHD behaviours, although both were possibly a result of the trauma of being rejected. He struggled to see the impact of his behaviours and the perspectives of others. He also lacked impulse control and consequential thinking.

When he arrived at the school, Den had distanced himself from adult relationships. He caused a great deal of damage in his care home in order to push adults away and focused instead on material possessions. He often talked about designer clothes, and not always ones he had bought; Den had been caught shoplifting numerous times. He would use clothes to try to impress the other kids, but he had no close friendships.

He was referred to by the other children as 'funny' and 'mad', but he bounced from group to group, sitting with a different crowd each day at lunch. The overconfident show-off working the room as if laughter was fuel. He seemed more interested in a quick laugh than anything meaningful, and he treated others more as an audience rather than peers.

Den had built some positive relationships with staff. He shared a love of mountain biking with the head teacher, which helped to create trust, and his office became a safe place for him to go. His general mood was low and he would get overwhelmed at times, but on the whole he managed his emotions well. He responded to the structure and consistency of school and was interested in learning, although he was far below where he should have been.

Outside school he would overcome the negative feelings with short-term buzzes, doing stupid and outrageous things to get the attention of peers and escape what he was feeling. There were different risk-taking behaviours each week – jumping trains, shoplifting, drinking, drug-taking and underage sex – but unless he was missing from the care home, he would come to school and cope fairly well. He would brag about his escapades and get some attention, but not as much as he really wanted.

We took Den on a residential, which gave him a chance to bond with the group. His risk-taking could be managed through activities and he could gain shots of approval by showing off his skills. He had already escaped what awaited him at home, so he could relax a little and the children saw a different side to him. They were more interested in his mountain biking than his mad weekend in Blackpool.

Sadly, Den was moved to a care placement out of the area before we could complete the work we were trying to do with him. However, if we could have had more time with him, I believe we could have built on that camp experience. We had some green shoots of belonging that I wish we could have nurtured.

We see bravado in children all the time; when it is coupled with rejection it may exist for a good reason.

# What NARM has taught me

Just as with every other aspect of behaviour as communication, the elements are rarely neat and tidy. However, by monitoring common behavioural responses and personality traits, we can take an educated guess at what is causing a child's behaviours. The more information we have, the more likely we are to select the right antidote, and thereby speed up the process of boosting self-esteem and ditching shame.

Of course, there will always be some children with a very complicated backstory, so having some set strategies and a universal scaffold to support all pupils is always going to be advantageous. The sequential approach in the next chapter is designed to do just that.

## Recipe for seeing behind the mask

Ingredients:

- An understanding of NARM
- Curiosity
- Determination to see past the mask

Don't:

- Just take behaviour at face value.
- Assume.

- Attempt to diagnose.

Do:

- Acknowledge and set about meeting children's core needs.
- Recognise that different trauma experiences create different personality traits and behaviours.
- Prioritise emotional safety.
- See past the mask or front.

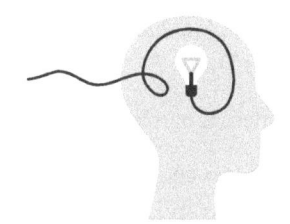

## Chapter 19

# Expectations and values

## No blame or shame

The purpose of this book so far has been to offer an understanding of what might be behind challenging behaviour. Not in a way that requires us to identify or diagnose, but to increase our empathy and understanding and help us to challenge mindsets in a positive way.

My hope is that readers will reflect on past and present pupils and find that some of their behaviours make more sense. I look back at things I have done in the past and wish I could undo or redo them, but if the point of the book is reflection and helping children to see mistakes as learning opportunities, then it would be wrong to blame and shame ourselves.

It is easy to be overwhelmed by all the possible causes for behaviour, whether it is:

- An uncontrolled short-term response led by survival instincts (Chapter 4).
- A masked challenging behaviour that is a form of avoidance, possibly driven by low self-esteem, fear of rejection or fear of failure (Chapter 9).
- An overwhelmed response caused by a child's inability to self-regulate (Chapter 12).

- Additional needs such as autism, ADHD, language or processing difficulties (Chapters 14–15).

- ACEs and early developmental barriers (Chapters 17–18).

Or, as is very commonly the case, a cocktail of different causes. Whatever is triggering the behaviour, there is still a child in front of us who still has needs. Therefore, whatever the dozen possible reasons for the challenging behaviour, we just need to accept that there is one. What we don't need is a dozen different responses, but we do need a strong school ethos and to provide children with a scaffold to help them to improve.

If we suspect that a young person needs specialist support, we should seek out that help. However, in the current system, this can take a long time. In the meantime, there are lots of things we can do to both help the child in the short term and prepare them for the transition to a specialist setting. Even when help is available, there is no guarantee that the child will be in a position to engage, so we have to help them. A child has no good reason to trust an adult if their experiences tell them that adults can't be trusted. It doesn't matter if it is a CAMHS practitioner or a therapist, they are just another professional who will let them down. Therefore, at the very least, we need to strengthen the young person's faith in adults.

## Values

I often use slides in my presentations including photos of my own kids. I haven't done so in this book because my eldest are 19 and 21 and have made it clear that they don't want their faces in 'some boring education book'. Nothing like a bit of family support!

When I am delivering training, I talk about them and their different settings where someone else has a duty of care over them. Whether it is Ethan's workplace, Morgan's college, Max's high school or Daniel's special school, I have expectations of each setting, and I expect their values to correspond with my own.

I then ask the group to think about their children, nieces/nephews, elderly parents/grandparents or even pets, and to reflect on their own values. Similar themes come up time and time again:

- Safe.
- Cared for/loved.
- Listened to.
- Treated as an individual.
- Nurtured.
- Basic needs met.
- Learning.
- Boundaries.
- High expectations.
- Social skills.
- Kind.
- Happy.

Topics that have yet to come up are stronger discipline, more punishment and more compliance. If the expectation is that our own children should be safe, happy and loved, then shouldn't that be the case for all children, regardless of how challenging they are?

Our values have to be for *all*. They have to be our ethos and what the school stands for. We can't choose different values for other children because they defy us.

> You cannot teach children to behave better by making them feel worse. When children feel better, they behave better.
>
> **Pam Leo, Connection Parenting: Parenting Through Connection Instead of Coercion, Through Love Instead of Fear (2005)**

Imagine if we took this quote by Pam Leo as representing our values. By seeing challenging behaviour through this lens, we would focus on making the distressed child feel better rather than the naughty child conform.

I often work with people employed in children's care homes and have explored the importance of shift changeovers. How the leaving staff member hands over plays a huge role in how the next shift goes. When it is positive and the person says, 'What a great shift it's been!' the incoming staff member is also positive, expects the best and invariably has a good day. When the changeover consists of 'Best of luck – she's been on one all morning!' the person is immediately more anxious, which changes the mood and how the child is approached. It is the same in schools. The adults set the mood: when we are positive from the beginning, we create safety.

For the vast majority, it is as Bruce Perry (2008) observes: it isn't therapists who heal children, it is human connection and love. Teachers often feel awkward about the word 'love', but what is important isn't whether we actually love the children (although it does make things easier); it is about making pupils feel loved when they are in school. If we look at the list of values above – cared for, nurtured, meeting needs, kindness, listened to – they all come under the umbrella of love. Dave Whitaker, author of *The Kindness Principle* (2021), might use the term 'unconditional positive regard' instead, and I agree that it is a brilliant ethos. He would also say that we must deliver this with relentless consistency. Sometimes, however, it is useful to have a scaffold to run alongside a great ethos.

## The sequential approach

I have been developing a working scaffold for some time; it was originally designed as a post-COVID-19 support tool. It has proved relevant throughout primary, secondary and SEMH (both moderate and severe learning difficulty) schools and even in children's care settings.

My book *Building Positive Behaviour* (2020) is centred around the sequential approach (see Figure 19.1). It was heavily influenced by Abraham Maslow's (1943) work on the hierarchy of needs and Bruce Perry's

Neurosequential Model of Therapeutics from *The Boy Who Was Raised As a Dog* (2008), as well as the work I do with schools and my own successes, and especially failures, from the past.

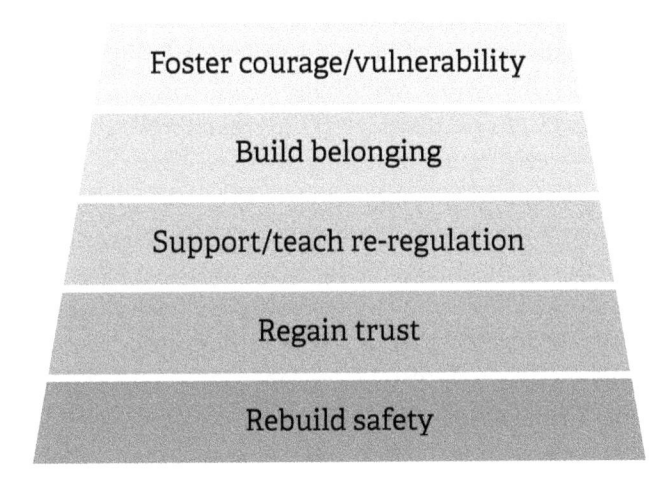

```
Foster courage/vulnerability
Build belonging
Support/teach re-regulation
Regain trust
Rebuild safety
```

Figure 19.1. The sequential approach

My SEMH school had some fantastic practice going on – for example, a strong focus on relationships, a multitude of skilled de-escalators and interventions, and high-quality emotional literacy and social skills support. For the majority of our pupils, the school's ethos and relational values were enough; however, for others, the ethos alone didn't work. To be successful, the work we did needed to take place in a specific order, and we had to scaffold and secure each building block in turn. There will always be crossovers; it isn't that you can't do higher stage work until the lower stages have been confidently achieved. It is about giving yourself the best opportunity of success with those pupils who need a little extra help and having a consistent focus for all staff.

As educators, we want the best learning opportunities for our pupils. To achieve this we need to create the best learning environment built on the strongest foundations. This chapter started with a bullet point list of potential causes of poor behaviour; the sequential approach has worked for all of them. Those children may have had different starting points and some may have progressed faster than others, but it is a process that involves following the sequence described below. A positive outcome will only be achieved through relentless consistency. If the child's trauma or additional needs require outside professional help, then being halfway up this scaffold with a child who already trusts adults will help enormously with their engagement. If a child has no trustworthy adults in their life, why would they engage with a stranger?

Often, the building blocks of life are wobbly or even missing; very few people's foundations are rock solid. When we experience setbacks, we will be propped up by our relationships. If the ground really shakes, then we all struggle; however, the more missing blocks we have, the more wobbly we are likely to be and more propping up will be required. The sequential approach offers a sturdy scaffold to manage those shocks, which doesn't rely on others and, most importantly, keeps us strong when those who shore us up are no longer around. Sometimes, the reason that transitions from primary to secondary fail is a reliance in primary to prop up the children and do things *for* them. If we can empower the child by doing it *with* them, they stand a better chance of becoming a successful adult.

When following the sequential approach, each stage must be secure before we move on. However, other people may have done some of the groundwork for us, so we just need to strengthen their footings. What we can't do is to start building from the top without a firm structure underneath.

# 1. Rebuilding safety

When we explored safety in Chapter 4, it wasn't about the environment being safe but the child feeling safe. If pupils are going to be inhabiting the right part of the brain for learning, we have to create emotional safety. Although school environments are physically safe, they are not necessarily emotionally safe.

There are many things we can do to help improve emotional safety:

- **Positive touch.** Even though we are still adjusting to the implications of the COVID-19 pandemic, physical contact remains a basic human need. The principle of high fives, fist bumps and handshakes has been brilliantly adapted in many school settings.

- **Voice.** Giving children a voice is essential. At the start of the book, we established the importance of validating children's feelings, and one of the key ways we do this is by listening to them.

- **Meet and greet.** The importance of meet and greet is the one thing on which both sides of the traditionalist and the progressive debate agree. However, the tone it sets may differ. The power of convincing a child that you want them there, that you are pleased to see them and that you expect the day to go well is as close to magic dust as you will ever get.

We also have to convince children that we aren't going to give up on them, that they are not their behaviour and that if they break something, not only can it be fixed but we should insist on it.

## Connor

Connor used to really frustrate staff. Every time they thought they were making progress with him, he would do something extreme. He was capable of aggressive behaviour and unpleasant language. He would often start with defiance and escalate if challenged. He would assault staff, threaten with weapons, destroy displays, spit and threaten your family. The bile that would emit from that innocent freckled face would need to be aired long after the 9pm watershed, despite Connor being just 10 years old.

Afterwards, he would be very remorseful, engage in restorative practice and make a plan for how things were going to be different next time. Then the next day he would do exactly the same thing. Staff began to feel that Connor's remorse was fake and that he was simply paying lip service. They argued that the restorative process was pointless because it didn't change anything and he wasn't sorry. The call for increasing sanctions and exclusion was great.

The truth is that Connor didn't feel safe. His home life was unsafe, so why on earth would school be any different? The adults he lived with didn't care about his welfare, so why would the adults at school? He had to fend for himself at home, so why was everybody always telling him what to do at school?

We can have all the plans, group work and counselling sessions in the world, but if we don't make a child's environment feel safe, then none of it matters. The remorse was genuine, the plan was genuine and the wanting to be better was genuine, but if Connor can't remember these things when the fear takes over, they can't help him.

When we perspective-take Connor's position – when we understand why the behaviour might be happening – our focus becomes safety. Now, we don't see defiance, we see fear. We don't prioritise getting the work completed, we prioritise making him feel safe. Once he felt safe, we could progress. Whether we view the purpose of education as solely about learning or as more holistic, we will achieve neither unless we are working with the child's prefrontal cortex and the nervous system's social engagement mechanism. Neither of them are activated by threat, so threatening this child will never work.

## 2. Regaining trust

We have seen how attachment and the child's early experiences of adults can influence how they behave and how they anticipate other adults will behave. If the primary adults in a child's life are inconsistent, untrustworthy or abusive, then it makes good sense to expect that from all adults.

It isn't only experiences related to primary caregivers that can impact on the child in a negative way. For some children, it will be their encounters with authority figures. Molly in Chapter 13 was a perfect example of this. If we insist on class work, or work on managing outbursts or social skills with a child like Molly before trust has been established, it is highly likely to fail. They have to believe what you are telling them, and that only happens if there is trust.

I have no doubt that relationship is the biggest power we have as educators, but to quote Uncle Ben's apocryphal advice to the young Peter

Parker, 'With great power comes great responsibility.' It can be used to lift up but equally to knock down.

I don't believe it is the job of educators to repair the most complex traumas – external professional help is often needed – although we have a major role to play. However, if we haven't helped the child to get to a point where they can trust adults, they are unlikely to engage with those professionals.

It is all too easy to point at the referrals we have made and be satisfied that we have done our job, but if the child isn't ready to access the help on offer then we have achieved nothing. I have been guilty of this myself, and then felt frustrated and infuriated when the child has refused to engage and been discharged. Someone in that child's life has to start changing the narrative, and for many children that will need to be educators.

This is the point at which a great number of children get stuck: we are trying to build belonging before we have taught them how to self-regulate (see Figure 19.2). Children who desperately want to belong, and therefore have a significant fear of rejection, can be hypervigilant, easily overwhelmed in social situations and often lash out. Other children are rightly wary of them, which only adds to their hypervigilance.

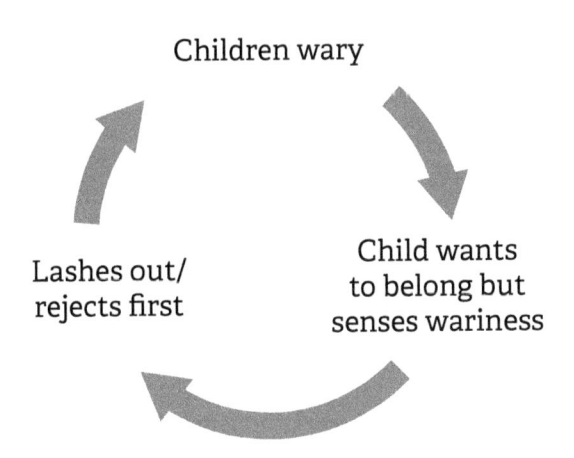

Figure 19.2. Sabotaging belonging

- Children wary
- Child wants to belong but senses wariness
- Lashes out/rejects first

It is a difficult cycle to break. Social skills work can help, but only after we have taught the child how to self-regulate. Staff at my school made this mistake regularly, particularly after reading paperwork suggesting that a child had social difficulties. The solution seemed obvious: putting the child in a controlled group, talking about body language and facial expressions. The child understands, answers the questions and you think you have cracked it. Then the child leaves the room, somebody says something that upsets them, they switch away from their thinking brain, forget everything they have just learned and let fly. We might assume that the child has been paying lip service to the social skills work, but the truth is that without impulse control and emotional regulation, they will continue to self-sabotage.

# 3. Supporting/teaching re-regulation

I suspected I had struck on something when I started sharing the sequential approach with schools, but I was totally unprepared for the number of young people I came across who were sabotaging their relationships with peers. Of the children in Chapter 11 who weren't school ready, many hadn't experienced the co-regulation necessary to be prepared for school life. One such example was Jamali.

### Jamali

Jamali was a Year 1 pupil. He was struggling and often getting into trouble for hurting other children. When I arrived in his PE lesson, he was already dysregulated. He was moving around the room, taking other children's equipment and lashing out. This continued for about 10 minutes and then he asked if he could leave.

The class teaching assistant took him down to the classroom, at which point I could see Jamali's body language relax noticeably, his interaction with the staff member become more positive and they started to talk about a map of the world. It was pupil-led talking about what animals lived where. When the other children returned from PE, Jamali's body language changed again. He very quickly got into conflict and was no longer interested in the map.

Jamali was doing lots of social skills work, and he performed brilliantly in these groups. However, when he left the room he would immediately find himself in conflict. Breaks and lunchtimes were especially difficult, and the temptation was to keep Jamali inside to prevent incidents. This became common for Jamali. He continued to behave and learn well one-to-one, even in adult-led paired or small group work, but he found it very difficult in situations when he was with large groups of other children.

As with Molly, we might assume that Jamali is simply going through the motions and not really listening or learning in his social skills sessions, but that couldn't be further from the truth. Jamali took it all in, but the moment he left the safety of his trusted adult, he became dysregulated and wasn't in the right part of the brain to access what he had learned. There would be no progress until we taught him self-regulation.

Whether it is staff-led or pupil-led, individual or group, planned or reactive, every time we co-regulate a child, we are showing them how to self-regulate. Every period of dysregulation is an opportunity to learn for next time. In the same way that a baby is comforted by a caregiver and learns to slow their heart rate, so we can recreate this process with soothing music, gentle tapping or even exercising – fast to begin with and then slowing down. We need to help children recognise the process and what is happening in their body, how they felt before the activity and how they feel after; how it has changed them.

The excellent regulation work being done in some schools is being followed up with some equally brilliant emotional coaching work. Teaching children to name their feelings means they can learn to control them and reduce their power. It is what Professor Steve Peters might call 'managing their chimp' in *The Chimp Paradox* (2012). Becoming dysregulated is aligned with letting our emotions take control. Giving those emotions a persona – like a chimp, which might be impulsive or irrational – can help children to train it, and if they train it they can control it.

> Having a chimp is like owning a dog. You are not responsible for the nature of the dog, but you are responsible for managing it and keeping it well behaved.
>
> **Steve Peters, *The Chimp Paradox* (2012)**

There are so many variables in a school day that to expect a staff-led, pre-emptive intervention every time a child shows any sign of distress is impossible to sustain. Having built-in plans for individual children who are known to struggle at certain times of day can help enormously, as can group activities at known flare-up points, like first thing in the morning. These will benefit all the children and create a calmer learning environment.

Few educators would argue that these issues aren't important or beneficial, but the reasons for not taking action are always the same: 'We haven't got enough staff/time.' 'What about the other children?' 'We aren't counsellors.' However, teaching the skills to all the children together initially means they can all develop the skills to use independently. That extra time at the start means the children can learn to self-regulate, which will save us so much intervention time later on. The payoff for that invested time is huge, both for future learning and well-being.

We wouldn't support a child who can't read by simply handing them some books and expecting them to get on with it. Equally unrealistic is the idea that a staff member would read to them for the entirety of their school life, which is an immediate solution to a short-term problem rather than a long-term solution to an underlying problem. What schools should be doing, of course, is teaching the child to read, because they know this makes sense in the long run and empowers the child's learning.

Let's stop short-term thinking around behaviour. Let's teach it and let's empower those children to control their own emotions, behaviour and learning potential. Self-regulation is acquired through co-regulation and emotion coaching, so this is where the focus must be before we expect social skills support to work. It also has to be experienced and put into practice.

A simple solution for a child who can't cope with conflict is to ensure they are not exposed to conflict, but this is neither helpful nor sustainable and doing *for* the child. Supporting careful exposure is key. Starting with pairs and then progressing to small groups, gradually withdrawing the levels of adult support, reminding children of their successes and using regulatory activities can all help with the process. When the lashing out stops, the other children have fewer reasons to be wary, there is less potential for the child to perceive rejection and belonging can actually begin.

## 4. Building belonging

It isn't always fear that causes social difficulties. And it isn't a child's unpredictability, angry outbursts or deliberately pushing away of other children that damages belonging to the group. Instead, it is their lack of understanding with regard to the social environment: children struggling to understand how their actions make others feel, their perceptions of others' intentions or reactions, empathy, differentiating jokes from seriousness. It is easy to get these things wrong and misperceive the emotions of others as potential rejection.

We are now at the point in the sequential approach where the child has developed some emotional regulation skills, so we can begin to tackle their social skills problems and create belonging.

### Gordon

Tall and thin with messy blond hair, Gordon was awkward and clumsy both physically and verbally. He found all elements of social communication difficult. He had experienced huge amounts of conflict in the past which made him hypervigilant. At school, he was safe and cared for, he had good relationships with staff and regulated his emotions during class time. However, he found any unstructured time unmanageable.

Gordon regularly perceived rejection and aggression from peers and would often instigate quarrels, believing he was about to become the victim. Similar conflicts happened at home. Although he often started the argument, he would end up getting hurt by older children and this added to his narrative of victimhood. On many occasions, we had to separate him for his own safety, only for him to make offensive hand gestures out of the window at the people we had separated him from!

During social skills work, it was clear that Gordon understood the theory, but he couldn't put it into practice. His own perceptions made it difficult for him to put himself in the shoes of others. We had to do a huge amount of restorative work, which entailed both him and the other children involved accepting some of the blame. He needed to be taught how his actions had affected others and how their reactions, even though inappropriate, were due to how they had been made to feel. This also gave the other children an opportunity to see that Gordon's actions weren't premeditated, and that by reacting negatively to it they were making everybody's job harder. Over time, they stopped reacting in the same way.

Gordon will always struggle, but what was once a fight every break time and lunchtime became a very infrequent occurrence. A lonely child progressed to being a young man who managed his unstructured time, had a small group of friends and even played for the school football team. Every term, it got easier and he was more accepted.

Again, the easy option – and the one initially favoured by many staff – would have been to keep Gordon in at break and lunchtime for his own safety, but this wouldn't solve the problem. It would hide it. Acceptance for Gordon meant that his self-esteem and confidence rose. This newfound belief also had a big impact in class.

# 5. Fostering courage/vulnerability

By following the sequence and providing a scaffold for our children, we have made them feel safe, we have built strong relationships with them, we have taught them how to self-regulate and we have helped them to be accepted by their peers.

By giving a child a feeling of acceptance, we have gone a long way to removing the fear of failure, rejection and humiliation – all issues we have discussed throughout the book. Yet, on a daily basis, we ask children to be vulnerable and courageous learners, to learn about topics they have never encountered before and respond to questions which they may not know the answer to.

It is so much easier to use poor behaviour to avoid, rather than to face, these exposing situations. So, the safer we make our classrooms, the more chance we have of children putting themselves out there. Even then, they may have previous failures they will need to overcome. Although what others think about them matters, it will never be as important as what they think about themselves.

## Nisha

Nisha had been on a long journey from the child who used to break down, self-harm and adopt the foetal position when in crisis. She had responded to the support she was given and those moments were a distant memory. The secretive child with Hermione Granger hair who had come to school, now had some friends and a little self-confidence.

We had repaired the damage with Nisha, we had taught her to manage her emotions and we had got her to a point of acceptance and friendship, but she was still terrified of the work. She was terrified when she didn't know all the answers. She would rather not do something than to get it wrong because every time she made a mistake it proved to her that she was stupid. Even though she had less fear about what others thought of her, she still had a fixed mindset of perfectionism.

How do you convince a child like Nisha that everyone makes mistakes and that making mistakes is the best way to learn? For us, it was by showing her. It was by unpicking all the other areas in her life where she had previously been failing, but was now succeeding, and demonstrating that she was doing that by learning from her errors. It was by using examples from our own lives of when we had failed and learned from the experience, both academically and whatever else we were prepared to share. It was by tapping into things she loved doing (in Nisha's case it was dance) and had therefore persisted through setbacks. We also identified her role models and pointed out the times they had overcome initial disappointments.

Nisha sat her GCSEs and went to college. She still has a way to go but she has achieved plenty.

We have to convince children to believe in themselves, but it is about more than telling with a child like Nisha. We have to show them they can be successful, and we have to make them believe it. In her many books and talks, Brené Brown observes that every good thing in your life happened because you made yourself vulnerable. Without reminding a child of the times when having the courage to be vulnerable has helped them, they will continue to play it safe in their learning.

Self-esteem isn't built in the short term using achievable targets. It is built over time with reminders of those times when they expected to fail but succeeded. It is the drip, drip effect of filling the child's experiences bag (see Chapter 13).

With children like Nisha, it is tempting to set work that is easy for them to get right or targets that are not hard to achieve, but this is the opposite of high expectations and the opposite of creating resilience (see Chapter 16). In fact, it is failing the child by creating learned helplessness in order to make our own lives easier.

For Nisha, who had started the process broken and with extremely shaky foundations, to gradually secure each layer of the pyramid step by step and to be on the verge of being a successful adult, is why I am so passionate about this model. The only way Nisha will be successful going forward is if she has the internal belief and motivation to do so. Sitting exams because this is expected of her is one thing, but continuing to progress after leaving school, when external expectations are taken away, will only happen if she has learned that she can be successful.

> ## Recipe for meeting expectations
>
> Ingredients:
>
> - Shared values
> - A sequential approach
> - Willingness to meet children where they are
> - Patience
>
> Don't:
>
> - Expect children without safety and trust to engage with outside support.
> - Do social skills work with children who can't self-regulate; they will often self-sabotage.
> - Expect children to be courageous learners without a foundation or reason to be so.
>
> Do:
>
> - Have the same values for the children at school as the ones you have at home.
> - Meet and greet every child.
> - Gain trust. It won't be given easily by some and you will be tested.
> - Co-regulate. It takes time but it will pay back in spades. The child won't feel they belong without regulation.
> - Accept that avoidance is survival for some children. It takes time to change this.

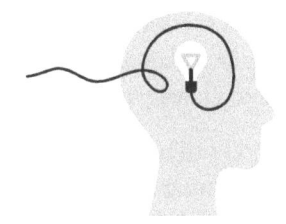

## Chapter 20

# Enforcing external control versus teaching self-control

There are some phrases I have heard many times, including: 'There was no trigger!' or 'They just kicked off for no reason!' I am not denying that the process from calm to crisis may move extremely quickly, but in 20 years I am yet to find an extreme behaviour that didn't have a catalyst. Many times, I didn't know what it was, and many times I made situations worse by trying to find out.

What I have realised since is that pinpointing the trigger can come later on. In the moment, the most important point is accepting that a reason does exist. So often, the message we have been given about behaviour is that we must know *everything*, but usually we don't know, often we can't know and sometimes we never will know. And that is okay. We are able to accept experiences and feelings we don't know about without all the details, so we need to have a very open mindset.

Having said that, we should try to learn as much as we can. We can only do this by talking to a calm child, but we shouldn't expect them to know the reason for their behaviour. Often, one of the biggest problems following an incident is getting the child to discuss what happened. It is much easier to avoid the conversation and carry on or punish the behaviour. Taking a child back to the event – back to the heightened feelings and shame – undoubtedly risks sending them back to crisis, if we have timed it wrong and they are still outside their window of tolerance, but it is well worth the risk because it is where the teaching and learning is done. This is our chance to make a plan together, to identify the feelings that drove the behaviour and to identify triggers.

I have gone through this process thousands of times during my career and very few are the same. The timing is difficult (and often age dependent): too soon and they won't be ready, but leave it too long, especially with younger children, and they may have forgotten what happened. In busy secondary schools, where children are seen less frequently, this step can be easily passed over, but if we are going to develop a genuinely restorative process then we need the repair. It is what prevents negative experiences filling up the child's experiences bag and counteracting good work done elsewhere.

As a pastoral lead, it is impossible not to consider punishment as making the job harder. If you are putting time and effort into challenging a child's feelings of shame and proving to them that they are a good person, then someone else consistently showing them they are bad makes the job much tougher.

If we are taking the time to talk to the child about logical consequences and repair, it makes good sense to also talk about prevention. If we are going to steer children away from shame, we have to separate the action from the feeling – and this is our opportunity to do so. Too many schools see the process from calm behaviour to challenging behaviour to consequence as three discrete stages, and a lot of schools see only two (preventing it and dealing with it). The best schools see it as one process repeated over and over, sometimes successfully, sometimes not. However, the de-escalation support doesn't stop at crisis; it keeps going all the way through to repair. This book contains many elements and each in isolation has its merits, but it is only when they are drawn together in a holistic way that we really begin to change things for young people.

# Joining it up

Anyone who has listened to Mark Finnis speak about restorative practice will know the passion with which he describes the social discipline window and how it affects children. We looked at the four ways model (i.e. with, to, not, for) in Chapter 7, but to recap: in order to help children learn how to change their behaviour, we have to support them to gain autonomy over themselves rather than forcing or doing it for them. To prevent poor behaviour, we have to support self-regulation and teach self-control. To change the narrative, we have to combat shame. If we don't teach children self-regulation and self-control, and concentrate instead on punishment, the child will continue to be without self-control and each incident will see them sink deeper into shame.

Kim Golding discusses the two hands of discipline in 'Connection Before Correction: Supporting Parents to Meet the Challenges of Parenting Children Who Have Been Traumatised Within Their Early Parenting Environments' (2015). The first hand provides connection with warmth and nurture, giving the child appropriate autonomy matched to their developmental and emotional age, whilst the second hand provides structure, supervision and boundaries.

Connection and correction provide a useful foundation that fits well alongside the social discipline window. Too much focus on relationships without boundaries creates too many excuses and is doing *for* the child, whilst too many boundaries without a relationship means a no-excuses culture and is doing *to*. It is only when we combine them and work *with* the child that we are truly successful.

To relate this model to what we want to see in schools, the first hand provides boundaries and high expectations. They are vital if we are going to use repair to cancel out rather than add to negative experiences after a behavioural mistake. With the second hand, we utilise the relationship we have developed with the child to build up their self-esteem. When we do these things separately the impact is limited, but when we add them together they lift the child out of shame.

If the school system is consequence led; behaviour A = consequence B, then the two hands are working against each other and any work being done to build self-esteem is being undone by the system.

It is this ethos and our school culture that dictate whether children thrive. Some children will succeed no matter what, others may fail in spectacular style and many are somewhere in-between. One of the big decisions schools must make about their ethos is whether they want to be a place of equality or a place of equity. Should all children get the same, or should they get what they need?

The counterargument to this is always fairness. Parents may ask, 'Why is that child getting more than my child?' and other adults and even children may ask, 'Why is that child getting away with it?' The answer to the first question is, 'Because they need more and because we are an equitable school.' Giving the same thing to children with completely different needs and experiences isn't fair, and it certainly isn't equal. The answer to the second question is, 'They aren't getting away with it, they just aren't being publicly punished.' There is a big difference.

## Ignoring low-level behaviour

Around five years ago, I nearly got banned from a leading teaching university. Well, perhaps banned is a bit strong, but let's say they haven't invited me back. I was asked to do a two-hour seminar on behaviour to the outgoing NQT cohort who had just qualified. Before I did my session, the course leader offered two pieces of advice:

1. **I don't want to see you smile until Christmas.** This took me by surprise as I thought this authoritarian message had gone away decades ago. It offers no benefit whatsoever to children. Consequently, I went on to talk in great depth about the very opposite being true – the importance of relationships and building everything from the foundation of safety.

2. **Ignore all low-level behaviour.** Although this is potentially a more dangerous message, I can see the thought process behind it. Dealing with every tiny misdemeanour would not only prevent a great deal of teaching but it would also be exhausting and unnecessary, especially as the majority of children occasionally wander off task and quickly return without adult intervention.

Now, I probably wasn't as diplomatic as I should have been in my attempts to dispel both points because I do understand where they are coming from. Whilst I wholeheartedly challenge the first point about not smiling, which I actually believe to be very detrimental to relationship-building, it is advice that is still more effective than trying to be too friendly. As for turning a blind eye to low-level behaviour, it makes sense for the majority. Most children will dangle a leg out of their window of tolerance, be off task briefly and then self-regulate. However, for a child with the potential to resort to more extreme behaviour, ignoring early signs of distress is paving the way for escalation, so we must step in and help them.

Acknowledgement is possibly the most important tool we have in terms of preventing the most challenging behaviours. Closing your eyes to warning signs because it might not get worse is a false economy, not a plan, and it doesn't support the young person. When did hoping for the best become an acceptable behaviour strategy? Doing nothing or leaving the intervention too late and then punishing the child for the outcome is the very definition of doing *to*.

# When children floor us

## Jamie

The paperwork told me that Jamie had ADHD. He was also defiant, aggressive and extremely destructive. His 0–60 behaviour acceleration meant there were no warning signs. He hated school, failed to build relationships and didn't respond to rewards or sanctions. He had been punished by having break times taken away, exclusion and had even been stopped from playing for the football team, but nothing made a difference. He hurt staff regularly, put himself in danger and had caused thousands of pounds worth of damage.

What the paperwork didn't tell me about Jamie was that he was funny, kind and had a lot of leadership potential. He was a great athlete, artist and a phenomenal musician. He had experienced childhood trauma, didn't trust adults, found self-regulation very difficult, was hypersensitive to how he was perceived by other children and terrified of rejection. He didn't believe he had earned rewards and expected punishments because he had been continually told that he was bad, both directly at home and through the actions of his educators.

People expected Jamie to be avoidant, to be violent and to smash stuff, so he did.

The threat of sanctions had no effect on Jamie because, when he was dysregulated, it was what he expected to happen. Punishment was normal and part of the shame loop. When attempts were made to reward him, he simply didn't believe he deserved it. His experience of adults was that they said things they didn't mean, or said they were going to stay but didn't, or were inconsistent and/or aggressive.

Nobody taught Jamie to self-soothe as an infant, so his focus ever since has been avoidance or punishment. Other children looked up to him because he was a good footballer, but he feared that if they found out how stupid he was they wouldn't (he was very far from it but this was how he perceived himself). We quickly managed to scaffold him through the creation of safety and to trust adults in school, and he made great strides on his self-regulation. He was able to articulate his fear of rejection better than any pupil with whom I have ever worked.

## Jamie's explanation

I had been Jamie's pastoral lead for two years at this point, and I had worked very hard to establish a relationship with him. The impact I could have very much depended on how early I could support him, otherwise it was an exercise in picking up the pieces. This was the same for many staff in school.

Following this particular outburst – flipping three tables and throwing a laptop at his English teacher – I had worked hard to get him to calm down. The incident began when she asked him to write the date and he threw his pen on the floor. She picked it up and firmly told him to write the date. Fairly standard practice; in many cases, he would have been told to pick up the pen as well. It certainly didn't warrant the destructive response it received.

It was easy to punish Jamie's extreme reaction. He would need a consequence for his actions – but that would come later. The point of this debriefing was to see what we could learn from it.

I asked Jamie about what had happened. I was surprised when he said he had been scared. I put a pen on the table in front of him and asked, 'What's scary about this pen?' He explained to me with absolute fluency (although slightly more colourful language): 'The pen means I have to write. My writing is rubbish, and everyone will see, so they'll think I'm stupid.' He went on: 'When we're out of class they'll make fun of me, which will make me angry and I will end up fighting with them, and then I'll be on my own.' Finally, he took a breath and said: 'It isn't safe being on my own – if I'm on my own I'll get jumped and killed.'

From pen to death in under a minute. It isn't about whether it is a real or logical threat; it is about a perceived threat. We don't create safety by making an environment secure. We create it by making it feel secure. I can't excuse Jamie's behaviour, and in fairness to him he didn't want me to. However, I could now understand it. I could explain it to staff and we could work on removing that fear. I was lucky on this occasion that Jamie could express himself so well. Many children feel this way but either don't understand or don't speak up.

After I had picked my jaw up off the floor, we approached learning differently with Jamie, but we had a lot to undo.

Going back to the social discipline window, we had three potential responses to Jamie and his behaviour: doing to, doing for and working with him.

## Doing to – high expectations/low support

To ignore Jamie's feelings and experiences and to just see his behaviour. To respond in the same punitive way each time. To not look for early signs of distress or anticipate triggers – to pretend that they didn't exist. To see his behaviour in a very binary way – as good or bad, conforming or not conforming – giving him very little wiggle room. This all creates conflict for a child who doesn't need much invitation. When it inevitably goes wrong, we then focus on the outcome, not the cause, believing that more punishment will make a difference. This can lead to a cycle of more poor behaviour and more shame.

### Jamie's high school experience

Jamie became dysregulated when faced with high written work expectations, when his behaviour would deteriorate. Rather than being supported and regulated, Jamie was reminded of those expectations and threatened with consequences.

Gradually, Jamie became even more dysregulated and aggressive. The consequences for hurting and damaging gave him no opportunity for repair and made him believe he was bad. Once this became Jamie's narrative, his senses were heightened on entering every class and the smallest instruction would tip him over the edge.

One of the things I asked Jamie's high school was what he was good at:

School: We've heard he is good at music.

Me: You've heard?

School: He hasn't behaved well enough to earn music yet.

I'll just leave that one there. Jamie was excluded at the start of Year 8.

## Doing for – low expectations/high support

It would be understandable to empathise with Jamie's experiences and want to protect him. To insulate him from potential stressors by making his work really easy, to not expect him to do it or to do it for him. To keep him entertained and away from others to reduce social pressures. It might also be tempting to excuse his behaviours and avoid talking to him about them for fear of a repeat incident. However, this is simply avoiding the problem and teaching learned helplessness. When the high levels of support are removed, the child hasn't been taught to manage their stress.

> ### Jamie's primary experience
>
> Jamie's fear of the classroom, dysregulation and aggression had been apparent throughout primary school. Having sought external support, but received very little, the school had managed Jamie as best they could by insulating him from stress. He went into very few classes, often working one-to-one. Nevertheless, getting him to complete work was still challenging and a trigger, so it was simplified or largely done *for* him. This had a positive effect in respect of reducing the number of behaviour incidents and kept people safe, but it didn't give Jamie any of the tools he needed for high school. His primary school spoke positively about Jamie and his many skills, despite him being a very challenging pupil.

## Working with – high expectations/high support

Having a good understanding of the roots of challenging behaviour enables us to react differently. Responding with logical consequences based on repairing what has been broken neither excuses the behaviour nor makes the action the priority. Working with the child to understand what they were feeling allows us to validate it and not make the feeling the problem. No child can help what they feel; it is what we do as a result of the feeling that is significant.

How many children believe that feeling angry or frustrated is bad? How many of those children also believe that they feel angry or frustrated because they are bad? The truth is that they have no control over their feelings, and believing they are bad for feeling that way is a breeding ground for shame. If we can work with the child to separate feelings from behaviours, we can stop the shame loop. Feeling angry isn't bad; punching someone is. Feeling frustrated isn't bad; ripping down a display is. When we separate the feeling from the behaviour, we shift from shame to guilt. Behavioural mistakes can be repaired.

We can also use some of our own emotion coaching and natural empathy to help the child: 'Sometimes, when I get angry, I find that going for a walk really helps me. Do you think that would help you? What would be better for you?' 'Do you know what, I get frustrated all the time. I find that breathing in for five seconds and out for 10 really helps me. Shall we give it a try, or is there something else you think might work?'

Stress feeds on negative feelings, and unless we can learn to control them, they will take over. Insulating children from stress only gives it more power when it happens, so we have to tame and control stress. When we work *with* children, we can regulate how much stress they experience and we can support its impact, but we still need them to be exposed to stress to reduce its potency.

## Jamie after exclusion

Jamie continued to struggle and continued to have serious behaviour incidents. We weren't striving for the elimination of incidents or expecting perfect engagement in lessons, but we were hoping for improvements in both areas. It actually took a relatively short amount of time to create safety and trust. He'd had this throughout primary school, and although his secondary schooling had been difficult, his experience of adults was mostly positive.

We were surprised by how the other children were drawn to Jamie. They looked up to him and he often dictated the behaviour of other pupils in the class. If the teacher could engage Jamie, the other children would often follow suit. However, doing this was easier said than done.

One of my roles in my SEMH school was inducting new pupils. I was the first person they would meet, so I was the first impression (I'm not sure how I ended up with that responsibility!). As always, I was keen to find out what Jamie was good at and what he enjoyed. I have observed several times, but especially in Chapter 12, that the common denominator with our children was low self-esteem. The intention was always to use this information to build the child up rather than attempting to knock them down with punishments.

Jamie was open about his love of football and computer games, but he was a very nervous and anxious boy in front of me. Then I asked him about music and told him that his primary school had said he was very gifted. He became a little more animated, so I pointed at the piano (which just happened to be in the room) and said, 'Can you play?'

What happened next still makes me feel emotional to think about and write about. I was expecting a bit of 'Chopsticks' or maybe a theme tune, but he played the piano fluently for about five minutes. This child 'who hadn't earned music' was the most talented musician I had ever seen, and he didn't even own a keyboard.

Not only was he a brilliant pianist, but it took him to another place. The nervousness and anxiety disappeared. It was obvious that music was going to be the vehicle to changing Jamie's narrative. We set about doing everything we could to get Jamie as regulated as possible before classes, often using music in the mornings. We welcomed him into classes, we identified triggers and we used the piano for regulation at times. We got him involved in whole-school projects and used this to lift him and build his self-esteem. Meanwhile, writing lyrics became a tool to build his confidence in the classroom.

Jamie still had his wilder moments but they lessened. When they did happen, everybody knew about it, but we were able to find ways for reparation. Jamie could regularly be found with a staple gun repairing the displays he had torn down in an angry moment. This combatted his shame because he had made amends and cancelled out a bad action with a good one.

When we see behaviour as binary, the obvious choice is to focus on the crisis behaviour, on the pain or damage – that is, on the things everyone is likely to know about. However, this means that we miss the big increase in engagement, quality of work, independent learning and growing self-confidence. For a child like Jamie, when it does go wrong, it often goes very wrong, but that should always be offset by how often it goes right. We have to balance those hands in order to build resilience. It was brilliant to see Jamie start to believe in himself and control his actions.

When systems are built around external control, children like Jamie don't stand a chance. The behaviours he displays are because he can't control his emotions. Threats and deterrents don't teach emotional control, so they are never going to change those behaviours. Not every child is as explosive as Jamie, but every child needs to be able to manage stress and control their emotions. In school regimes where everything is micromanaged and externally controlled, I fear this skill is not being taught enough.

### Recipe for teaching internal control

Ingredients:

- A willingness to give up some control
- An open mind
- Patience

Don't:

- Insulate children from all stress.
- Rely on systems where behaviour A = consequence B.
- Expect overnight changes.
- Let big incidents count double or treble; one behaviour failure is one behaviour failure.

**Do:**

- Join up restorative responses with building self-esteem. Draw it all together.
- Be patient. If a decade of experiences has created a narrative, it can't be changed in 10 weeks.
- Control a child's exposure to stress – make it gradual.
- Emotion coaching.

## Chapter 21

# Less is sometimes more

## Prevention is always better than cure

As we saw in the previous chapter, I struggle to understand the benefit of waiting for negative behaviour before intervening, especially under the guise of preventing lost learning time.

If a child is starting to show early signs that they are leaving their window of tolerance, and setting the class a quick discussion with the person next to them whilst the teacher dedicates two minutes to perform a small intervention with that pupil, to show them they care and to make them feel safe, we have lost very little.

If we ignore it and wait until they have left their window of tolerance, the behaviour will have escalated and now everyone is being disrupted. At this point, we have got to give them our public focus, perhaps wait for the on-call staff member to remove them, resettle the class and then do a follow-up consequence.

This isn't better for anyone. Of course it isn't fair on the other 29 children to interrupt their learning to focus on just one pupil, but neither is that pupil escalating and the learning loss being far greater. The easy option is to exclude troublesome pupils from the classroom, but that is morally questionable and certainly not inclusive. The fact is that for many young people, pausing a lesson to support them will only be needed to begin with; once they know that you see them and will come to them, they will feel more secure. This will result in greater self-control and, in time, they will be able to wait for you to become available.

Spotting when timely support is needed is difficult, which is why we need good pupil behaviour plans in place. Disruptive behaviours are obvious, but they hardwire us to negative responses. Discerning initial signs of distress will only happen when we are well attuned and/or when we have a dependable plan. Secondary teachers encounter lots of children for short periods, so being highly sensitive to the subtle needs of every child can be difficult. All the more reason, then, to have the relevant information recorded on a simple plan to remind us what to look out for.

## Plans for the right people

I have recently found myself in the position of supporting schools with policy and planning. One of the biggest issues I find is that often we are producing them for the wrong audience. I regularly go into schools and come across 17-page behaviour policies and three-page pupil behaviour plans. I understand why this happens: it is because we are writing them for external sources. There is a perception that Ofsted expects schools to include everything they possibly can in a whole-school behaviour policy in order to tick the right boxes.

I have no problem with schools box-ticking to protect themselves from the horrible system in which we find ourselves. However, those overcomplicated framework documents aren't fit for purpose: they aren't easily digestible by busy teachers and they aren't practical. Hefty documents for outsiders is fine, but staff need condensed versions. My advice is that behaviour policies are no more than a few pages and individual behaviour plans are no more than one page.

This is my example, which schools ask for after nearly every session I do. I suggest that no more than 10 words are used in each box.

| Pupil's name: | | | Date: | |
|---|---|---|---|---|
| | Inside | Partly out | Out | Crisis |
| 1 Presentation | | | | |
| 2 Strategies | | | | |
| 3 Distractions | | | | |
| 4 Triggers | | | | |
| 5 Re-regulators | | | | |

## Five rows

Row 1 consists of the issues covered in this book: how the child presents at each stage of the journey from inside the window of tolerance to crisis. This doesn't need to include lots of information, just the main things to expect.

Row 2 comprises the strategies we have available at each point. The further the child is outside their window of tolerance, the fewer strategies we have available to us once that prefrontal cortex is offline.

Row 3 contains information about special interests or skills that we can use to distract the child. It needs to be specific and individualised. Noting down something generic like 'Music' isn't very helpful. What type of music – African folk music? German electropop? We need to know their favourite singer or band, whether they have ever been to a concert, if they like to sing or can play an instrument. If they are interested in football, what team do they support? Who is their favourite player?

We are looking for something that will spark a conversation. One of the best purchases I have ever made was a set of Pokémon socks. Whenever a certain child was struggling, I could flash my Bulbasaur socks and change the direction of his bell curve. It can also be important to do our own learning about the child's interests.

Row 4 is about identifying triggers and hotspots. It is important that we look for patterns in behaviour. This allows us to be pre-emptive rather than reactive when it comes to that child's bell curve.

Row 5 is about identifying the child's most effective individual re-regulation activities, whether they are physical, sensory, mindful, arty or musical.

## Nisha

We first met Nisha at the end of Chapter 19. The journey ended well for her but it started in an extreme fashion. There were daily crises, and we were often having to stop her from hurting herself. In my 20-year career, I have seen few children more distressed than Nisha. Sometimes, she was so emotionally overwhelmed that it was extremely difficult to calm her. However, the more we learned about Nisha, the easier it became to avoid a crisis. And as we identified ways to co-regulate and create safety, crisis gradually became a thing of the past.

What we learned with Nisha was that as she started to leave her window of tolerance, she regressed emotionally and became more child-like. The best thing to talk to her at about this point on her bell curve was My Little Pony. Now, My Little Pony wasn't an area of specialty for me, so I had a choice. I could try to engage her in conversation about the things I can talk about at length (although her interest in football and golf was limited), or I could learn about My Little Pony. So, I got on to YouTube and watched a few episodes. I learned enough to know my Fluttershy from my Twilight Sparkle, so when Nisha heated up I could easily distract her. It allowed us to keep her inside her window of tolerance and paved the way for her progress. I have to say I got quite into the *Equestria Girls* series – it is underrated!

## Five columns

Behaviour plans often include a bank of strategies from which teachers can pick. However, the success of the strategy will vary dramatically depending on where the child is in relation to their window of tolerance. Something like 'limited choices' might work brilliantly when a leg is being dangled out of the window because the prefrontal cortex is still engaged, but using it after they have left the window just means two ways to refuse. We need to match up the behaviours to the strategies.

I always go row by row when I ask adults to complete a behaviour plan, but I don't complete the columns in order. Years of work in this area have taught me that it is far more effective to go backwards. Having said that, I start with column 2 (inside), which is often missed out completely. Typically, we are creating a behaviour plan because things are going wrong, so there seems to be no purpose in including the child's good points because they aren't the focus. However, it is crucial to remind ourselves that this *is* a good child and what we would like to see from them. This also helps us later on in the plan.

Next, I skip to column 5 (crisis). When we have a child in crisis, their behaviours are likely to be defiant, either physically or verbally, or both. We won't be able to reason with them. Learning has been lost for everyone and we may need to get the child out of the classroom, so our responses are limited. Withdrawal and regulation may be the only things we can do at this point. It may take over an hour to get the child back into a state where they are ready to learn and the consequences aftermath is likely to be high.

If we now work backwards and look at column 4 (out), we can see that as the child approaches crisis we will encounter undesirable behaviours, probably challenging ones, which are telling us that if we don't act fast the child will be in crisis. We have no choice but to stop teaching and address the disruptive behaviour, which is likely to be shouting over, walking around, distracting others or messing about with equipment. In the moment, it will feel a bit like the child is saying, 'I'm doing this – what you gonna do about it?' and sometimes they are. But, often, the child is saying, 'I'm starting to lose control now – I need you to see me and help me!' It necessitates another subtle shift in the mindset of the adult, so that it becomes simpler to see a distressed child rather than a disruptive one. In practice, we don't really have many more options than we had at crisis point, although it may be easier to withdraw the child and require less time to calm them down.

Next, we come to column 3 (partly out). The reason for going backwards is that we are now in a position where in column 2 we have a child who is calm and content, in column 4 a child who is outside their window of tolerance and column 5 on the verge of crisis, so what goes in that column 3 gap? We probably aren't looking for a behaviour. Instead, we are looking for an initial sign that something is amiss, that something is different from their behaviour in column 2. They may be more fidgety, quieter/louder, more/less withdrawn, more red in the face/paler, have a funny look in their eyes or sunk back in their chair – the list goes on. If we can identify these indicators at this point, when we have more strategies available to us, this will require less time to be spent on them.

In terms of simplicity and usability, noting down just 10 words in each box means we have everything we need to know about effectively supporting that child in just over 100 words. The plan is also quick and easy to update, which is vital because new information will come to light and their interests will change. If you are unfamiliar with the child, the middle column tells you what to look out for, how to respond and how to engage them in conversation. Many escalations can be prevented when these powerful pieces of information become the focus of our interventions. It is the difference between being proactive and reactive.

If we understand the process, if we have a plan and know the plan, then the emphasis can be on prevention and small interventions, rather than waiting for things to go wrong and creating a lot of extra work for ourselves.

## Recipe for a good plan

Ingredients:

- Knowledge of the individual
- Flexibility

Don't:

- Put too much in the plan.
- Solely focus on what is going wrong.
- Develop a bank of strategies that aren't linked to the window of tolerance.
- Produce a show document that never gets updated.
- File the plan away in a folder that is never accessed.

Do:

- Include the child's positives in the plan.
- Identify behaviours at individual stages of the window of tolerance and have responses for each stage.
- Intervene early.
- Make it a workable document.
- Write it as a team.
- Make it accessible.
- Write the plan for staff, not for Ofsted.

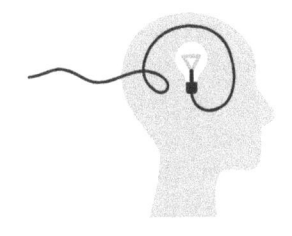

# Conclusion

I hope that this book has provided clarity about the importance of developing a holistic approach to behaviour. Having knowledge of a theory without the experience to implement it is no better than ignoring the theory and expecting rules and boundaries to be sufficient. It has to be both. Schools are only truly inclusive when we are curious, determined and flexible enough to support all children.

This does not mean lowering our expectations or letting children off; equity does not mean unfairness or losing our deterrent for other children. It means that every child matters. It means that children are viewed as individuals and responded to as such. It means that reasonable adjustments don't happen just because an EHCP says so.

Of course, working in a more holistic and restorative way can be resource heavy in the beginning; early intervention, changing mindsets (of adults and children), building self-esteem and properly teaching behaviour takes time. However, the time invested at the start will save hours of repeated cycles of poor behaviour and lost learning in the future.

Education is full of false economies. Some children become collateral damage at the altar of academic achievement, but there is little evidence that this improves the learning of those left behind. Behavioural approaches that inhibit pupils can result in children who are more focused on masking their feelings than academic learning. Quantity of academic learning may be all that matters for the Department for Education; however, it is safety and ensuring that children are inhabiting the right part of the brain for learning that will increase quality. You can pour as much data as you like into a child, but the simple fact is that if the lid is still on, none of it goes in.

There is no evidence that traditional disciplinary approaches are the only way. Education has to move forward, especially after COVID-19. Many schools have relied on systems which accept that a small percentage of children will struggle and, therefore, they are predominantly the responsibility of the pastoral team. These schools are now realising that the number of children struggling is much higher, and those systems are imploding because pastoral teams are overwhelmed.

Behaviour has to be everyone's responsibility, not just the pastoral team or the senior leadership team. There are already too many children outside of education, and this number has to stop increasing.[1] Pushing parents towards elective home education should not be acceptable (I am not against it as such, but it should be a choice, not the only option). If the system no longer works, it is time for a new one. It is time for brave leadership and time to make understanding children's behaviour and meeting their needs a priority. Schools exist to serve the community of pupils and parents, but somewhere along the way this has been lost.

I observed at the beginning of the book that there could be over a dozen reasons for the same behaviour. We cannot just wait for a behaviour to happen and then respond in an identical way, especially when it is obvious that the same things keep happening. If we taught using the same method repeatedly, and the children couldn't understand, that would be regarded as inadequate teaching. It would not be seen as the children's fault. The expectation would be that we should teach in a different way to improve learning. And that must include behaviour too. The definition of madness is said to be repeating the same process over and over and expecting a different result, but that is what happens in rigid behaviour systems.

In this book, we have explored resilience and where it comes from, and, more importantly, why it is missing for some children. We have looked at the barriers pupils continue to face – from additional needs and trauma to shame and being completely underprepared for the school experience. Everything comes back to that experiences bag and children's narratives of themselves. Create a culture where children aren't afraid and they will develop resilience and achieve their potential. Create a culture of fear and many will fail. Is it such a strange idea to lift children up rather than

---

[1] According to Whittaker (2022), up to 1.8 million pupils are persistently absent from school in England.

continually beat them down? Being feared certainly wasn't why I became a teacher, and the disconnect between what I thought I had to be and what felt right was the reason I almost left the profession after a year, believing that I was a bad teacher.

Much of this book has been about repairing and boosting children's self-esteem following behavioural failures. We can't affect children's pre-school experiences, so for some we are always working from a deficit, but the truth for the many is that it doesn't need to get to that point. Prevention is always better than cure, so let's do that! The bell curve should be a staple of initial teacher education; the idea that we should ignore low-level behaviours is a stunningly misguided message. Refusing a child a few minutes when they are unsettled because of potential lost learning, and then spending time dealing with the challenging behaviour when they escalate, or getting the child withdrawn, or trying to settle the class back down again makes zero sense. Add to that the inevitable consequence and five minutes has become over an hour, the child has another failure to add to their experiences bag, their self-esteem has taken another hit and the shame cycle is further strengthened.

We can't prevent everything, and I certainly don't expect every low-level behaviour to be picked up, but they should not be disregarded for those young people with the potential to go into crisis. Ignoring these children when they dangle a leg out of the window of tolerance is equivalent to giving them a shove. If they are out of the window, then we must see it as an opportunity. We hold the cards after they have recovered, so why would we want to hand them on to somebody else? Again, time invested here will pay back tenfold. The class teacher being present for the rupture, but letting someone else do the repair, doesn't create a safe classroom. Instead, it leads to a self-fulfilling prophecy because, rightly or wrongly, the child will perceive that the class teacher doesn't care. We must prove otherwise. Showing children the door 'because we care' is fooling nobody, especially the child.

Avoiding difficult situations is a perfectly acceptable approach for adults, so why don't we allow children the same concessions? Why are expectations higher for them than they are for adults? No child needs our assumptions. We can't claim that it isn't our job to diagnose children, and then diagnose them as 'just being naughty'.

An explanation is different from an excuse, but our consequences must be designed to teach new behaviours. Rigid systems fail the same children because not every child is a nail, so using a hammer for every child is useless, unless you are selective and only intake children who are nails. An educator's tool box should contain more than just a selection of hammers; we need to understand the nature of the job before selecting the tool. There are poor teachers and there are poor leaders, but I have worked with tens of thousands of educators and the vast majority are trying to support children with one hand tied behind their back. Change requires brave leadership, but there are examples of schools successfully using trauma-informed, relational and restorative practice all over the country.

The sequential approach of getting from safety to happy children is tried and tested. If we combine that scaffold with the bell curve to avoid creating work for ourselves and focus on building self-esteem, then all children can succeed both behaviourally and academically. If the most important thing is the learning, then let's make it holistic. The goal is to provide children with an equitable scaffold that will teach them how to manage their own behaviour rather than teachers having to do it for them. In our quest to use our precious time well, embedding internal control will always require fewer resources than managing it externally. I sometimes wonder whether it is the adults who are scared to give up their power.

I hope readers of this book will use it to reflect on behaviour plans and who they are for. We all have to play the Ofsted game, but the child still has to be at the centre. The plan needs to be designed to prevent the behaviour whilst, yet again, saving us valuable time.

When I look back at my career, I know I have helped a lot of children, but there are a million things I would do differently. Reflection is valuable, but dwelling on mistakes doesn't help anyone. If we are going to see children's mistakes as learning opportunities, then we should do the same for ourselves. Build a school with this ethos and everybody can succeed.

# Bibliography

Alghamdi, Yasser (2016) Negative Effects of Technology on Children of Today [unpublished research proposal]. Available at: https://www.researchgate.net/publication/318851694_Negative_Effects_of_Technology_on_Children_of_Today.

Barkley, Russell (2012) *Executive Functions: What They Are, How They Work, and Why They Evolved* (New York: Guilford Press).

BBC (2020) Marcus Rashford Welcomes School Holiday Support Climbdown (8 November). Available at: https://www.bbc.co.uk/news/education-54841316.

Bennett, Tom (2020) Rebooting Behaviour After Lockdown: Advice to Schools Reopening in the Age of COVID-19. Available at: https://tombennetttraining.co.uk/wp-content/uploads/2020/11/Lockdown-Behaviour-1.pdf.

Blakemore, Sarah-Jayne (2018) *Inventing Ourselves: The Secret Life of the Teenage Brain* (London: Doubleday).

Bombèr, Louise (2020) *Know Me to Teach Me: Differentiated Discipline for Those Recovering from Adverse Childhood Experiences* (Duffield: Worth Publishing).

Breaux, Annette and Todd Whitaker (2009) *50 Ways to Improve Student Behavior: Simple Solutions to Complex Challenges* (Abingdon and New York: Routledge).

Brown, Brené (2012) *Daring Greatly: How the Courage to Be Vulnerable Transforms the Way We Live, Love, Parent, and Lead* (New York: Avery/Penguin).

Brown, Brené (2018) *Dare to Lead: Brave Work. Tough Conversations. Whole Hearts* (London: Vermilion).

Carpenter, Barry and Carpenter, Matthew (2020) A Recovery Curriculum: Loss and Life for Our Children and Schools Post Pandemic, *Evidence for Learning* (23 April). Available at: https://www.evidenceforlearning.net/recoverycurriculum.

Chatterley, Graham (2020) *Building Positive Behaviour: Returning to Learning Using a Sequential Approach* (n.p.).

Condliffe, Emma (2021) 'Out of Sight, Out of Mind': An Interpretative Phenomenological Analysis of Young People's Experience of Isolation Rooms/Booths in UK Mainstream Secondary Schools. Doctoral thesis, University of East Anglia. Available at: https://ueaeprints.uea.ac.uk/id/eprint/82288.

Desautels, Lori (2021) *Connections Over Compliance: Rewiring Our Perceptions of Discipline* (Deadwood, OR: Wyatt-MacKenzie Publishing).

Dix, Paul (2017) *When the Adults Change, Everything Changes: Seismic Shifts in School Behaviour* (Carmarthen: Independent Thinking Press).

Dix, Paul (2021) *After the Adults Change: Achievable Behaviour Nirvana* (Carmarthen: Independent Thinking Press).

Doidge, Norman (2007) *The Brain That Changes Itself: Stories of Personal Triumph from the Frontiers of Brain Science* (New York: Penguin).

Don't Exclude Me (2021) Episode 2, *BBC Two*. Available at: https://www.bbc.co.uk/programmes/m001046t.

Dweck, Carol S. (2006) *Mindset: The New Psychology of Success* (New York: Random House).

Eanes, Rebecca (n.d.) Debunking Myths About Positive Parenting – Myth #3: Does Positive Parenting Reward Misbehavior? *Creative Child*. Available at: https://www.creativechild.com/articles/view/debunking-myths-about-positive-parenting-myth-3-does-positive-parenting-reward-misbehavior/1.

Felitti, Vincent J., Anda, Robert F., Nordenberg, Dale, Williamson, David F., Spitz, Alison M., Edwards, Valerie, Koss, Mary P. and Marks, James S. (1998) Relationship of Childhood Abuse and Household Dysfunction to Many of the Leading Causes of Death in Adults: The Adverse Childhood Experiences (ACE) Study, *American Journal of Preventive Medicine*, 14(4): 245–258.

Finnis, Mark (2020) *Restorative Practice: Building Relationships, Improving Behaviour and Creating Stronger Communities* (Carmarthen: Independent Thinking Press).

Finnis, Mark (2021) That Behaviour Show, *Teacher Hug Radio*, episode 1. Available at: https://teacherhug.co.uk/listen-again-that-behaviour-show?r.

Finnis, Mark (2021) Restorative Practice: Placing Relationships at the Heart of Teaching, *SecEd* (20 April). Available at: https://www.sec-ed.co.uk/best-practice/relational-and-restorative-practice-at-the-heart-of-your-teaching-restorative-justice-behaviour-relationships-schools-classrooms-teachers.

Foley, Colin (2022) What Conditions Can Co-Occur with ADHD?, *ADHD Foundation* (May). Available at: https://www.adhdfoundation.org.uk/wp-content/uploads/2022/05/What-conditions-can-co-occur-with-ADHD-Colin-Foley.pdf.

Golding, Kim S. (2015) Connection Before Correction: Supporting Parents to Meet the Challenges of Parenting Children Who Have Been Traumatised Within Their Early Parenting Environments, *Children Australia: Consilience in Action – Lessons from an International Childhood Trauma Conference*, 40(2): 152–159.